Famous and For[gotten]

Albert Goldthorpe and A[lbert Rigg] – rugby footballers

The parallel playing careers of two Yorkshire rugby icons

Robert Gate

London League Publications Ltd

Famous and Forgotten
Albert Goldthorpe and Archie Rigg – rugby footballers

© Robert Gate

The moral right of Robert Gate to be identified as the author has been asserted.

Front & back cover design @ Stephen McCarthy.

All photographs are from private collections unless credited to the photographer or provider of the photo. No copyright has been intentionally breached; please contact London League Publications Ltd if you believe there has been a breach of copyright.

Front cover photos: Baines cards of Albert Goldthorpe and Archie Rigg.
Back cover photos: Ceramic by Ted Underhill of Archie Rigg when he was the first Northern Union captain of Halifax; photo of Albert Goldthorpe; Yorkshire Northern Union County Cap 1895–96.

This book is copyright under the Berne Convention. All rights are reserved. It is sold subject to the condition that it shall not, by way of trade or otherwise, be lent, resold, hired out or otherwise circulated without the publisher's prior consent in any form of binding or cover other than that in which it is published and without a similar condition being imposed on the subsequent purchaser.

A CIP catalogue record for this book is available from the British Library.

Published in February 2024 by London League Publications Ltd, PO Box 65784, London NW2 9NS

ISBN: 978-1-909885-35-6

Cover design by Stephen McCarthy Graphic Design
46, Clarence Road, London N15 5BB.

Editing and layout by Peter Lush

Printed and bound in Great Britain by CPI Group (UK) Ltd, Croydon CR0 4YY

Introduction

Albert Goldthorpe, alias 'Ahr' Albert. Sounds a bit like an old-time music hall comedian but facing him on a rugby pitch was definitely no joke. 'Ahr' Albert and Archie Rigg – Albert and Archie – equally sounds like a variety theatre double act, two comics for the price of one. The two rarely operated together on the field of play, but what a nightmare that pairing would have represented for any opponent.

Albert and Archie were both famous in their time. Somehow Albert's fame has survived the passage of a century and more, but Archie has slid into the murky realm of the forgotten. Archie Rigg is in the Halifax Rugby League Hall of Fame, but that does not really resonate far in the great scheme of things. Similarly, Albert Goldthorpe is in the Hunslet Rugby League Hall of Fame. However, Albert is also now firmly placed in the Rugby League Hall of Fame, which counts for an awful lot as the ultimate accolade the sport can offer.

Albert is in fact the only player in the Hall of Fame whose career spanned the years immediately before and after the Great Schism of 1895, which gave birth to the Northern Rugby Football Union. Almost inexplicably, he is the only player who represents the first decade of the sport that became known as rugby league. That is something which should be addressed by the game, because other men from that early period certainly deserve consideration for admission.

Indeed, it was something of a surprise that Albert was elevated into the Hall of Fame before James Lomas, the great Cumbrian centre-cum-half-back. Lomas arguably outshone all other players in the early years of the game. He captained Lancashire, Cumberland, England and the first Lions tour to Australasia, established all manner of scoring records and enjoyed a first-class career slightly longer than even Albert's. That is not to claim that Albert does not deserve his place in the Hall of Fame. He assuredly does. It merely highlights the fact that other men from the earliest period merit consideration – Jim Leytham (Wigan), Joe Ferguson (Oldham), Jack Fish (Warrington), for example, are just three of many candidates.

The modern journalistic tendency to employ rampant hyperbole has sometimes enveloped Albert Goldthorpe and he would certainly have disapproved of it. In the *Yorkshire Post's* Saturday Magazine (18 July 2015) it was stated that "Albert Goldthorpe was the first great rugby superstar in Yorkshire". The statement is demonstrably untrue. Men such as Dickie Lockwood (Dewsbury and Heckmondwike), Fred Bonsor (Bradford), Tom Broadley (Bingley and West Riding) and Teddy Bartram (Wakefield Trinity) are just some who would justifiably nullify that claim.

In Bryan Smith's splendid book *Four Cups to Fame* (2008) it is claimed, "Albert Edward Goldthorpe was the first sporting Superstar. He was, is and always will be Hunslet's first local hero". The latter proposition may well stand scrutiny. The first clearly does not – just think, for example, WG Grace (cricket), Fred Archer (horse racing), Arthur Gould (rugby union) and any number of other cricketers, boxers, athletes and footballers. The same work also claims, "Albert Goldthorpe was the game's first playmaker". Albert did not even move to the 'playmaking' role of half-back until 1901 and there were certainly innumerable playmaking half-backs in union and league before that time.

However, Albert was a truly extraordinary figure in northern rugby circles in that nebulous period before and after the Great Schism of 1895. From his Hunslet debut in 1888 he became famous for his peerless kicking skills, his educated boots settling countless matches. Although an expert place- and field-kicker, he earned his greatest glory from his mind-boggling expertise in the art and/or science of dropping goals, a priceless asset in his earliest days when a goal beat any number of tries. For the first dozen or so years of his career, he operated at centre, effectively enough to win Yorkshire caps in both codes. However, he was never really in the running for international honours, despite what some people have written down the years. Basically, Albert was judged to be too slow for international rugby and by some to be over-obsessed with dropping at goal. Indeed in his early career there was plenty of debate about whether he was even the best centre in the city of Leeds. Many critics gave that particular palm to Tommy Summersgill, who ruled the roost at Headingley and certainly scored a lot more tries than Albert.

Moving to half-back in 1901 did not curb Albert's drop-goaling proclivities, but it did provide him with more opportunities to dictate play. History shows that he succeeded dramatically in that respect. His greatest triumphs are enshrined in the events of 1907–08, by which time he was 36 and his career was in its dying embers. Albert famously captained Hunslet to All Fours Cups in that season, the first time that it became a possibility. He also became the first player in the game's history to kick a century of goals in a season. It is for these two distinctions that his place in the sport's pantheon will remain immutable, not forgetting his inspirational qualities as a captain and his high reputation for sportsmanship.

Albert never won international honours even after converting to a half-back. The Northern Union did not stage its first international match until 1904 by which time Albert was probably even slower than he was in his rugby union days, while the newer game was even quicker.

Lack of international status has, however, never detracted from Albert's legendary status as an icon of rugby league. Indeed, this book's genesis began in the 1980s. Albert Goldthorpe had fascinated me almost from the commencement of my interest in the game's history in the 1960s. Back then, even though Albert had been retired for half a century, people still talked and wrote about him. He was firmly embedded in the game's folk-lore, even though only septuagenarians and even older fans would ever have seen him in action. I decided to write a piece about Albert, possibly for submitting to *The Rugby Leaguer* for publication. It quickly became obvious that the material was far too extensive for a mere article. So in the end I wrote a pretty large essay on Albert basically for my own interest. This was so long ago that the original manuscript was typed on an old Brother *deluxe* manual type-writer and the spare copy was on carbon paper, festooned with liberal amounts of Tippex. No hi-tech home computers in those days!

The Goldthorpe manuscript was filed away for over 30 years but on 30 November, 2010, I began work on this book. At least that is what my computer tells me. Three decades on much water had flowed down the Aire and the Calder and I had done a lot more research on the early history of rugby union and rugby league. My club loyalty to Halifax had been a life-long pleasure, but as a historian it had always presented a nagging problem – the fear of being regarded as biased. This even extended to my role as a selector for the Rugby League Hall of Fame. I could never propose a Halifax player for entry into that most prestigious company. That was, however, a fortunate coincidence because, wonderful as many Thrum Hallers had been, I never believed any Halifax player quite merited that ultimate accolade. However, the world changes and over 30 years have elapsed since the first nine Hall of Famers were inducted. The Hall has since swollen to more than three times that figure and I would now happily support a couple of players nurtured by Halifax – Colin Dixon and Archie Rigg.

Plenty of league followers will remember Colin Dixon, of course, or know about him, whether they actually saw him play or not. Practically none will have a clue about Archie Rigg, who has simply dissolved in the mists of time. Archie Rigg died in 1951, just five years before I began to frequent Thrum Hall, where multitudes had venerated him. His name would still crop up occasionally when the old-timers reminisced on the terraces or in the stands, especially when the blue and whites fell short of expectations. It dawned on me early on that Archie Rigg must have been some player, but it also became apparent that no one ever wrote about him in the wider rugby league community. Effectively he became lost to history. Yet in his time Archie Rigg was just as big a name as Albert Goldthorpe, if not bigger. That is why I decided to link Archie and Albert in this single volume.

Archie and Albert were exact contemporaries; Albert was just 15 months the elder. Both enjoyed successful careers extending over two decades in both codes of rugby. Both earned public adulation for their outstanding qualities of leadership, sportsmanship and match-winning prowess. Both excelled as half-backs and centres, although they occupied those positions in reverse order, Archie starting at half-back and Albert at centre. Both won Yorkshire caps before and after the 1895 breakaway, but both were denied international honours despite their towering reputations.

Rigg and Goldthorpe were obviously similar but different. Archie could kick goals but clearly not as well as Albert. He could dictate play from half-back, when he operated in that position from 1891 until about 1900, when the game he directed was union until 1895 and remained essentially the same for several years afterwards. Albert's days as a controlling half-back began after 1901, by which time the Northern Union game was evolving into something entirely different. Albert's style was influenced to some extent by his lack of pace, which was offset by his footballing intelligence. He had what it took between his ears. Archie was altogether more of an eye-catcher. At 5 feet 10 inches, he was a couple of inches taller than Albert and a bit heavier. He was also a lot quicker, more elusive, dynamic and spectacular, capable of scoring tries from anywhere, in profusion and in many ways.

These two paragons of ancient rugby history operated in the same spheres, enjoyed similar triumphs, suffered similar disappointments, established club records and were renowned for fair play and durability. Albert Goldthorpe represented Yorkshire eight times as a union player (1891 to 1892) and six times under the Northern Union (1896 to 1903). Archie Rigg won 19 Yorkshire RU caps (1893 to 1895) and 13 NU caps (1895 to 1902). At a time when representing Yorkshire was almost as prestigious as playing for England, the captaincy of the county represented a supreme achievement. Rigg led Yorkshire for the first five seasons of the Northern Union, an extraordinary recognition of his qualities. Goldthorpe's solitary captaincy of the county was against Cheshire in 1892, when the Yorkshire team was essentially a Second XV.

Statistics and facts, lies and opinions – history and mystery, truth and stretching it. Sometimes there is no answer. Was Archie as good as Albert? Why are some characters remembered and some forgotten? Albert's fame has endured; Archie's has withered away.

Albert's continued fame may be attributable to several reasons. His name has lived on for more than a century through the annual schools rugby league competition in Leeds, the Goldthorpe Cup, inaugurated in 1904. Arguably, the fact that Albert lived, worked and played within the Leeds area afforded him greater prominence in Yorkshire's Leeds-centric press and the Goldthorpe name remained in the public eye through the writings in the *Yorkshire Evening News* of his journalist brother James, who became secretary at Leeds RLFC.

If Albert's fame was fading, it received a massive, if totally unexpected, unwelcome and inaccurate boost with the release of the Australian film, *The First Kangaroos*, in 1987. No doubt Albert is still spinning in his grave in Hunslet cemetery! Much more benignly and appropriately, Albert's memory has been celebrated since 2008 in the annual player-of-the-year awards, the Albert Goldthorpe medals, instituted by League Publications Limited via their trade paper *Rugby League Express*. Finally, Albert's elevation to the Rugby League Hall of Fame in 2015 fixed him immovably as a star in the rugby league firmament.

The difference between fame and anonymity is sometimes a genuine conundrum. If Archie Rigg had not been such a modest man, his fame may have endured like Albert Goldthorpe's, an equally modest man. Yes, I know that does not make sense and what about the bloke in chapter 7?

Robert Gate
October 2023

Acknowledgements
Thanks to: Peter Benson, Steve Calline, Tony Capstick, Trevor Delaney, Harry Edgar (Rugby League Journal, Phil Fearnley, Michael Inman, Richard Lowther, Dave Makin, Graham Morris, Barry Rennison and Graham Williams.

Select Bibliography
VAS Beanland, *Great Games and Great Players* (1945)
Andrew Hardcastle, *Thrum Hall Greats* (1994)
Les Hoole, *We've swept the seas before, boys* (1991)
Thomas Kitchen, *History of the Halifax Cricket & Football Club* (1900)
Bryan Smith, *Four Cups to Fame* (2008)
Frank Williams, *Thrum Hall through six reigns and three wars* (1954)

London League Publications Ltd would like to thank Steve McCarthy for designing the cover and the staff of CPI Group (UK) for printing the book.

Archie Rigg's benefit

Many years ago, the author acquired a small (3 inches x 8 inches) black notebook, which someone had used as a scrapbook in late Victorian and early Edwardian times. It was just wide enough to accommodate solitary newspaper columns and its contents varied from politics, hangings and West Riding local history to sport. Included is the following article, probably from a Bradford newspaper, dated Friday 22 January 1904, covering almost four pages (28 column inches), highlighting the following day's match between Halifax and Huddersfield, which was Archie Rigg's benefit match. Apart from extolling the virtues of Rigg, appropriate and due reverence is directed to his long-time friend and foe Albert Goldthorpe.

ARCHIE RIGG'S BENEFIT - HALIFAX FOOTBALLER'S CAREER
HIS SERVICES TO CLUB AND COUNTY – SOME INTERESTING REMINISCENCES

Since the halcyon days when the doughty football deeds of Fred Bonsor used to thrill the heart of every sport-loving Yorkshireman, no man has arisen to more captivate the public eye of this county than JA Rigg, the popular Halifax player, who is to be honoured tomorrow with a public benefit. As a great sportsman, a prolific scorer, and a judicious captain, he has been for over a dozen years not only the idol of the Halifax club, but probably the greatest favourite in Yorkshire.

In expressing so bold an opinion in unrelenting type one does not forget the long-sustained services of such men as Albert Goldthorpe and Tom Broadley. Comparisons are odious, but whilst remembering the creditable accomplishments of many other Yorkshire players during the last decade, still more credit goes to Rigg, by reason of his long reign as captain of the county team, and of his record as the greatest scorer who has ever played for his county. At the zenith of his career he was undoubtedly the finest half-back in the North of England - a worthy rival, indeed, to Bonsor in his best days – and as such he emblazoned his name among the list of Yorkshiremen who did so much to establish the fame of the county in the world of football. It is a matter of regret that he never secured international rank – but more of that anon.

James Archer Rigg – to give him his full name, though he is popularly known as 'Archie' – is shy, unassuming, and a man of modest mien. Modesty, indeed, in him may be a weakness as well as a virtue. He tells his story without the slightest idea that he deserves any credit for the way he has borne his part. If he were to have his way, the insatiable printer would probably never have the satisfaction of displaying in all the glowing publicity of newspaper ink the record of his wonderful deeds. To talk of one's self he calls 'advertising'. We cannot let such modesty go unrewarded, and we take the risks of publication on our own heads. Let us at once say, however, that, like most modest men, 'Archie' Rigg possesses true gentlemanly instincts. Albert Goldthorpe is such another, and we know of no two players whose popularity is more deserved. Between them they have given to the calling of a professional football player a tone of dignity and respect of which it has often stood in need.

'Archie' Rigg has not always been a professional. In the old days, before the advent of the Northern Union made the payment of players a legal proceeding, he cherished his amateur status quite as much as the most punctilious of University 'undergrads'. After a match no sovereigns were to be found in his boots – a remark which will be appreciated by some players who were, perhaps, not so scrupulous as he. But that is another story, as Rudyard Kipling would say.

The beginning of his career

To come to Rigg's football 'history', though, as he is still playing a fine game, it will be many a long day before the last chapter can be written. It was at Halifax that his career commenced, and it is with Halifax that he has played throughout the last 13 years. It will thus be seen that apart from his own inherent abilities which would have made him a success in any team, no small credit attaches to the Halifax club for having, to use a common aphorism, "brought him out". He first started to play with the Albion-street Gymnasium. Here such enthusiastic lovers of gymnastic pursuits as Mr JH Whitley, MP, Mr EH Hill (the coroner), and Councillor Howard Clay were interested in him. If one might digress for a moment, one might point out the effect which this early gymnastic training had upon Rigg's future career. He was taught for one thing that the practice of gymnastics required abstention from all intoxicants, and it is to his always having been a teetotaller that he attributes his fitness and staying powers today. This is a fact which leaders of the Band of Hope societies will no doubt read and inwardly digest and after this we may read of Rigg being asked to pose as a teetotal lecturer. But if not a teetotal lecturer he is at present time an instructor of physical culture at some of the Halifax evening schools, and frequently engages in exhibition wrestling and boxing contests.

When he joined Halifax

Rigg captained the gymnasium football team for three seasons, a club comrade of his being Joe Arnold, who afterwards partnered him at half-back on many an historic field. It was on September 12th, 1891, that Rigg first turned out as a youth of eighteen with the Halifax second team against Rochdale Hornets second. He was at once a pronounced success, for he scored three times. Naturally he was at once drafted into the first team, his first match being against Bradford, at Park Avenue, the following week. A subsequent match at Park Avenue, probably the following season, he remembers very distinctly. That was the day on which the new method of scoring by penalty goals came into operation, and Percy Illingworth – whom rumour has it, is to become a Member of Parliament at the next election – won the match for Bradford by claiming a penalty kick when Bob Winskill got off-side in the scrimmage. This was only one of many memorable club matches of that period in which Rigg played and distinguished himself. Halifax found that they had unearthed a treasure and, of course, made much of him. But the head of this fine, well-built, young athlete was as insensible to flattery as his body was to the rough and tumble of a fierce forward maul, and on November 2, 1892, we find him figuring in the Probables and Possibles match at Leeds, after which he played in the county team on and off for a period of ten years.

A 12 years' performance

Up to the beginning of this season Rigg had scored for Halifax no less than 61 goals and 145 tries, without naming the excellent work which he did on behalf of his county. We believe it is a fact that in his 10 years experience of county football he scored more points for Yorkshire than any other player who ever donned the white jersey. During the first four seasons of the Northern Union regime, he captained the Yorkshire team, and had the satisfaction of leading his men to championship honours in two successive seasons. As a memento of this unusual service, he was presented by the County Committee with a gold medal, inlaid with the White Rose of Yorkshire in diamonds. In the light of his great achievements and of the more than local fame which he attained, it seems inconceivable that Rigg never got his international cap.

Missed his international

It was in 1892 that a vacancy occurred in the English half-back position, and Rigg was fancied for the place. Just about then was played the great match at Richmond between Yorkshire and the misnamed Middlesex 'Invincibles' which ended so much to the credit of the Yorkshire men. The Middlesex side included 11 internationals among whom were such names as AJ Gould, the hero of 30 internationals, Stoddart and Orr. It was in that match that Donald Jowett scored a marvellous never-to-be-forgotten goal. 'Dicky' Lockwood, who was captain, expressed the fear that Donald would never land the ball but told him, anyhow, to kick it as far as he could. So Donald did and the result was a surprise. It was the longest place kick that Rigg ever saw, but it was a successful one. Rigg distinguished himself greatly in the match by scoring two tries and, after the exhibition which he gave, it seemed impossible that his claim for the international position could be ignored. But the Bradford club had great influence with the England Rugby Union committee at that time, and Horace Duckett was selected instead. Rigg, it was held, was inexperienced, which seemed a strange thing to say when it was his superior play that had mainly frustrated and turned into a rout the combined attacks of English, Welsh, Irish and Scotch internationals on the field of Richmond.

It was several seasons later, however, that Rigg was seen at his best. A real 'class' player, and a man of great resource, he was much to be feared when near an opponents' line. Indeed, as a scorer, he acknowledged no peer in the land. Today – now that he has come back to his old position after two seasons among the three-quarters – he is as agile, resourceful and strong as ever, and spectators may be as well entertained by his play today as they were in his best days.

He comes as near the ideal of what a footballer ought to be as any man we know, combining as he does ability to play with the true instincts of a sportsman and a gentleman. When Mr JH Whitley, MP, spoke of him last week as "one of nature's gentlemen" he spoke with the knowledge of 15 years' close acquaintance with the man, and the expression, we venture to say, is one with which no one will differ. His fame as a sportsman and a gentleman stands today unblemished, and nowhere in England can a footballer be found who, on the grounds of true sportsmanship, has a greater claim to public esteem. May his benefit tomorrow be a bumper.

Previous publications by Robert Gate

Gone North: Welshmen in Rugby League (vol 1) [RE Gate], 1986
The Struggle for the Ashes [RE Gate], 1986
Champions: A Celebration of the Rugby League Championship 1895-1987 [RE Gate], 1987
Gone North: Welshmen in Rugby League (vol 2) [RE Gate], 1988
The Rugby League Quizbook [Mainstream], 1988
Rugby League: An Illustrated History [Weidenfeld], 1989
The Hall of Fame Brochure [Rugby Football League], 1989
An Illustrated History of Saints v Wigan Derby Matches [Smiths Books (Wigan)], 1990
The Guinness Rugby League Fact Book [Guinness], 1991
They Played for Wigan [Mike RL Publications], 1992, with Michael Latham
There Were A Lot More Than That: Odsal 1954 [RE Gate], 1994
When Push Comes to Shove (vol 2), [Yorkshire Arts Circus], 1995, co-editor with Ian Clayton and Ian Daley
The Official Rugby League Centenary Magazine [Grandstand Publications], 1995, with David Howes
The Struggle for the Ashes II [RE Gate], 1996
Bradford, Northern and Bulls [Tempus], 2000
The Great Bev: The Rugby League Career of Brian Bevan [London League Publications Ltd], 2002
100 Greats: Cumberland Rugby League [Tempus], 2002
Rugby League Hall of Fame [Tempus], 2003
100 Greats: Thrum Hallers, Halifax Heroes 1945-1998 [Tempus], 2004
Trevor Foster: The life of a Rugby League Legend [London League Publications Ltd], 2005, with Simon Foster and Peter Lush
Neil Fox: Rugby League's greatest points scorer [London League Publications Ltd], 2005
Rugby League Lions: 100 Years of Test Matches [Vertical Editions], 2008
Billy Boston: Rugby League Footballer [London League Publications Ltd], 2009
Building the family game: A Rugby League Memoir [London League Publications Ltd], 2014, with Maurice Oldroyd
Harold Wagstaff: A Northern Union Man [London League Publications Ltd], 2019, with Graham Williams

The author also contributed all or most of the material for the following brochures/booklets:

Ronnie James 1971 (benefit brochure)
Gordon Baker 1975 (benefit brochure)
John Martin 1977 (benefit brochure)
Dave Callon 1981 (benefit brochure)
Halifax RLFC Centenary Year Magazine 1973
Wales and Rugby League [International Rugby League Supporters Federation], 1981
The Rugby League Foundation Clubs' Centenary Brochure, 1995
The Rugby League Clubs Millennium Brochure, 2000

Contents

Albert Edward Goldthorpe (1871 to 1943)

1. 'Ahr Albert' – the greatest of drops ... 1
2. Into the Northern Union ... 17
3. Cobblers & Kangaroos – a tarnished reputation ... 45

James Archer Rigg (1872 to 1951)

4. Archie Rigg – the most gentlemanly player ... 51
5. Archie and the Northern Union ... 69
6. Bradford Northern – new club, new game ... 99

And now, someone no one remembers ...

7. James William Bulmer, Knight of the Realm ... 111

Appendices

1. A Chat with the Northern Union Football Champion ... 129
2. Club career records ... 131
3. Yorkshire County records ... 133
4. Appearances in major finals ... 135
5. Halifax's double-winners season 1902–03 ... 139
6. Hunslet's All Four Cups season 1907–08 ... 140

"In every town or village in Yorkshire or Lancashire where the Rugby football is kicked, the name of Albert Goldthorpe is one to conjure with. It is no figure of speech to say that Albert Goldthorpe is the most popular footballer in Yorkshire. Every ragamuffin in the street regards him as a personal acquaintance. No matter where he goes, he cannot escape recognition."

Yorkshire Evening Post, 28 September 1907

"Rigg has been one of the smartest half-backs going, and in the height of his form was one of the most dangerous men who ever stepped onto the field. There was a pleasing incident when Archie led his men onto the field. The King Cross band struck up 'Auld Lang Syne' and there was general cheering. Meanwhile, Rigg looked the bashful fellow he is. I quite sympathise with him."

Halifax Evening Courier, 23 January 1904, on Archie Rigg's benefit match

The trophy is the Yorkshire Senior Competition Shield

Yorkshire versus Cumberland at Leeds Parish Church rugby club on 28 January 1899. This is one of the few occasions that Goldthorpe and Rigg played together on the same side.
Back: H Robinson, T Wilkinson, J Ramage, H Hutchinson (Hon Secretary), A Starks, A Kemp, W Dale, H H Waller (President);
Middle: T Broadley, A Goldthorpe, A Rigg (Captain), J Gath, J E Parker;
Front: J Metcalfe, A Hambrecht, F W Cooper, M Sutcliffe.

1. 'Ahr Albert' – the greatest of drops

It was a typical winter's day on a wet and windswept rugby league ground in south Leeds and the match was dying on its feet. It was not exactly resuscitated when a New Hunslet player recklessly, foolishly, tried to drop a goal from about 40 yards. He hadn't a hope in Hell. It might have helped if he had possessed the technique. The effort was doomed from the start and the crowd vented its spleen - those who were not falling about laughing, that is. It was 1978 and dropping at goal from rifle range on the second tackle was not too bright tactically. It probably did not help that, uniquely and barmily, New Hunslet had American Football goals, which may have disoriented the bloke taking the pot shot.

"Who the bloody 'ell do you think you are then?" screamed a middle-aged man, who was clearly not best pleased. "Albert bloody Goldthorpe? Give it a rest, for God's sake!"

The strident supporter obviously had a high opinion of Albert Goldthorpe but he was hardly old enough to have seen "Ahr Albert" in the flesh even though he was clearly pushing toward retirement age. "Ahr Albert" must have been some player because our distraught supporter could only have been dredging the depths of his subconscious for this reference to a man who is now little more than a folk lore memory to rugby league followers.

Modern rugby union fans will think fondly of Johnny Wilkinson, Dan Parks and Dan Carter as the bee's knees when it comes to dropping goals and an earlier generation will similarly venerate Ollie Campbell, Gareth Davies and Jean Lescaboura. There is no disputing that all of them were magnificent practitioners of the art. Rugby league fans who were around in 1978 when the hapless New Hunslet player made a fool of himself would sing the praises of Nigel Stephenson, Norman Turley and Harry Pinner as drop-goaling match-winners. They might even mention the record 29 goals dropped by Lyn Hallett for the Cardiff City Blue Dragons in the 1983–84 season.

However, the drop-goal is not universally popular in league circles as it tends to get in the way of the rugby. For long enough it was almost extinct as unlimited tackles offered no incentive to risk the loss of possession by taking speculative pots at goal. In the two decades following the Second World War drop-goals were conspicuous largely by their absence. True, there were occasional memory-jerkers – most notably Jeff Stevenson's gem that carried Leeds to Wembley in 1957 after a 10–9 victory over plucky Whitehaven in the semi-final war of attrition at Odsal. Neil Fox's unparalleled feat of dropping three goals in Wakefield Trinity's 1962 Wembley triumph over Huddersfield caused a sensation because it was such a novelty.

The introduction of the four-tackle rule in 1966, later extended to six, brought the neglected drop-goal back into fashion and literally everyone seemed to be having a go, often to comical effect. From 1897 until 1974 the drop-goal had been worth two points and its return to the sport, encouraged by the limited tackles laws, was at first welcomed but the novelty soon wore off as people railed against the absurd proliferation of drop goal attempts as soon as the play-the-balls ran out. Its devaluation in 1974, perversely, did nothing to reduce the rash of goals dropped. In fact, the reverse applied with the figures rising from 49 goals dropped in the First Division in 1974–75 to 147 in 1980–81. In the Second Division the figure rose from 36 in 1974–75 to a monstrous 254 in 1983–84. For 20 or more years the drop goal was transformed from what was almost merely a figment of some old-timers' imaginations to an exercise in overkill.

The mania for dropping goals has diminished somewhat through the 1990s and first decade of the 21st century. That has been the result of changes in the laws - the four point try and handover in 1983, the emasculation of scrimmaging from 1989 onwards, the ten metre law in 1992 and subsequent alterations to the play-the-ball laws and the increasing use of substitutions. All have combined to radically alter the game. Teams now rarely bother to kick two-point penalty goals, never mind one-point drop goals. Despite the constantly trumpeted mantra that the modern game is characterised by awesome defences, it is in fact all too easy to score tries, so why bother chasing a solitary point, when four or six will be along shortly?

Of course, it was different back in the mists of time, when rugby football was in its infancy. In Victorian days goals alone decided the outcome of matches and the drop goal was a major match-winning device. When a points system was at last adopted by the Rugby Football Union in 1891–92 the drop-goal was fixed at four points - twice the value of a try, while a conversion counted three points. It was not until 1893–94 that the try was set at three points and the conversion lowered to two. Until 1897–98 the Northern Union retained the four-point drop-goal before reducing all goals to two points. The RFU persisted with the four-pointer until 1948–49.

At the dawn of rugby, therefore, the drop-goal was accorded almost paramount importance and its value reflected the degree of difficulty deemed to be inherent in its successful execution. In December 1882 *The Yorkshireman* noted in its *Football Chat* column: "There is a discussion now going on in a London weekly journal – entirely devoted to football topics - about the desirability of adopting the round in place of the oval ball for Rugby Union rules. Several football celebrities are in favour of the change on the grounds of dribbling being thereby facilitated; but surely that department of the game ranks second to drop-kicking, and everyone who has the right to an opinion admits the difficulty of dropping the round ball, while it is almost impossible to place-kick with it." Aesthetically, the goal dropped from the hand was considered more delightful to the eye than any amount of balls being carried over the goal-line, which, after all, were only the prelude to a "try at goal". Consequently, a proficient drop kicker in the Victorian era was worth his weight in gold and was often the archetypal "game-breaker".

There was no greater game-breaker than Albert Goldthorpe, whose drop-kicking exploits have possibly never been equalled in first class union or league. He was, arguably, the most deadly drop-goaler that either code of rugby has ever produced. Anyone wishing to refute such a claim would have a hard time producing evidence to the contrary. Modern claimants have the advantage of improved boot, ball and pitch technology, not to mention kicking coaching gurus. Goldthorpe was regarded as the greatest of "drops" in the epoch when drop-goaling was held in its highest esteem and when that art was fiendishly difficult in relation to the overall state of pitches, the wide variety of ball shapes and weights and the more claustrophobic nature of the game itself.

Goldthorpe's career was remarkable in that it spanned the years 1888 to 1910. It ran from the days before scoring values were adopted and when professional rugby was simply unthinkable, through the momentous breakaway of the Northern Union from the parent Rugby Football Union in 1895, to the game now recognisable, warts and all, as rugby league.

Albert Edward Goldthorpe was born on 3 November, 1871, nine months after the Rugby Football Union was founded. He was born into a family, which owned Urn Farm at Rothwell Haigh, Stourton, south of Leeds, and he worked on the land for most of his life. Sadly, James Goldthorpe, his father, died, aged 44, in 1876, leaving his wife Grace as head of the family and in charge of the farm, which encompassed 133 acres, according to the 1871 census. By the following census in 1881 the farm was recorded as stretching to 186 acres, employing six men.

Ahr Albert was the youngest but one of five brothers, all of whom played rugby for Hunslet. The eldest was William (born 28 August, 1864), the least distinguished as a player. He was followed by James (born 1 October, 1867), who developed into a dashing three-quarter and later became a first-class referee and secretary of the Leeds club, while also dabbling in rugby journalism. John Henry (born 26 September, 1869), also a three-quarter, played for Hunslet and Leeds Parish Church, then a power in the game. Youngest of the Goldthorpe clan was Walter (born 9 January, 1874), a full-back turned three-quarter, who fell little short of Albert's stature as an all-round footballer. Walter won 11 Yorkshire caps as a rugby union player after making his debut against Durham in 1891 at the tender age of 17 years and 10 months. Walter gave Hunslet almost two decades of sterling service before crossing the city to join Leeds, where he enhanced his reputation by helping the Loiners to lift the Challenge Cup for the first time in 1910.

All the boys attended Leeds Parish Church School. James actually taught at the school for a time and played briefly for the Leeds Parish Church club. Attendance at the school necessitated walking there and back twice a day, which no doubt aided their fitness regime. It was said that Albert also had to milk the cows before he left for school.

Of his introduction to the game of rugby Albert related in 1899: "We had a field and a ball of our own on my mother's farm down Pontefract Road and my four brothers and myself used to take what opportunities we could – and they were not a few – of practising football kicking and football tactics. That is the simple origin of the Goldthorpe family's connection with the game. For myself, goal-dropping, though partly a natural art, was perfected by long and constant practice."

He continued: "It was Alf Stephens … who was instrumental in introducing me to the Hunslet club. Stephens, who afterwards played with Leeds Parish Church, was then a member of the Hunslet second team, and played at three-quarter back. Being lame, he asked me if I would take his place in the team, and I did so, with the result that I dropped a goal, won the match, and received an invitation to play with the first team the following week."

A week later on 6 October, 1888, a month short of his 17th birthday, Ahr Albert made his debut in first-class rugby against Wortley. He turned out at full-back, a position he retained throughout the season.

Albert's debut at Wortley was hardly headline material because the newspapers were agog with stories concerning the meeting in Vienna of the German and Austrian Emperors, of yellow fever in Florida, of floods in France and Switzerland, of Jack the Ripper's horrific Whitechapel murders and of the Prince of Wales' meanderings in Bucharest. The sporting world's interest lay not in a young farmer from Stourton but in the visit of the first rugby touring team from New Zealand, quaintly referred to by one writer as "our kinsfolk of the under world."

The *Yorkshire Post* reported Hunslet's victory "at Oldfield Lane before several thousand spectators" by two goals, three minors to nil but gave no mention to Albert in the actual match report. He did, however, warrant his first press comment in the accompanying column devoted to a review of the principal Yorkshire matches. It simply noted, "A young recruit called Goldthorpe was tried at full-back and not found wanting." For the next 22 years Albert was rarely to be found wanting on the rugby field.

Albert's club Hunslet was barely five years old and had been the result of an amalgamation of two local clubs, Albion and Excelsior. They had been induced to share Hunslet Cricket Club's ground at Woodhouse Hill in 1883 but had moved to a new ground at Parkside just eight months before Albert's debut. Hunslet was widely regarded as a working men's club at a time when fixtures were often arranged on the perceived social status of an organisation. Consequently, they had to work hard to obtain fixtures against the elite clubs of Yorkshire and beyond. Hunslet were amongst the ranks of the second class clubs, meeting local rivals such as Kirkstall, Holbeck, Bramley and Morley, sometimes going as far afield as Selby and York, but not encountering the elite teams of Yorkshire such as Bradford, Dewsbury, Halifax, Huddersfield, Leeds St John's and Wakefield Trinity.

In the 1889–90 season Hunslet shook up the established order in Yorkshire rugby by reaching the semi-finals of the Yorkshire Cup. On the way they dispatched Dudley Hill, Ossett, Castleford and Halifax. Albert had become so indispensable to Hunslet that he was persuaded to play in the semi-final on 29 March 1890, against Huddersfield at Dewsbury, despite being so lame that his ankle was immersed in cold water for half-an-hour before taking the field. On this occasion there was no happy ending as Huddersfield ran away with the game, scoring five goals, three tries and four minors to Hunslet's one try and 10 minors – a massive victory margin.

It was in this, his second season at Parkside, that Albert moved into the centre position and began dropping goals in earnest, landing 18 from his new position. In the six seasons remaining to him as a rugby unionist he dropped no fewer than 73 goals, his most productive campaign being 1891–92 when he potted 19 for Hunslet.

Such was his propensity for winning matches that he was soon a marked man. At St Helens in 1890 it was reported that "from a drop-out Goldthorpe made his mark exactly on the centre-line and after going a few yards back dropped a magnificent goal from within his own half."

18 January 1890: Albert drops a goal from halfway to draw a game against Heckmondwike. 10,000 supporters were present. (Both cartoons from *The Yorkshireman*)

22 March 1890: Albert drops a goal in a Yorkshire Cup tie against Halifax. A record crowd for Parkside of about 26,400 attended.

Some observers asserted that Albert specialised in dropping goals from close range, often following scrummages, but match reports over the whole of his career frequently describe goals dropped from half-way or beyond, left and right-footed. In 1945 the distinguished sports writer, VAS Beanland wrote of Goldthorpe's dropping abilities: "His gift of seizing the opportunity and his accuracy of aim have never, in my experience, been equalled. The expansive smile and the little flick of the hand as the ball sailed over the cross-bar will always remain with me as a memory. I have so often seen them both." (*Great Games and Great Players*, WH Allen & Co)

One team that Albert belaboured even more than most with his match-winning drops was Brighouse Rangers. In a game played in 1891 the Brighouse three-quarter, Lewis Brooke was given the task of watching Albert to ensure that he did not drop any goals. Albert, true to form, landed a couple and after the match it was put to Brooke that he had not watched his opponent closely enough. Brooke's reply was irrefutable: "Oh, yes, I did. I saw him drop both the goals!"

On 24 October, 1891 Albert dropped no fewer than five goals, placing two more into the bargain, in a 36–0 victory over Kendal at Parkside, his best haul of drops. Apart from his artistry as a goal-dropper, he was also a wonderful place kicker. His greatest performance in this respect occurred on 1 March, 1890, in a Yorkshire Cup-tie against Dudley Hill, when he landed 14 conversions from 15 attempts – seven in each half. For good measure he also ran in four tries. Under modern values Hunslet would have won 88–0 and Albert would have amassed 44 points. If the scoring system introduced a year later were to have operated, he would have scored 50. The *Yorkshire Post*, not normally given to sensationalism, contented itself by declaring, "this is truly prodigious" as "Hunslet cut the record."

Soon enough Ahr Albert was catching the eye of the Yorkshire Rugby Union selectors. That in itself was a high compliment as the playing power base of the English international team lay in the northern counties in general and in Yorkshire in particular. The wearers of the white rose carried almost all before them in the period 1889 to 1896, failing to win the County Championship only in 1890–91, when Lancashire took the title. Albert made his Yorkshire debut against Durham at Hull on 14 November, 1891, 11 days before his 20th birthday. The Yorkshire team for his debut was: Walter Goldthorpe (Hunslet); Lockwood (Heckmondwike), Albert Goldthorpe (Hunslet), Dyson (Huddersfield); Paisley (Huddersfield), Stadden (Dewsbury); Bedford (Wakefield Trinity), Bradshaw (Bramley), Broadley (Bingley), Bromet (Tadcaster), captain, Dewhirst (Bradford), Fletcher (Halifax), Jowett (Heckmondwike), Nicholl (Brighouse Rangers) and Toothill (Bradford).

Albert placed three goals in a comfortable 17–7 victory. Despite the result the critics were not too enthralled by Yorkshire's display, apparently expecting miracles every time the Tykes took the field. Albert was not treated too harshly, however, one reporter writing, "As to A Goldthorpe, he received three passes from the scrimmage side, one going over his head and the other two along the ground. It would be unfair therefore to pass any decided opinion upon his capabilities except just to say that he negotiated three places and dropped well, though not always into touch. Personally we think he did creditably considering the four three-quarter opposition he had to contend against."

Two points from this quotation are worthy of explanation. First, the reference to the fact that Albert "dropped well", not at goal but in general play, is a reminder that drop-kicking was regarded as the mark of a stylist. Punting the ball had still not been accepted as quite the done thing. In other words, it was decidedly not stylish, perhaps even "bad form". For a player to be described as "a good drop" or to have "dropped well" was a high compliment, which persisted well into the era of the Northern Union. Secondly, Albert was literally "the" centre three-quarter as Yorkshire still clung to the three three-quarter system, a system which had been discarded by the Welsh and some of the English teams of the north-east in favour of the four three-quarter line. Although Yorkshire's forward power was still stiflingly effective – nine men still in the pack – even the *Yorkshire Post* was moved to say after Yorkshire's 5–5 draw with Glamorgan at Fartown in November 1892 that "the days of long slow passing have gone by, sharp rushes and quick half-back play being most effective and greatly appreciated from an onlooker's point of view." In that game Albert had rescued Yorkshire from defeat against the upstart Welsh by creating and converting a try for the English international wing, Jack Dyson, ten minutes from time.

In his second game for the county Albert found himself elevated to the captaincy. England were due to play Ireland on 6 February, 1892, the same day as Yorkshire were to engage Cheshire at Birkenhead. With several Tykes in the England XV the Yorkshire committee decided to select an entirely new team and placed Albert in charge, just three months past his 21st birthday.

This "Second XV" did Yorkshire proud, going down only 13–12 in the last minute, the county's only defeat in nine games that season. Of the young captain the *Yorkshire Post* noted, "Goldthorpe shone, for when a smart drop was required he was always to the front."

A fortnight later he was Yorkshire's centre three-quarter in a famous 4–0 victory over England at Headingley, Yorkshire having again taken the County Championship. The photograph of Albert in the Yorkshire XV, alongside such icons of the game as Dickie Lockwood (Heckmondwike), Harry Bradshaw (Bramley), Tom Broadley (Bingley) and Jack Dyson (Huddersfield), portrays a young man of cherubic countenance, who hardly looked old enough or robust enough to withstand the rigours of so fearsome a recreation as rugby football. A massive crowd of 20,479 packed into Headingley on a fine, but frosty, afternoon.

Albert's brother Walter was Yorkshire's full-back and Albert's two wingers were Lockwood and Dyson. Donald Jowett (Heckmondwike), Yorkshire's famously massive forward, scored his side's first try close to the posts just before half-time but Albert unaccountably missed the conversion. He may not have felt so bad, however, when Lockwood missed a similarly easy conversion after forward Billy Nichol (Brighouse Rangers) scored Yorkshire's second try. In truth though, Albert, who had come in for the originally selected Tommy Summersgill (Leeds), did not perform as well as expected. The *Yorkshire Post* reported, "Albert Goldthorpe spoiled the whole combination. He dropped and dribbled well at times, but at others his running was painfully slow, and besides his passing was almost a dead letter, the tenacious manner in which he stuck to the ball losing Yorkshire two capital chances of scoring."

In the following season, 1892–93, Albert found time to represent Leeds in the Yorkshire Tradesmen's Challenge Cup competition, which was played on Thursday afternoons.

Hunslet 1892 Yorkshire Cup winners. Standing: Bennett, J Goldthorpe, Moore, Skirrow, Groves, W Goldthorpe; Seated: Liversedge, A Goldthorpe, Kaye, Lapping (capt), Mosley, Rathmell
Front: Townsend, Gilston, Wright

The Yorkshire team (County Champions) who beat England by two tries to nil in 1892.
Back: J Toothill, E Dewhirst, W Nichol, D Jowett, F Wood, W Goldthorpe, Barron Kilner (President);
Middle: H Bradshaw, H Varley, WE Bromet, T Broadley, E Redman;
Front: A Briggs, J Dyson, RE Lockwood, A Goldthorpe.

Left: Albert had his own visiting cards in 1892, for business (left) and as a Yorkshire County rugby footballer (right).

1892 Yorkshire Cup semi-final at Halifax: Hunslet (white jerseys) versus Liversedge.

Yorkshire versus Lancashire 24 November 1894 at Manchester. Standing: Hirst (Secretary), Donaldson, Barraclough, Nowell, Jack Riley (Halifax), Walton, Miller (President) Seated: Broadley, Arnold, Tooting (captain), Jackson, Dobson, Firth; Front: J Riley (Leeds), Rigg, Cooper, Ward

Similar Tradesmen's Cups were staged in other Yorkshire and Lancashire towns – usually under the local half-day shop closing arrangement. At a higher level, Albert represented Yorkshire against Lancashire, Durham, Devon, Glamorgan and Northumberland, amassing three tries, six conversions, a penalty and four drop-goals, as Yorkshire retained their title.

However, he again experienced a harrowing afternoon against Durham at Hartlepool as Yorkshire continued to persist in playing three against four three-quarters. Even so, Yorkshire won, 13–7.

Fifteen years later Albert recalled the game in a *Yorkshire Evening Post* interview: "My most memorable county match was against Durham at Hartlepool. We were playing three three-quarters, but as Durham were playing four, I had opposite to me those two big players Alderson [who was captain of England] and Bell. All the same I managed to [kick three goals] and get a try and we just won." Ironically, Albert was missing when Yorkshire easily beat Middlesex down at Richmond on 30 January, 1893 and operated with four three-quarters for the first time. Yorkshire finally abandoned the three three-quarter formation for the 1893–94 season, reputedly on the advice of Dickie Lockwood, the county's captain. By then Albert Goldthorpe had played his last county match under rugby union auspices, having gained eight caps.

Ahr Albert was one of those working men caught in the middle of the momentous controversy over "broken-time", which shattered the Rugby Union and gave birth to the Northern Union. When the rugby equivalent of Armageddon dawned in 1895 Hunslet and the Goldthorpe clan were in no doubt as to which way to jump. Hunslet had developed into a prominent club in the Yorkshire Senior Competition, which had unashamedly operated a league table since September 1892, the same year in which Hunslet carried off their first trophy by defeating their arch rivals Leeds 21–0 in the final of the Yorkshire Cup at Fartown. A crowd of 15,484 was ample evidence that competitive rugby could generate sufficient funds to reimburse players for broken-time. In fact Hunslet had played before a crowd estimated at close on 20,000 in the semi-final at Halifax, where they had defeated Liversedge 12–3, while Leeds had sneaked past Wakefield Trinity 2–0 at Bradford before 15,462 spectators. In the earlier rounds, Leeds had accounted for Wakefield St Austen's 70–2, Kirkstall 17–5, Halifax 9–6 and Bowling 26–2.

Hunslet had a relatively comfortable route on their way to the semi-finals. Their first tie, on 19 March, saw Birstall demolished 41–0 at Parkside, Hunslet running riot with 15 tries. The goal-kicking was, however, lamentable. Albert managed just two conversions from seven attempts. His brother James added another. Walter Goldthorpe did convert a try "but the referee blowing his whistle for no charge, he failed at the second attempt!"

The following week, Bramley were beaten 24–0 at Parkside after a scoreless first half. This time Albert's kicking was immaculate as he improved all four of his side's tries, while Walter Goldthorpe dropped a four-point goal "from the centre". On 2 April Hunslet journeyed to Belle Vue, Wakefield where they encountered Alverthorpe. The Three Hunslet three-quarters were Goldthorpe, Goldthorpe and Goldthorpe – James, Albert and Walter. Hunslet won 30–2, largely due to the brothers' scoring. Albert kicked four conversions and a penalty, James bagged a hat-trick of tries and Walter added a try and conversion.

The quarter-final, on 9 April, pitted Hunslet away to Brighouse Rangers, who fully expected to oust the Parksiders from the tournament. In perfect conditions Hunslet completely turned the tables, their forwards pushing, rushing and wheeling their opposing pack to distraction. Four Goldthorpe brothers took the field together. Walter was full-back, Albert centre and James and John on the wings. Hunslet scored three tries to two in a 13–4 win, Albert booting two conversions in a engagement that was far easier than any Hunslet follower could have hoped for. One press report declared, "Brighouse had paid the penalty for over-training."

As outlined above, the semi-final against Liversedge at Halifax ended in a comfortable victory for Goldthorpe & Co. After falling behind to a sixth-minute penalty goal from Ben Sharpe, Hunslet quickly established domination in the forwards and Liversedge's defence was found wanting. James Goldthorpe set Hunslet on the right path with a magnificent try from his own half but it was generally agreed that Albert was the best back on view. He gave Hunslet the lead when he kicked a penalty after being obstructed as he chased his own kick and with a minute to the half-time whistle, he grabbed a loose ball near half-way and engineered a clever try for James Goldthorpe. Albert tacked on the conversion to stretch Hunslet's advantage to 8–3. In the second half Hunslet added two unconverted tries without reply from Liversedge. The first was due to an enormous kick by Albert from a scrum. He followed up and nailed Lister, the Liversedge full-back, on the "25". The ensuing scrum saw Hunslet forward Skirrow dashing over for the try. Another mistake by Lister resulted in the final try, half-back Charlie Lapping charging down his clearance kick and scoring an easy try.

The final, on 23 April, 1892, was a something of a clash of cultures. Hunslet, south of the River Aire, working class, industrial, and with no pretensions to grandeur at homely Parkside, were pitted against Leeds, north of the river, who had moved into stately Headingley in 1890, having evolved from the former Leeds St John's club. Leeds had plenty of money, patronage and high ambitions. In a way it was the plebs *versus* the toffs, the hoi poloi against the hoity-toity, David against Goliath. None of which mattered because Hunslet still started as favourites. It was reported that 4,863 people travelled on special trains from Leeds to Huddersfield, most of whom must have been from Hunslet, according to the newspapers, who said that the Leeds fans at Fartown were markedly outnumbered.

The Goldthorpes contributed in no small measure to Hunslet's annexation of the Yorkshire Cup. All but William had played in the semi-final – one of only two occasions on which four of the brothers played together for the club. In the final Albert and Walter each scored a try, while James got two, one being a sensational effort covering almost the length of the Fartown pitch. Albert also converted three of the team's five tries.

The Parksiders turned out in "spotless white" jerseys and knickers with magenta stockings, which provided a vivid contrast to Leeds, who sported "blue jerseys and green pants". Although Hunslet had looked the better team, surprisingly no score had accrued at half-time. Albert had failed with three drops and a penalty attempt, but after the break the floodgates burst open. The *Huddersfield Examiner* reported admiringly: "Every [Hunslet] man seemed as strong as a horse, as fast as a deer, and as tough as a rhinoceros, and every man did his full share of work, both in and out of the scrummage ... It was as fair and square a licking as anyone could wish to see."

The Yorkshireman was equally enthusiastic and commented, "Four tries among three brothers is a fair contribution to an afternoon's work, and shows the value of a family combination. The best try of the day was James Goldthorpe's great run from his own '25', but Albert's sprint through the Leeds backs was not much behind in point of merit. Poor Tommy Summersgill was completely outshadowed for once, and the 'great rivals' controversy ended in a big triumph for Albert. The success of the latter was very soothing to Hunslet nerves, no doubt. But the question arises, what would Tommy have done behind the same forwards? Don't ignore that question, ye jubilant Parksiders."

Albert's stock was sky high and, even though he was still a mere 20 years old, a reporter at the 1892 Yorkshire Cup Final noted, "Hero-worship in the football world is a candidly admitted fact. One player for instance has his biography written and sold in the streets for the small price of one penny. It is a tempting biography if there was much space for quotation. Albert Goldthorpe, who did such splendid service for Hunslet on Saturday, is, we are informed, 'undoubtedly one of the finest centre three-quarters that ever donned a football jersey'. His admirers are, of course, legion and are to be found among people who, 'though they delight to see the Hunslet lads get licked, yet they cannot but acknowledge that the Hunslet crack plays a game that delights not only his friends, but also those who turn up with the hope of seeing his team get the knock'."

Albert's status seems to have been confirmed in the evening of the match when the team took the Yorkshire Challenge Cup to their headquarters, The Anchor Hotel: "Several thousand people had collected there, and it was with considerable difficulty that the players could make their way from the waggonettes into the building. The scene was of the wildest enthusiasm. The appearance of Albert Goldthorpe at one of the upper windows was the signal for a thunderous cheer, which was renewed with equal vigour on Lapping [the captain] exhibiting the challenge cup."

For Albert and for Hunslet the 1892 Yorkshire Cup triumph represented the high-water mark of achievement under rugby union laws. As alluded to above, the 1892–93 season brought the innovation of league rugby, as the leading clubs in Yorkshire and Lancashire set up the Yorkshire Senior Competition and the Lancashire Club Championship. Both comprised 10 clubs. In Yorkshire, Hunslet vied for the title with Batley, Bradford, Brighouse Rangers, Dewsbury, Halifax, Huddersfield, Liversedge, Manningham and Wakefield Trinity. The clamour for league competition was such that a Yorkshire Second Competition was also formed consisting of 10 more clubs – Bramley, Cleckheaton, Elland, Holbeck, Kirkstall, Leeds Parish Church, Morley, Otley, Pontefract and Wortley.

Hunslet put up a good show in the inaugural Yorkshire Senior Competition. They finished runners-up to Bradford. The top four finished:

	W	L	D	F	A	Pts
1 Bradford	14	4	0	106	76	28
2 Hunslet	10	5	3	135	76	23
3 Halifax	10	6	2	92	57	22
4 Batley	9	6	3	98	77	21

Hunslet were intent on keeping the holy grail of the Yorkshire Challenge Cup. On 7 February, 1893 *The Yorkshireman* noted, "Joe Moore, the genial boniface of the Anchor Hotel [Hunslet's headquarters], recently gave his annual treat to the Hunslet players, several friends being also there. A good spread was made upstairs in the club-room and festivities followed galore. There have been doubts expressed about Hunslet retaining possession of the Cup. Just go up to Boilerdom and ask if there is any question about it there. The old tin-pot is safely ensconced in a walnut box with a glass front in the smoke room of the Anchor, and it has got its likeness taken too. Hunslet believe in keeping a thing once they have got it."

Hunslet's high hopes were maintained when their attempt to retain the Yorkshire Cup began with a 2–0 home win against Huddersfield on 18 March, 1893, followed a week later by a 4–0 win at Leeds Parish Church in the second round. However, April Fools' Day saw a 10–2 knock-out for Albert's team at Manningham in the third round. The trophy was removed from its walnut sanctuary and returned to the Yorkshire Rugby Football Union, from where it would soon find its way to Halifax, who beat Batley in the final of 1893.

Albert made 33 appearances in all games (YSC and friendlies), kicking 40 goals, 13 of which were dropped. He also scored 11 tries, his best return in his entire career and the only time he reached double figures as a try-scorer.

Hunslet disappointingly dropped to seventh in the Yorkshire Senior Competition in 1893–94, when Hull and Leeds were admitted to the elite competition, having shied away from it the previous season. Manningham and Brighouse Rangers tied at the top with 33 points from their 22 fixtures. Hunslet had mustered only 21 points (9 wins, 3 draws and 10 defeats). A play-off to decide the title was arranged at Halifax on 14 March, 1894 but a scoreless draw ensued. Manningham finally became champions, when they won the replay 9–3 at Wakefield five days later.

The Yorkshire Cup also provided disappointment for Hunslet. A trip to Ripon in the first round on 17 March was easily negotiated with a 31–11 victory. The following Saturday for the second round Hunslet confidently journeyed east to meet Hull Kingston Rovers, who were a third tier club, operating in the lower reaches of the Yorkshire Intermediate Competition. A crowd of 12,000 was astonished but joyous as Rovers caused an enormous shock by winning 9–3. Still, that was what the Yorkshire Cup was all about – giants crushing dwarves, or in this case, minnows gobbling the big fish.

Albert Goldthorpe had a decent season with Hunslet, however. His 38 appearances had yielded 38 goals (8 dropped) but only four tries. On the other hand, he had lost his place in Yorkshire's XV, an indication perhaps of Hunslet's comparative fall from grace. Hunslet's only county man during the season was their stalwart forward Owen Walsh, who appeared in all eight of Yorkshire's fixtures.

On 26 March 1894, Hunslet played Belfast Albion at Parkside. It was notable for being the last time Hunslet would play an Irish XV. They had first played Belfast Albion, holders of the Ulster Challenge Cup, on 22 April, 1889, also at Parkside, before a crowd of "fully 5,000". Hunslet's victory was large – three goals and three tries to a solitary try. Albert had played on the wing against the Irishmen and landed a conversion. In 1891 Albert had been in Hunslet XVs, which had beaten Lansdowne 12–0 in Dublin on Tuesday, 27 October, Albert contributing two conversions, but then lost 0–4 two days later against Belfast Albion at the North of Ireland Grounds.

Albert retained happy memories of such trips. Of the 1891 jaunt, he recalled years later: "I remember the Hunslet team going on tour in Ireland one time. We had been doing very well, and when we appeared against Belfast Albion we had got very 'big heads'. But weren't we humiliated! We dropped across 'Sammy' Lees, the Irish International, in his best form, and didn't he make us look like school kids!

Talking about that Irish trip, it used to be the custom with Hunslet to have at least one tour every season. That, of course, was in the amateur days, though nobody, of course, objected to receiving wages for broken time whilst on tour. We had some splendid times. I don't think any Hunslet man of the period will ever forget those lively trips we had to Belfast, Galashiels and the Isle of Man. They could always get together two good teams in the Isle of Man in those days, and Arthur Paul, the old Swinton and Lancashire county man, used to be one of their best players.

Stories, do you want? I could tell them for hours but this I think is the best. It was at the Imperial Hotel in Belfast. A Hunslet player asked the waiter to bring him a serviette. His neighbour, a burly forward, not to be outdone, called back the waiter, and this is what he said: 'Here! Bring me two, lad. If he can eat one, I can manage two'.

I suppose I had better give you the parallel story, the scene of which is laid in the Metropole at Newcastle. A waiter asked me whether I would have cod or sole. I took cod and enjoyed it. Presently the footballer on my right was asked whether he would have cod or sole. 'Nayther', he said, 'Bring me a bit a fish like Albert's hed'."

The 1894–95 season was an improvement on the previous campaign. Hunslet jumped a place to sixth in the Yorkshire Senior Competition. Liversedge (34 points) just edged out Manningham (32) to win the title. They were followed by Bradford (28), Leeds (25) and Halifax (24). Hunslet also totalled 24 points (11 wins, 2 draws, 9 defeats) but had an inferior points average to Halifax.

The Yorkshire Cup brought some joy and a lot of trouble to Hunslet in 1895. Skipton were hammered 26–0 at Parkside on 16 March, 1895 in the first round, Albert notching three conversions. Pudsey were downed 7–0 in the second round, also at Parkside. The latter game was an extremely rough affair. Pudsey would shortly be crowned Champions of the Yorkshire Third Competition and normally would have been considered easy meat for a team of Hunslet's status but put up a terrific fight – literally. The game was so heated that Hunslet's minutes book posed the question as to whether it would be possible to discover if there was any truth in a claim that a Pudsey player had been paid to injure Albert Goldthorpe. Albert had left the field almost as soon as the game began after being kicked on the thigh. In his absence Robinson scored a brilliant try for Hunslet. Albert returned before half-time just in time to end the scoring with a four-point goal from a mark.

The third round took Hunslet back to Hull Kingston Rovers on 30 March but this time Hunslet held their nerve and emerged 13–7 winners in a much more civilised encounter. The Rovers played above themselves but conceded three tries, two of which Albert improved. The fourth round – the quarter finals - on 6 April, brought Brighouse Rangers to Parkside. Rangers had finished one place and one point below Hunslet in the YSC, so a tight game was likely. It was certainly a dramatic affair with Hunslet forward Mosley being sent off after one of the Rangers half-backs was clobbered. Soon after the dismissal Brighouse got the only points, a try from their England international forward Billy Nichol condemning Hunslet to a 3–0 defeat. If the result was bad enough, the repercussions of a fractious match were disastrous for Hunslet. Or they would have been had fate, in the shape of the Northern Rugby Football Union, not come to the rescue.

The game ended in chaotic scenes. Many Hunslet fans were incensed about the referee's handling of the game. Mr W Rayner (Batley) had penalised Hunslet to distraction. Half-back Jack Mitchell had persisted in feeding the scrum crookedly, despite being told that he would be penalised every time he did it. Imagine that – a referee actually penalising a scrum-half for putting the ball into his own forwards' feet at a scrum. How quaint. As Mr Rayner left the field he was struck on the shoulder as spectators milled about him. Players, officials and 21 policemen, under Inspector Vincent, escorted him to the cricket pavilion. The trouble did not end there for he was struck by a flying piece of iron when he crossed the cricket field. He got into a waggonette, accompanied by police and Brighouse players and officials. A mob of about 300 was still on his tail and a half brick whizzed into the waggonette, hitting half-back George Schofield on the head. A couple of policemen were also injured by flying stones,

Inevitably, there were serious consequences. Five spectators, all aged between 17 and 28, were arrested. All appeared in court and got the choice of 21 days jail or a £2 fine. Hunslet and Brighouse were summoned to appear before the Yorkshire Rugby Union Committee at their Green Dragon Hotel headquarters in Leeds on the evening of Tuesday, 9 April. The upshot was the suspension of Parkside until November. The cup-tie against Brighouse thus became Albert Goldthorpe's last game of rugby union at Parkside, as well as the club's. Hunslet were, however, scheduled to play their final games of the season away from home. On Tuesday, 16 April, a local derby at Leeds Parish Church, which Albert missed, resulted in a 4–0 defeat for Hunslet. Hunslet's final game as a rugby union club took place at Lancaster on Saturday, 27 April, 1895. Fittingly enough, Albert dropped a goal in Hunslet's 7–3 victory. An era had ended.

A Baines card featuring Albert Goldthorpe.

As well as playing rugby, Albert was an accomplished cricketer and captained Hunslet Cricket Club.

2. Into the Northern Union

The Great Schism of 1895, which spawned rugby league, legitimised payment to players for broken-time. It did not yet represent open professionalism – no more than six shillings was allowed – but it was, inevitably, the thin end of the wedge. The satirical magazine *The Yorkshireman* (2 November, 1895) remarked, tongue in cheek, as usual, "Kidnapping is being gradually promoted into an enterprise in Northern Union football. It is remarkable how many men are being brought into Yorkshire – for six shillings a week."

Albert's view of the new-fangled Northern Union was clearly stated in an interview published in 1899 in *Yorkshire Chat, A Weekly Journal For All Yorkshire Folk*, in which he said, "I think the formation of the Northern Union was a fine thing for Yorkshire. It has made all above board, and done away with the 'sailing under false colours' that was carried on to such an extent by clubs in the old Rugby Union in regard to paying players. There is now none of the humbug that we had to contend with. It is a question (if professional, of course) of paying players openly, which is considerably better for all concerned. Then, again, the alteration of the rules has made accidents to players less liable, especially so when the referee rules with a stern hand; and, so far as I am concerned, I can assure you that I prefer the Northern Union in every way to the fast declining old Yorkshire Rugby Union."

His views had not changed by the time he approached retirement. In 1907 he told the *Yorkshire Evening Post*, "I was a pure amateur for a long time. All I got was 18 pence for my tea when we were away from home, and, personally, I think I had no other desire than to continue as an amateur. I could see, however, what a sham it all was. I myself was offered a big inducement to leave Hunslet, and play for another big Yorkshire club, who would have paid me well. When, therefore, the open professional movement was started, I was hand-in-glove with it. I don't believe in this hypocrisy, and I believe today, that professionalism, with all its alleged failures, is the best thing that could have happened to Yorkshire football. I can certainly speak of the good effect professionalism has had upon players. Take, for example, our players at Hunslet – many of them teetotallers, who are encouraged to lead a steady and sober life, because they know if they abuse themselves, they will be dropped out of the team.

From a sentimental point of view professionalism may not be 'the thing', but there can be no doubt that it has improved Yorkshire football in many ways. Of course, if I had my way, there would be no professional footballers, who did not also follow a regular occupation. The man who plays football on a Saturday and lounges about the rest of the week is apt to get into bad ways, and his money disappears quickly. I know the system in vogue now [1907] gives men a licence to play football without working, and that is one of the evils of the present Northern Union rules; but, at the same time, open professionalism, as we have it today, is far better than the veiled professionalism of the old days."

By 1895 Hunslet was one of the top clubs of Yorkshire, at least in the playing sense. Since the Yorkshire Senior Competition's foundation in 1892–93, Hunslet had figured prominently in it. As we have seen, in the YSC's first season Hunslet had been runners-up to Bradford, subsequently finishing seventh in 1893–94 and sixth in 1894–95 and thereby cementing their status as an elite club. When 22 northern clubs seceded from the Rugby Football Union on 29 August 1895, Hunslet were among them. They had a bigger incentive to join than most because of the RFU's decision to suspend Parkside from hosting matches until November. The suspension would certainly have cost the club hundreds of pounds in lost gate revenue. Hunslet fared well in the early years of the new game and Albert established himself as one of its leading lights. Oddly enough, Albert missed Hunslet's historic first fixture in the Northern Union, a 5–4 loss at Warrington on 7 September 1895, as he was still playing cricket.

Ironically, Hunslet's only score in the match was a four-point drop-goal kicked by his brother Walter. Albert's Northern Union debut followed the following Saturday, 14 September, when he began making up for lost time by landing two conversions and a penalty in a 16–8 home win against Oldham. In the first eight seasons of Northern Union football figures show that he dropped 125 goals, his biggest haul being 29 in 1897–98 and 21 issuing from his magic boots in 1900–01.

By January 1904, Albert was reliably reckoned to have dropped 204 goals in his career for Hunslet under both codes and, although subsequent records are incomplete, it is evident that he must have landed 250 to 300 drop-goals by the time he retired in 1910. Incidentally, Albert retired or threatened to retire almost as often as Frank Sinatra is supposed to have done, but kept coming back for more. The last four-point drop goal that Albert negotiated came in a 7–0 victory over Batley at Parkside on 13 March, 1897, a game in which he scored all the points. Four days later it fell to him to kick Hunslet's last three-point penalty goal in an 8–3 home defeat by Hull. Albert's drop goal figures are taken from an article that appeared in the *Yorkshire Evening Post* on 30 January 1904. They apply to Hunslet matches only.

Rugby Union

Season	Drop-goals
1889–90	18
1890-91	9
1891–92	19
1892–93	13
1893–94	8
1894-95	6
Total	**73**

* (1903–04 at 23 January 1904)

Northern Union

Season	Drop-goals
1895-96	5
1896–97	7
1897–98	29
1898-99	16
1899–1900	13
1900–01	21
1901–02	16
1902–03	18
1903–04*	6
Total	**131**

Hunslet 1895–96: Back: A Mawson, O Walsh, H Barraclough, J Deacon, W Eno, J E Hughes, T Leach, W Greenwood; middle: W Goldthorpe, R Rubry, A E Goldthorpe, W Hannah, E Kaye; front: H Robinson, J W Wright, T Gillings, J Mitchell, E Fletcher, W H Gilston (President).

Left: A Baines card of Charlie Lapping and 'Ahr Albert'.

Right: An 1899 drawing of Albert Goldthorpe.

Around 1925, a decade and a half after he had retired from playing, Albert told an interviewer, "I was always trying to drop goals, for in my early days they were of more points value than today, and you know you can sometimes drop goals when it is impossible to score a try. There is no royal road to success in goal-kicking, and my advice to the aspirant is to persevere and practise. One great essential is to be able to kick with either foot. Unless you attain this, opportunities will be limited. Another necessary factor is confidence. Keep on the look-out for opportunity and you will find that goal-kicking is a pleasurable and profitable pastime."

The interviewer noted, "In his playing days Albert Goldthorpe was a farmer. His work took him into the open, and his job was undoubtedly a healthy one." In response, Albert commented, "I believe in a player's following some useful occupation during the week. A player who follows a regular and steady occupation need not worry overmuch about special preparation for Rugby football. Have regular habits. Only eat and drink what you know by experience agrees with you – not what you like, bear in mind. I always cut out smoking on the morning of the match, for smoking directly before a game affects the 'wind'."

The latter remark contradicts what many have written or said about Albert's virtues, i.e. that he was both a teetotaller and a non-smoker. They may well have had the former right but presumably not the latter.

The establishment of the Northern Union, though financially recompensing working men, prevented players with international aspirations from fulfilling them. The first Northern Union international match was not staged until 1904 by which time Albert was almost 33 and no longer the whilom, flaxen-haired youth depicted in the photograph of the Yorkshire XV of 1892. Nonetheless, he retained his fitness to a marked degree throughout his career. Never the fastest of players, his weight was recorded at 12 stones 3 pounds in 1899 and by 1908, when he was 37, it had risen to only 12 stones 10 pounds, his height being 5 feet 6 inches. Albert's fitness was probably a major factor in his imperviousness to injury. In 1904, after 16 years of top-grade rugby, it was reported that he had only twice suffered injuries of any severity – a small fracture of an ankle-bone sustained in trying to drop a third goal against Brighouse Rangers and a broken rib in a local derby against Holbeck at Elland Road. A pious comment by *Old Ebor* (AW Pullen), doyen of Yorkshire rugby scribes, asserted, "his immunity from serious damage is substantial proof that the men who play football well have nothing to fear."

Goldthorpe could certainly play football well. If anyone ever had educated feet it must have been Albert. Apart from his mastery of all forms of kicking, he was renowned for his skill as a dribbler at a time when that art still flourished. He captained Hunslet from their entry into the Northern Union until he retired 15 years later. VAS Beanland described him as "a considerate, courteous and able captain. He was quite unselfish and, though the easy dropped goal appealed to him so much, he was a great artist in making tries for others … A trim figure, with fair hair and a pleasant smiling face, he never seemed to be ruffled in the fiercest of fights, and in the very many matches in which I saw him play he never, so far as I could observe, lost his temper or descended to a shady trick."

In his days as a centre – he settled at half-back in 1901 – Albert often partnered a fine Cumbrian winger, Billy Hannah, whose association with Hunslet lasted even longer than his own. Hannah joined Hunslet in January 1895 and was granted a second benefit that realised £443 in 1945, when he was still on the training staff. With a name like Hannah, the winger was a ready source of mirth to the rugby fraternity, if not to his opponents. *Clito*, correspondent of the *Halifax Daily Guardian*, writing in the days when rugby reporters had space and licence enough to describe anything from the journey to the ground to the latest in scurrilous gossip about the players, wrote this of a Halifax-Hunslet game in 1897:

"'Sithee', said a Tup while the match was in progress, 'look at Ben Whiteley cuddling Hannah!' "

"'Wheear?' said an anxious beauty in female garb, 'Shoo must be a brazen-faced beggar wi all thee as fowk abaat'. And the girl could not be pacified until she was told that Hannah was a male man."

Hannah was "male man" enough to top the list of Northern Union try-scorers in 1896–97 and run in a career century of tries as a Parksider.

Albert's and Hunslet's first taste of success under the Northern Union was their lifting of the Yorkshire Senior Competition Championship Shield in 1897–98 when, after finishing level with Bradford at the top of the table, a play-off was arranged to decide the championship, thereby helping to start the mania that rugby league has slavishly developed for such matches. The tie was set for 30 April at Headingley. Such were the conventions of the day that the *Yorkshire Post* was moved to declare, "serious football on the last day of April is unnatural." It was also suggested that "a reduction in the competition programme is desirable." That cry has been heard ever since. It is interesting to note that the Yorkshire Senior Competition required the fulfilment of 30 fixtures, while the Lancashire Senior Competition entailed a mere 26 and the only other obligations the clubs had to meet were NU Challenge Cup-ties. One shudders to think what the founding fathers of the game would think of the fixture gluts of succeeding generations.

Whether or not the last day of April was an unnatural time for playing rugby, the elements disagreed and it was wet, cold and miserable with the Headingley pitch a mud heap. Despite the atrocious conditions, the game was wonderfully good and a vindication of the new rules, which were beginning to distinguish the new game from the parent form. Bradford, who had lost in the Challenge Cup Final to Batley on the same ground a week earlier, deservedly led 2–0 at half-time through a penalty kicked by their Welsh wingman, Fred Cooper.

The *Yorkshire Post* reported, "Hunslet practically had only two periods of attack in this half. In the one case A Goldthorpe would probably have scored had he not been unfairly tackled when he had dribbled past the opposition, an incident the referee failed to penalise. In the other, the same player had a drop at goal which went wide of the mark." Hunslet, however, were a trifle fortunate to win the match 5–2 on the hour mark, when a disputed "punt-out" from touch (the line-out having been abolished) resulted in their Scottish forward Jim Ramage dribbling from half-way for the winning try, to which Albert added the goal.

The *Yorkshire Post* summed up the game thus, "Though beaten, Bradford certainly had not the worst of the play, taking it all through. They are fully entitled to sympathy, yet at the same time no one can begrudge or question the merit of the Hunslet team's success." Of Albert's contribution, it stated, "Save for some good fielding and kicking by Albert Goldthorpe, the Hunslet three-quarter line by no means distinguished itself. On the other hand, Mitchell was a tower of strength in the last line of defence, and if he had not been reliable at all times Hunslet could not have won."

At the conclusion of the game, in front of the grandstand, Albert received the Yorkshire Senior Competition Shield from Mrs CA Brewer, wife of the chairman of the Competition Committee. His little acceptance speech was suitably diplomatic and generous. The *Yorkshire Post* wrote, "Mr A Goldthorpe ... said no one could be prouder at receiving the shield than he. His team had played well all through the season, and hard work had entailed much sacrifice on all the players. He thought it was a great pity there were not two shields this year, so that Bradford could get one. He could sympathise with Mr Broadley [Bradford's captain] very much, because he knew how disappointed the Hunslet team and he would have been if they had lost the day. (Applause)"

The following season saw Hunslet reach the final of the Northern Union Challenge Cup. After knocking out Maryport (home) 11–2, Swinton (away) 2–0, Castleford (home) 16–0, Hull (home) 9–0 and Salford 15–8 in the semi-final at Park Avenue, Bradford, they had qualified to meet Oldham at Fallowfield, Manchester on 29 April 1899. Their route to the final had not been a simple one. Albert had kicked at least one goal in all those ties and had scored a magnificent 75 yard try in the game against Maryport, which effectively won the match after Hunslet had performed extremely poorly.

The tie at Swinton was played in dreadful conditions. Albert decided the game with a late penalty out of the mud. The game was extremely ugly and Albert's opposite centre Bobby Messer, a diminutive Welshman, was sent off allegedly for deliberate kicking, while the referee further incensed the home fans by disallowing a try. Both the referee and Albert's team were pelted with mud and forced to flee to the railway station after the game. Swinton's ground was subsequently suspended until October.

The semi-final against Salford was even wilder. Salford had five men sent off and Hunslet one. Jack Smith, the referee, who also doubled up as Vice-President of the Northern Union, reported the entire Salford team for rough play and four of them received suspensions until the end of December! Conditions at Park Avenue were dreadful, heavy rain falling throughout the match and rendering the pitch a veritable quagmire. Hunslet took an early 5–0 lead when Tom Walsh scored from a forward rush and Albert converted. He was then "injured slightly," as one reporter noted "the tackling was unnecessarily severe". Eventually, shortly before half-time, Jack Rhapps, Salford's Welsh forward, was sent off for "foul charging", which would nowadays be called a late tackle.

The Leeds Mercury did not hold back: "So far as fair football was concerned, Salford had not a chance to win, and therefore brutally rough and wholly unnecessary charging was resorted to, and on several occasions the Salford men were heard exhorting each other to 'go for 'em and to knee the __'. Albert Goldthorpe was especially the mark at which violence was directed as if it was felt that something would be gained if he could be 'knocked out'. The swinging blow with the arm for which Rhapps was first cautioned might have dislocated a player's neck, for it was of sufficient force, with the Salford man going at full speed to lift Goldthorpe clean off his feet and double him up as if he had been shot. And it was utterly inexcusable, as Rhapps, following up, was so wide of the Hunslet crack that only the hand and wrist, with the arm fully extended, reached Goldthorpe's face.

Hunslet 1898–99: Back: J Bradburn, Lunn, W Goldthorpe, O Walsh; standing: J Lewthwaite (Secretary), J Ramage, H Wilson, T Young, W Glew, Field; sitting: Tibbutt, J Harrison, A Goldthorpe (Captain) J Mitchell, H Robinson; front: J Wright, F Kendall.

Hunslet 1901: Back: Lunn, Wray; second row: W Goldthorpe, Tunningley, Wilson, Shoot; third row: Hannah, Horne, A Goldthorpe (Captain), Glew; sitting: Wright, Whiteley, Gillings, Baggot, Brook; Committee (left): Biggins, Harrison, Walsh, Stones; Committee (right): Speight, Shenton, Barroclough.

A little later we saw another Salford player tackle and bring down Albert Goldthorpe only a short distance to the left of the press-box. In that there was nothing wrong, but with Goldthorpe prone on the turf and resting on his left hip and elbow, the Salford man caught his opponent on the back of the head with his right hand and banged his face on the ground. Instances equally bad could be multiplied, as could also those of insolence to the referee when that official found it needful to caution a player."

By half-time Hunslet led 8–0 and the later stages of the game became farcical as four more Salford forwards were dismissed. *The Bradford Daily Telegraph* described the Salford team as "the most ungentlemanly set of players ever seen on the Park Avenue ground", while *The Yorkshire Post* raged, "Of the Salford forwards it is only necessary to remark that some of them did not appear to think that the function in which they were taking part was a football match."

Of course, there was another view that none of the trouble was Salford's fault! The Salford chairman, Councillor James Higson, who had watched the game from a seat in the press-box, said, "Up to Rhapps leaving the field the game was as pleasant as any cup tie game I have ever witnessed, and my candid opinion is that after that the referee and touch-judges completely lost their heads." Higson accused Albert Goldthorpe of pretending to be seriously injured and staying down, which inflamed the situation – not withstanding the evidence of Albert's swollen eye after the tackle. The Salford chairman also pursued the argument that two Yorkshiremen should never have been chosen as touch-judges and had shown clear bias, despite the unsullied reputation of the pair, Harry Waller (Brighouse Rangers), founding President of the Northern Union, and Herbert Hutchinson (Wakefield Trinity), Secretary of the Yorkshire Union and Senior Competition.

Interestingly, even at this early stage of the game's development there was talk of taking the Cup Final to London with the Crystal Palace being favoured as the venue. For now, however, Albert would have to settle for a trip to Manchester, where Oldham were favourites to lift the trophy. Hunslet were lacking the services of half-back Tom Gillings, suspended following his dismissal in the semi-final – a big blow to the side. However, during the first half fortune seemed to favour Hunslet and Albert was the guiding light. After three minutes he landed a penalty, but after six minutes Hunslet trailed 5–2 after Albert's opposing centre Sammy Lees converted his own try.

A purple patch from Albert reversed the situation. First, he made the try of the match after intercepting an Oldham passing movement near half-way, drawing the Oldham full-back, Dicky Thomas, and sending in brother Walter for the try. After booting the conversion Albert proceeded to drop a towering goal from a penalty on the half-way line following an Oldham infringement at a "squash" (scrum). Holding a 9–5 interval lead Hunslet must have been confident but Oldham took the game by the throat and at one stage "the ball travelled from hand to hand for a couple of minutes before Hunslet could get a man held." Tries from Sam Williams and Jim Moffatt pushed Oldham into an 11–9 lead, at which point Walter Goldthorpe left the fray with a broken collar-bone. Oldham added another eight points to run out winners by 19–9, thereby becoming the first Lancastrian winners of the Challenge Cup. Albert Goldthorpe would have to wait nine years to play in another Challenge Cup Final. Meanwhile, he moved to half-back. His first appearance in the position was the local derby against Leeds at Parkside on 16 February 1901, when his partner was Herbert Robinson. *The Yorkshire Post* noted that "Hunslet tried the experiment of playing A Goldthorpe at half-back. The game, which was of a very moderate character throughout, was won by Hunslet with ease." The experiment was, of course, a resounding success, effectively giving Albert a new career. Hunslet won 16–0 with Albert kicking two conversions, one a brilliant effort from the touch-line, and scoring a try.

Despite his transformation into a half-back, Albert played a couple of games in the forwards in the 1901–02 season, against Swinton, won 11–3, and Oldham, won 9–6, both at Parkside. He particularly remembered the Swinton game. Apart from landing four decisive goals, he recalled in a 1907 interview with *The Yorkshire Evening Post*, "I shall never forget it, for in the scrummages, with Brookes behind me, it felt as if there was a steam horse impelling me forward." Billy Brookes was not known as 'Tubby' for nothing. Although he was only five feet six inches tall, he weighed 14½ stones, and sometimes more, which was very heavy for a forward in Edwardian days.

The last of Albert's six Yorkshire caps as a Northern Unionist was won in 1903 against Cumberland, a dozen years after he had won the first of his eight rugby union county caps. In 1898–99 he played in all three of Yorkshire's games, earning a County Championship winners medal.

Albert certainly did not expect to win that sixth and final Yorkshire NU cap. It was bestowed almost five years after his fifth, back on 28 January, 1899, when Cumberland were vanquished 8–5 at Crown Point, Leeds Parish Church's ground, the Yorkists' County Championship-clinching victory. Yorkshire travelled to Workington on 5 November 1903 to meet Cumberland and things went awry before they even left their own county. The team was to leave Leeds Midland Station at 10am, but a dense fog presented problems. All representative games for that season were played 12-a-side, as the Northern Union experimented in search of a more attractive game. When the train left Leeds, it was minus winger Wattie Davies (Batley) and forward JG Moffatt (Leeds), whose trains from Batley and Huddersfield were delayed. Wakefield Trinity half-back, Tommy Newbould, missed his train completely and Halifax forward Jack Riley telegraphed at the last minute, pulling out because of a family illness.

Even providing a 12-a-side team looked problematic for the Tykes. In the event Davies and Moffatt caught up with their colleagues at Carlisle, where the train for Workington was held up. The reserve forward, George Fletcher (Hull KR) filled Riley's spot and Albert Goldthorpe stood in for Newbould at half-back, the first time he had played there for Yorkshire in either code. Albert, according to *Flaneur* (*Leeds Mercury*), "was travelling into Cumberland on pleasure bent". It was a pure fluke that Albert took the same train as the Yorkshire party. Amazingly, Yorkshire won a dreadful game 11–0 in poor conditions and Albert claimed the last of their three tries, his first for the county in Northern Union. *The Yorkshire Post* remarked, "Albert Goldthorpe, if slow, did not play a bad game and the Yorkshire Committee must have felt very glad that he was present to help them out of the difficulty into which the befogged train service had landed them."

Hunslet versus Leeds 16 February 1901. Albert Goldthorpe is in the middle of the group.

The crowd at the Hunslet versus Leeds match on 16 February 1901.

Hunslet 1905 Yorkshire Cup winners. Standing: Glew, Wray, Jukes, Uttley, Hannah, Williamson, Everson, Walsh, Shooter; Seated: Eagers, Wilcox, A Goldthorpe, W Goldthorpe, Brookes, Wilson; Front: Jackson, W Ward, Place, C Ward.

Hunslet 26 October 1907: Back: H Cappleman, J W Higson, W Jukes, W Brookes, H Wilson, W Wray, W Goldthorpe; front: F Smith, W Batten, H Place, A E Goldthorpe (Captain), F Farrar, W Eagers.

A high acclamation of Albert and his brothers' contribution to the Hunslet club and community manifested itself early in 1904. On 15 January Mr TV Harrison presented a Cup, dubbed the "Goldthorpe Trophy", to the Hunslet Schools union on behalf of the Hunslet Cricket, Football and Athletic Club, to be contested annually amongst the local schools. The inaugural final, at Parkside on 28 April, 1904 resulted in a 14–0 victory for Bramley National School over Burley Lawn. Medals, purchased for four guineas, were presented to both sides. Albert and Walter acted as touch-judges and Albert's wife, Jane, presented the Cup. The Goldthorpe Cup is quite possibly the oldest schools rugby league trophy in the sport of rugby league, still contested to this day. In 2018 a competition for girls rugby league was introduced.

Later in 1904 Albert enjoyed a joint benefit match with his brother Walter, when 8,000 to 10,000 passed through the Parkside turnstiles for Hunslet's Christmas Eve encounter against Hull. The gate-money was in excess of £100. *Old Ebor* wrote in *The Athletic News:* "The pair [Albert and Walter] are the oldest players and the youngest-hearted men in the Hunslet team today." Hull were in a fine seam of form, unbeaten in their last six games and had not conceded a try in the last four. Hunslet were unimpressed, *Old Ebor* noting, "The two Goldthorpes seemed to be imbued with the idea that they were personally required to give the onlookers good value for their money, and right well did they play the part of entertainers-in-chief."

After winger Charlie Ward had given Hunslet the lead with an unconverted try, "Albert Goldthorpe compelled Hull to scrummage within their own '25', and the ball coming out to him, he ran a few yards, took aim, and with a curling drop sent the ball over and registered a goal." Shortly afterwards Albert kicked an easy penalty goal when Hull went off-side and then "the evergreen Albert, with a kick into touch, made Hull scrummage near their own line, and receiving the ball from the heels of his faithful forwards, he planted it over the line and scored a try." Albert's team led 10–0 at half-time and the only score of the second half was a try from Scottish forward Jim Ramage, created after Walter Goldthorpe intercepted a bout of Hull passing. A 13–0 victory went down pretty well with the benefit boys, if not with the chastened Airlie Birds.

Also in 1904, when Albert was 33, he featured in a series of articles in *The Athletic News*. It was written by Fred (FA) Marsh, who often wrote under the *nom de plume* 'Forward'. The articles went under the title "Northern Union Captains I have met" and its series number was XIV (yes, even before the supremely innovative Super League decided to list its seasons by Roman numerals – very contemporary!). Marsh wrote:

"Albert Goldthorpe is, perhaps, without exception one of the best known and most feared players in the whole Northern Union. Although a veteran as regards age and length of service, he is yet today a player who, if he decided to leave Hunslet, would be more than welcomed by any other club. Records innumerable have been made by him, but he is the same pleasant and unassuming individual he was in the days of his early struggles for fame, a typical broad-shouldered Yorkshireman, full of grit and determination, able to take a defeat with little variation of the smile of success. He stands 5'6", and his weight he gives as 12st 12lb. Born at Stourton, near Leeds, Goldthorpe confesses to having completed thirty-three years.

A TACTICIAN
Goldthorpe is a leader amongst the best of football tacticians. This is undoubtedly the secret of his success, despite the fame of his goal-kicking abilities, for are not these goals in the majority of cases the result of well-laid plans? He cleverly draws his opponents to certain positions, then comes the scrimmage, out comes the ball, and whilst some players are thinking, Goldthorpe performs and another goal is the result. Orthodox methods form no portion of his regular programme and though opponents may describe the goal-kicking business as 'no class', Goldthorpe's feats in this direction have many times proved the salvation of his side. One is reminded of a story respecting his early career, when he played at Whalley Range [Manchester]. He was even then known as a 'dead shot' but his success that afternoon startled the spectators and, figuratively speaking, paralysed the players. What could the best defence do against a man who seemed able to kick goals from anywhere on the field?

AN IDEAL CAPTAIN
One would be doing Goldthorpe a great injustice if a reference was not made to his defensive powers. Few players can so effectively 'spot' an opponent as can the Hunslet captain, and he has few superiors in the sure and hard tackle. He uses his weight with rare judgement, and pounces upon his man with surprising agility for one of his years. There is nothing of the gallery play about his movements, but all his work is of the finished order. He seems to direct the ball even on his own line with a coolness that draws admiration even from the most bitter opponent. As a leader he watches both his men and his opponents, and seems to know by instinct the weak spots on both sides.

THE MATCH OF HIS CAREER
As to the match of his career, Goldthorpe confessed to being undecided which to select. He rapidly thought of his long list, and then referred me to one of his officials, who had no hesitation in giving the game as the one between Hunslet and Broughton Rangers, which Goldthorpe's team won by seventeen points to ten. Naturally, one thought that the captain had done great deeds that afternoon; so the query was, 'And what did you do, Albert?' 'Nowt', he replied, with his usual smile. 'I only prevented the other lot from doing anything more'. The reply was characteristic of the man, and one learned that the Hunslet full-back on that occasion was at first woefully weak and presented Broughton with a couple of tries. Then the captain thought it was time to 'shut them up', and he did so in a fashion that surprised both friend and foe."

(The game referred to above was played on 23 November 1901, at Parkside. Seven days earlier Hunslet had lost their previous game 23–2 against the same opponents at Broughton. The unfortunate full-back was named Walker. He played no other games for Hunslet that season.)

Towards the close of the 1904–05 season, Albert announced his retirement, missing the last four games. Four games into the following season he made his come-back! By 1905–06,

Hunslet had laid the foundations of a very powerful side, with the reinvigorated Albert imperiously directing operations from half-back behind a dominant pack. The county cups were put up for competition for the first time under Northern Union auspices and Hunslet became first holders of the Yorkshire Challenge Cup after defeating Halifax 13–3 in the final at Bradford Park Avenue. Albert dropped three goals, while Walter placed two. Remarkably, four of the players in the 1905 Yorkshire Cup Final had played in finals in the old rugby union days. The Halifax forwards Bob Winskill (1893) and Jack Riley (1894) had finished on winning teams, as had Albert and Walter in 1892. The two brothers thus became the only men to have won the Yorkshire Cup in both codes. Hunslet also finished runners-up to Leigh in the Northern Rugby League Championship, winning 25 of their 32 fixtures. Their Challenge Cup hopes were, however, rudely shattered when Halifax crushed them 20–5 in the first round before a crowd of 16,950 at Thrum Hall.

When the playing of the game was revolutionised and its pace accelerated in 1906–07, through the abolition of the old knock-on law, the introduction of new play-the-ball regulations and the reduction in teams from 15 to 13-a-side, it would have been understandable and forgivable if Albert, pushing 36 years of age, had decided enough was enough. Amazingly, his greatest triumphs were yet to come.

Hunslet did not immediately find the new laws to their advantage, although Albert certainly got plenty of goal-kicking practice, as the number of tries scored rocketed. He broke his own club records with 74 goals and 163 points. Hunslet finished seventh in the Northern Rugby League, behind Halifax, Oldham, Runcorn, Keighley, Wigan and Leeds, but made no impact on the knock-out competitions, losing 6–0 at Halifax in the second round of the Yorkshire Cup and 20–6 at Wigan in the first round of the Challenge Cup.

On 28 September. 1907 *The Yorkshire Evening Post* ran an article on Albert, under the heading "My Football Career" in a series of "Weekly Talks with Leading Players". The interviewer wrote, "One cannot have a talk with Albert Goldthorpe without referring to his remarkable goal-kicking feats. Asked if he could remember a few goals which had brought off unexpected victories for his side, Albert said their name was Legion. 'The one I remember best', he said, 'was when on one occasion we played Manningham at Valley Parade. It had got to the last five minutes of the game, and I was having a shot to convert a try. If I kicked the goal it meant that we won the match and we did. No, George Lorimer was not playing that day. We never used to beat Manningham when poor old George was with them. He took the palm of all modern full-backs, did Lorimer. I have never seen his equal."

Tragically, George Lorimer had died of typhoid on 8 February, 1897, aged 25, having won eight Yorkshire RU caps and five Yorkshire NU caps. Albert went on to list more of the players he admired. He observed, "Of all the great players, I think the one who impressed me most of all was that great Irish international three-quarter, 'Sammy' Lees, though, of course, 'Dicky' Lockwood would always remain a vivid personality as a wing three-quarter. I would name a few forwards for you, but, upon my word, when I go back a dozen years, all the men of that day seem to have been giants! But if you want to know who I think are the best forwards of the present day, I will name [Ike] Bartle, of Halifax, and [Harry] Wilson, of Hunslet."

Season 1907–08, Albert's 20th with Hunslet, was to be his *annus mirabilis* and the greatest in the club's history. The strength of the team resided in its awe-inspiring pack, known to history as "The Terrible Six", a title since usurped by many. The six usually comprised Harry Wilson, Billy 'Tubby' Brookes, Billy Jukes, Jack Randall, Willie Higson and Tom Walsh, who were ably assisted when necessary by Walter Wray, Jack Smales and Charlie Cappleman. While much credit deservedly went to these titans, the back division was arguably as good as any that ever represented Hunslet, then known as the "Boilermakers", after one of the local industries. Goldthorpe's half-back partner was Freddie Smith, who became a notable test player.

The centres were Walter Goldthorpe and Billy Eagers, a Cumberland cap, who had also represented Yorkshire and England. Walter was steadiness personified, whereas Eagers was just as capable of playing a blinder or having a stinker! The wingers were the wickedly quick Fred Farrar, alias "The Farsley Flier", and the youthful Billy Batten, both of whom were to tour Australasia with the first Lions in 1910. Charlie Ward, a Yorkshire cap, filled in when any of the three-quarters was absent and behind them all was the imperturbable Herbert Place at full-back, who would go on to play for Yorkshire.

For the first time four trophies were potentially winnable. The Northern Union had decided to reinstitute the County League Championships for Lancashire and Yorkshire, which ran alongside the three existing competitions – the County Cups, the Challenge Cup and the League Championship. Although the achieving of a clean sweep was a mouth-watering prospect, most critics believed it would be a long time before any team would manage such a triumph. Indeed, just the previous season all the major competitions were won by different clubs – Bradford won the Yorkshire Cup, Broughton Rangers took the Lancashire Cup, Halifax lifted the Championship and Warrington were the Challenge Cup winners.

However, the season became a titanic struggle for supremacy between none of the above, but between Hunslet and a formidable Oldham side. Albert's team did not meet with defeat until 18 January 1908, when they went down 23–11 away to Hull Kingston Rovers. Hitherto, they had won 22 games out of 23. The only team not to succumb to them had been the New Zealand tourists who had gained an 11–11 draw at Parkside before a crowd of 19,000 on Boxing Day.

Even such an outstanding record as Hunslet's paled in comparison to Oldham's, which saw the Roughyeds win 28 and draw two of their first 30 fixtures and remain undefeated until they lost 5–0 at Salford on 22 February, 1908. Oldham had won the Lancashire Cup on 30 November, beating Broughton Rangers 16–9 at Rochdale. Three weeks later Hunslet met Halifax in the Yorkshire Cup Final at Headingley. The Terrible Six controlled affairs and Albert Goldthorpe was in his element, playing a selfless game and contriving to have a hand or foot in every score as his team won 17–0. Apart from kicking a penalty and dropping his customary goal, he scored a fine try dribbling from a scrum past three defenders. A reporter wrote, "One could not but admire Albert Goldthorpe's wonderful resource on the attack again and again. His club's victory was indeed largely another personal triumph for him."

Although the Parkside juggernaut stuttered alarmingly in January and February to lose five games in a row, the Yorkshire League Championship was clinched by March with Hunslet finishing nine points clear of runners-up Halifax. On the other side of the Pennines Oldham had already taken the Lancashire League Championship and finished seven points ahead of Broughton Rangers. Consequently, when the 1908 Challenge Cup began on 29 February both Oldham and Hunslet were in with a chance of lifting all four cups. The first round gave them both comparatively easy away ties. Oldham won 13–2 at Dewsbury, while Hunslet had the satisfaction of winning 14–5 at Headingley, where Leeds were having a wretched season, eventually finishing in 20th place in the table.

Albert landed only one goal and was struggling with a nagging thigh injury, which caused him to miss the next three games. Among those absences was Hunslet's most crucial game of the campaign. The second round of the Challenge Cup had pitted Hunslet against Oldham at Parkside on 14 March. In hindsight it was one of the most pivotal cup-ties in history. The winner could go on to create history.

A crowd estimated at 20,000 flocked to Parkside for this tie of ties. Oldham, probably a more talented all-round side, made light of Hunslet's home advantage and finished the first half 8–4 ahead. However, qualities Hunslet were not short on were stamina and spirit and on the back of their indefatigable pack they eventually wore down Oldham's resistance. Two tries from Freddie Farrar and one from Harry Wilson in the second half found no response and Hunslet progressed into the third round with a 15–8 victory. In Albert's absence, brother Walter landed two goals and Billy Eagers dropped one. The tantalising idea that Hunslet might indeed annex all four cups was now beginning to dwell within the realm of possibility.

Albert returned to action for the home game against Merthyr Tydfil on 23 March, landing a conversion to Jack Smales's try, which provided a 5–3 victory. Five days later he led Hunslet to an 8–0 win at Barrow in the third round of the Challenge Cup, contributing a drop goal. A few days after that, on April Fools' Day, Batley looked likely to make fools of Hunslet, but the Boilermakers were saved by Albert, whose two penalty goals gave his side a 4–3 win. No one at the time noticed, but Albert's second goal was his 87th of the season. He thus broke the Northern Union record of 86 goals, set by Salford's James Lomas in the previous season.

On 11 April Albert took his team to Wigan for the Challenge Cup semi-final against Broughton Rangers. Their opponents were a top-class side, with a few surviving members of their team which had become the first in the Northern Union to complete the Cup and League double in 1901–02. On their day they could beat any side. However, this was Hunslet's day and Albert schemed to such good effect that a 16–2 victory sent many of the 16,000 crowd home believing that the lifting of all four cups was now more than just a possibility. Their opponents in the Final would be Hull, who beat Leigh at Halifax in the other semi-final.

Hunslet were back at Central Park two days later for a league fixture against Wigan. In view of their tough final run-in, Hunslet wisely left out Albert and several other first team players and lost 36–0, after a run of 13 consecutive wins.

The Northern Union took a dim view of Hunslet's decision to field a weakened team and fined the club £10. It was not the first time such a sanction had been taken and many more such instances would occur around Challenge Cup semi-finals time in the future. The result did not affect Hunslet's position in the league table. They had already been assured of second place in the following top four:

	P	W	D	L	F	A	Pts	%
1 Oldham	32	28	2	2	396	121	58	90.62
2 Hunslet	32	25	1	6	389	248	51	79.28
3 Broughton R	30	23	1	6	421	191	47	78.33
4 Wigan	32	23	1	8	501	181	47	73.43

Thus for the Championship semi-final Hunslet had to renew hostilities with Broughton Rangers. Nevertheless, they were confident of winning, especially as they had home advantage and, in the event, simply overwhelmed their opponents 28–3. Hunslet bagged six tries and Albert kicked five goals, as his side swept through to the Championship Final. Predictably, their opponents would be Oldham, who disposed of Wigan 12–5 in the other semi-final.

Before that, however, was the small matter of the Challenge Cup Final on 25 April. Fartown was the venue and 18,000 went through the turnstiles. Hull had finished 16th in the league, but had put out Swinton, Salford, Wakefield Trinity and Leigh on their way to the final. Hunslet were clear favourites. For the first quarter, however, Hull held the upper hand but no scoring occurred. Albert broke the deadlock in the 22nd minute when he provided the space for Bill Eagers to drop a fine goal and Hunslet were on their way. Just before the interval Albert conjured a move from a scrum close to the Hull line, which resulted in a try to Fred Smith, duly converted by the captain, giving Hunslet a 7–0 advantage.

During the second half Hunslet doubled their score in spite of the snow, which fell throughout. Albert converted a try by Fred Farrar and kicked a goal from a mark called by Smith. Hunslet's 14–0 victory was clear-cut if not wildly entertaining. *Athleo*, of the *Hull Daily Mail*, commented somewhat sourly "The game could not be termed a scientific exposition and attempts to play 'class' football were conspicuous by their absence – being substituted by endless useless punting."

Still, Hunslet had done the necessary and a 14–0 victory was hardly to be sniffed at. Certainly the 20,000 or so people who jammed Leeds City Square and its environs to greet Albert and his men later that evening were happy enough. Three cups won and one to play for – one more game and one more victory was all that stood between Goldthorpe's Hunslet and sporting immortality. Or was it?

Next up were the doughty men of Oldham, who, remember, had actually finished above Hunslet at the top of the league. Clearly the best team in Lancashire, Oldham had emulated Hunslet in lifting both county trophies, but had fallen to Hunslet in the second round of the Challenge Cup. They were understandably bent on revenge. With Hunslet seeking "All Four Cups" and Oldham intent on taking their third trophy, the Championship Final between the game's two super powers at Salford on 2 May had all the makings of an epic. Bizarrely, a week after contesting a game in a snow storm, Hunslet found themselves having to contend with "well-nigh tropical heat", so much so that by the final whistle both of the behemoths of northern unionism could "hardly raise a gallop", according to the *Yorkshire Post*.

The same newspaper reported that, "It was a hard, tearing game, marked by a grim earnestness of purpose that severely taxed the stamina of both sides." At the end of the contest no-one was any the wiser, as a 7–7 draw ensued, Albert having scored all his side's points and drawn the following eulogy: "Hunslet were best served in the virile, telling game played by Albert Goldthorpe. His splendid judgement in attack was combined on this occasion with a most resolute defence. He expended himself to the uttermost, and his tenacity in tackling was marvellous for one of his years. A real leader was he both by precept and example."

Oldham had twice led, 2–0 and 4–2, thanks to two penalties from their international halfback Tom White. Following an infringement by Oldham forward 'Mad' Arthur Smith, Albert had landed a simple penalty to level the score at 2–2. Just before half-time he gave Hunslet a 7–4 lead, when he took advantage of a bad error by Oldham centre Billy Dixon near his own line. According to the *Yorkshire Post*, "Dixon fielded the ball and the two Goldthorpes had closed up when the Oldham centre rose. Dixon played the ball, and Albert Goldthorpe put his foot to it, sent it over the line, and scored, also adding a very easy goal." Oldham salvaged a draw with a second half try from forward Joe Wright, who forced his way over from a scrummage near the Hunslet goal-line. Hunslet were mightily relieved to see Tom White's conversion sail wide, as did two attempted drop goals by the same player.

The replay took place at Belle Vue, Wakefield, the following Saturday and this time there was no doubting Hunslet's superiority as they triumphed 12–2. Albert was restricted to a couple of penalty goals, but a drop goal by full-back Herbert Place and two tries to the indomitable Walter Goldthorpe saw off Oldham, who could only muster a second half penalty goal from White.

The *Yorkshire Post* remarked somewhat jingoistically, "As an exposition of the finer arts of Rugby football the game was very disappointing. As a display, however, of the manly British qualities of pluck, tenacity and endurance, the game was without peer in the annals of the Northern Union. Both teams fought hard to the finish under summer skies and a broiling sun, and although Oldham were beaten by a better lot they at least died hard and unyielding."

Oldham had all the early pressure, but contrived to miss four penalties before Albert broke the deadlock by showing them how to kick with "a fine penalty goal from long range". After Oldham missed another couple of penalties, Albert doubled Hunslet's lead when he "steered the ball over the bar with another fine penalty kick". As the interval loomed Hunslet struck a killer blow when Billy Batten shook the ball loose from opposing winger George Tyson in a jarring tackle. Walter Goldthorpe was on hand to hack the ball on, found a clear field, picked up, and ran to score near the posts.

Unaccountably his brother missed the simple conversion but Hunslet led 7–0. Albert's failure looked as if it might prove costly when White landed his penalty goal only three minutes into the second half. Oldham pressed strongly for a time, but Hunslet raised the siege when Place landed a lovely drop goal.

In the last few minutes Hunslet made the game safe when a burst from Batten was followed by an exquisite piece of interplay between Billy Eagers, Fred Smith and Walter Goldthorpe, the latter scoring his second try.

On Monday 11 May 1908, the *Yorkshire Post* noted, "In adding the League cup on Saturday to all the other trophies for which they competed, Albert Goldthorpe, Hunslet's captain, might well declare that it furnished the proudest event in his football career. Hunslet's success in a succession of championship finals this season has been as much a personal triumph for Albert Goldthorpe as a credit to the team as a whole. Never before has his experience and his presence as a leader had so much to do with Hunslet's fortunes. He has made records this season that will stand for a long time. He has completed 20 years' active participation in the game with one club, has kicked a century of goals in one season, and has brought his own aggregate of goals for Hunslet up to 810 [sic]. If he should decide to retire now he will do so with honours thick upon him, and with his glory at his zenith. We have reason to believe, however, that his career as a footballer is not yet over. He declared as much to the writer on Saturday evening. 'If I am fit and well', he said, 'next season will see me in my place', and for that assurance there will be many followers of the Hunslet club who will be devoutly thankful."

Hunslet's annexation of All Four Cups was a monumental landmark in the history of the game. Subsequently Harold Wagstaff's Huddersfield (1914–15) and Hector Halsall's Swinton (1927–28) emulated Albert Goldthorpe's team's ground-breaking achievement. However, with the demise of the County League Championship (1970) and the County Challenge Cup (1992) competitions, the days have long gone when such a feat could be accomplished.

A journalist later wrote of the All Four Cups Hunslet team: "Of the side it was written in those days that 'Hunslet swept the seas with a very clean broom, the handle of which was the back division, guided by Ahr Albert, while the brush was the pack' and of the back division Albert Goldthorpe once said, 'They were all sound catchers and good footballers. Everyone understood everyone else. There was strength in the middle and we had two grand wingers – Batten, full of courage and dash, and Farrar, with his speed and wonderful swerve. Every man could and did tackle'."

Thirty years after the triumphs of 1908 the *Yorkshire Evening Sports Post* ran an article recalling Goldthorpe's great team: "They knew the value of teamwork ... They were men who could handle the ball, they were men who could pass the ball, they were men who could back up in defence and attack, and they were men who could tackle, and here comes another echo from the days of long ago. This time the voice is that of Albert Goldthorpe, 'Those forwards, I tell you, were good in the loose. Every man could, and did, tackle – No asking the other fellow where he wanted tackling!'"

Apart from the unprecedented success of the team, the 1907–08 season had been notable for Albert in that he became the first man to kick 100 goals in a season. Appropriately enough, it was that first long-range penalty in the Championship Final replay that brought up his century. It was a feat something akin to breaking the four-minute barrier for the mile. In November alone he had banged over 29 goals, twice registering a personal best of eight goals in Northern Union matches against Bramley and Hull KR.

Although kicking 100 goals in a season, like the four-minute mile, later became almost routine, it was hardly dreamed possible in those far off Edwardian days – until Ahr Albert put his mind and feet to it.

Hunslet 1907–08 – the 'All Four Cups' season.

Hunslet beat Broughton Rangers in the Challenge Cup semi-final on 11 April 1908. Albert is seen knocking out opposing captain Bob Wilson and dropping a goal. (Cartoon from *The Athletic News*)

Since the Northern Union had sprung into being Albert had topped the goal-kicking charts in 1896–97 (jointly), 1897–98, 1898–99, 1900–01, 1902–03 and 1907–08.

He had set new NU records by landing 66 goals in 1897–98 and 67 goals in 1898–99. In turn Broughton Rangers' Willie James – 75 goals in 1901–02 – and Salford's James Lomas – 86 goals in 1906–07 – had extended the record before Albert broke the 100 goals barrier. Albert's record was surpassed in 1910–11 when Hull KR full-back Alf Carmichael booted 129 goals. Nor had Albert lost a smidgeon of his prowess in dropping goals. No fewer than 27 of the 101 goals he booted were dropped and he dropped a goal in 22 of the matches he played; 17 times a single goal and five times two goals.

Albert did, as predicted, carry on playing as Hunslet began the 1908–09 season in good style. The first three months of the season gave hope that more tangible success would bless the Boilermakers. By 18 November, when Hull were beaten 16–7 at Parkside, the team had won seven, drawn one and lost once, 18–10 at Wigan, in the league, were high in the table and had eliminated Keighley, York and Dewsbury in qualifying for the Yorkshire Cup Final. Their only other defeat had been by the Australian tourists on 7 November, when they went down 12–11 at Parkside. Albert had been an ever-present and had showed his kicking was as good as ever by landing 21 goals.

The game against the Australians would 80 years later gain undeserved notoriety, when a film, *The First Kangaroos*, was released (see following chapter). Among its many and various misrepresentations was a spurious vendetta between Albert and Dally Messenger – something which could hardly have been more preposterous. The game was, in truth, a desperately hard-fought affair in which both sides played almost to their full potential. *Flaneur*, in the *Leeds Mercury*, reported, "Though there were few brilliant pieces of play on either side, it was a display that appealed strongly to the real lover of the handling game. Sound, vigorous forward play, in which no quarter was asked or given, determined tackling by the backs, and fine fielding in the face of impetuous forward rushes were the leading features, and the interest and excitement never abated for one minute of the game. There were times when the keenness of the players bordered on actual roughness, but it was not a dirty game, though it was marred by several stoppages for injuries, and one regretted that Messenger was off the field on at least two occasions, and was handicapped by both a damaged leg and a knock on the head. Yet this great player never lost his pluck, and his defence played a big part in giving his side the victory."

Hunslet scored three tries to the Kangaroos' two, but Albert was not in his best goal-kicking form. Late on he had the misfortune to hit the post with a long-range penalty, which would probably have won the match, had it not bounced the wrong way. It was also reported, "The home team had other chances that were bungled, and late in the game Albert Goldthorpe showed fatal hesitancy near his opponents' line, when, had he shown his usual intuition, the game might have been won. The fact is that in the critical final stage of the game the Colonials were the cooler side and nothing could have been finer than the way in which their backs fielded the ball in their own quarters in face of the tearaway rushes of the Hunslet forwards." The 6,000 onlookers certainly got their money's worth.

Even when Albert, Fred Smith, Jack Smales and Harry Wilson were missing from the side at Crown Flatt on 21 November, when Dewsbury racked up a stunning 23–2 victory, no one was unduly perturbed. Everything would surely be well for the Yorkshire Cup Final against Halifax the following week at Wakefield. After all, Hunslet had beaten Halifax twice in the final in the first three years of the competition. Perhaps it would be the start of another All Four Cups journey? In the event that dream evaporated at the first obstacle. Albert's men were confident enough. They knew how to win big games. Halifax might have been third in the league but Hunslet were only two places lower. The result was Halifax 9 Hunslet 5 but the 13,000 spectators knew early on that there would only be one winner. Hunslet did not get on the score-board until the 67th minute, when Albert converted Jack Randall's try. *Rambler*, a Halifax newspaper reporter, observed, "The game had not been long in progress when it became apparent that the cup would not return to Hunslet ... their 'terrible six' had lost their terror, or rather were not permitted to display their powers." The correspondent of the *Athletic News* asserted, "Never have I seen Hunslet more thoroughly beaten in any of their great games, and the adverse margin of four points rather flatters their defence."

Hunslet were certainly off colour and no longer invincible. With Albert conspicuously missing, Halifax emphasised Hunslet's decline when they hammered them 31–0 at Thrum Hall on Christmas Day. However, he was back in the side on Boxing Day in a welcome 21–5 home win over Leeds, kicking five goals, his best tally of the season. For the first time he played in an opposing team to his brother Walter, who had transferred to the Loiners in November. Coincidentally, Walter's last appearance for the Parksiders, on 3 October, had been in Hunslet's 13–10 victory at Leeds. Undoubtedly the loss of Walter contributed to Hunslet's continuing fall from grace. Walter's contribution to Hunslet's cause had been monumental – over 400 games since the founding of the Northern Union, in which he had amassed 479 points from 75 tries and 122 goals.

Six wins from seven games up to the beginning of February raised hopes that Hunslet might be back on track for the Challenge Cup-ties, only for losses away to Hull, 11–0, and Batley, 9–0, to provoke scepticism. However, on 27 February Mid-Rhondda were dispatched 25–5 at Parkside in the first round, a game which Albert missed and in which Billy Batten scored four of his side's five tries. The second round on 13 March brought Leeds and a bumper crowd of 22,000 to Parkside. Albert slotted a drop goal with his left foot and Hunslet swept into the third round with a 15–9 win. Sadly, Hunslet's inconsistency was underlined with three consecutive defeats to Wigan, 12–0, York 26–11 and Oldham 14–7 in the league but there were still high hopes of Challenge Cup glory. Wakefield Trinity at Belle Vue in the third round on 27 March was a tough nut to crack, but Hunslet's pedigree in crunch games gave the local fanatics enough encouragement to predict victory.

The optimists were badly mistaken as 16,000 saw Trinity coast home 19–0. The *Wakefield Express* observed, "With a sadly disorganised back division Hunslet were completely overthrown by Wakefield Trinity on Saturday, and thus lost their hold on the last of the four trophies so well won last season. Hunslet's defeat surprised few people, though it was much more decisive than had ever been anticipated. Very little excuse can be made for the Parksiders, for they were beaten in every department, even 'the terrible six' being overwhelmed by the resolute efforts of 'the old brigade'."

Left: Fred Smith was Albert's half-back partner in the 1907–1908 season. He went on to win international honours and was a Lions tourist on the 1910 tour of Australia and New Zealand.

Below: Bramley National School were winners of the 1911–12 Goldthorpe Cup.

Page 41: Article from *Yorkshire Chat*, 1899

CHATS WITH
Celebrated Yorkshire Footballers.

No. 6—ALBERT GOLDTHORPE.

Albert Goldthorpe is, without doubt, one of the most popular players in Yorkshire, and has for a number of years occupied a unique position as an all-round player, although he has undoubtedly proved best as a drop-kick. Many a time has he pulled matches out of the fire by his extraordinary abilities.

"Ahr Albert" has for years been a household word in the Leeds district, and there are few, if any, notabilities that are more respected than the popular Hunslet three-quarter. It would go hard with any rash individual who dared to speak disparagingly of him.

Few players have assisted in more benefit matches for any unfortunate footballer, and it was solely on account of his generous disposition that he became associated with the Hunslet Club.

He was accustomed to practise with a lot of youths at Stourton who were not in a position to afford goal-posts, corner flags, &c., the absence of which, however, mattered very little. Coats and waistcoats were taken off and put in bundles to take the place of the posts, the same as can be seen amongst the youngsters at the present time.

It was whilst playing with these youthful aspirants that Alf. Stephens, who did good service for both Hunslet and Leeds Parish Church, asked Albert if he would play in his place on the following day, Stephens not having recovered from an injury sustained in the week previous. The genial one at once acceded the favour asked, and played with the "A" team against Morley "A."

In reply to my query as to how long he played with the second team, Mr. Goldthorpe replied—"The following week 'A. Nother,' a popular way at that time of selecting a new man, appeared as full back on the first team list, and I was asked to fill the position. I consented to do so.

"My performance, which was against the Wortley Club, must have given satisfaction, for I continued to play full back until we were knocked out of the cup ties by Halifax.

"After that," continued Albert, "I played centre three-quarter, a position I have filled ever since."

The famous drop-kick at this point apologised for not being able to give me dates and detailed performances, the book containing same having got lost.

"I think it was in 1890 that I got my county cap, playing my first match against Durham at Hull."

"This would be about the time that the controversy in regard to the claim of Summersgill and yourself for county honours occurred?" I ventured to remark.

"Yes," he replied, at the same time smiling all over his face; "that was a rare bit of fun for Tommy and I, who have always been the very best of friends, both on and off the field. Neither of us were ever aware that we had so many faults, failings, and capabilities until we read the comments of our opponents and partisans respectively that appeared in the Leeds papers, which at the time were perhaps hard up for matter to fill the space, there not being any warlike movement or attempts at yacht racing to fall back upon."

County football did not seem very palatable to the Hunslet player, it being very awkward for him to leave business when matches were played, say, down south, and he had been compelled to ask off on several occasions.

He spoke with the greatest of pleasure in regard to several of the tours of the Hunslet team, and expressed surprise that most of the Yorkshire clubs seemed to have dropped these annual outings.

During a tour in the north the Hunslet players and friends played a match at Newcastle, and after the game a most sumptuous dinner was provided at the Hotel Metropole. One of the waiters asked Albert whether he would have cod or soles, and he asked for the former. His right hand neighbour, who had never been at anything of the sort before, was also asked, "Cod or soles?" "Naither!" he murmured; "I'll hev some fish, like Albert." The waiter and those around nearly collapsed, and whenever the individual is asked any question in regard to fish it is similar to showing a red shawl to a Spanish bull.

It is needless to chronicle the wonderful performances of the Hunslet Club, but still the high position they have attained must be attributed in great measure to Albert Goldthorpe.

During a cup tie match against Dudley Hill in 1890 he placed 14 goals out of 15 attempts, which, I believe, to this day stands as a record.

"What do you think of the Northern Union?" I asked him.

"Well, I think the formation of the Northern Union was a fine thing for Yorkshire. It has made all above board, and done away with the 'sailing under false colours' that was carried on to such an extent by clubs in the old Rugby Union in regard to paying players. There is now none of the humbug that we had to contend with. It is a question (if professional, of course) of paying players openly, which is considerably better for all concerned. Then, again, the alteration of the rules has made accidents to players less liable, especially so when the referee rules with a stern hand; and, so far as I am concerned, I can assure you that I prefer the Northern Union in every way to the fast declining old Yorkshire Rugby Union."

Albert is not the only footballer in his family, no less than four of his brothers having assisted Hunslet. That he is popular all round will be understood when I state that, on his marriage a public subscription, unconnected with his club, was got up by his admirers, and the handsome present of a valuable piano and other articles was made to him and his good lady.

Next Week:
ARCHIE RIGG.

Albert Goldthorpe.

Hunslet's demise was now complete. All Four Cups had been wrested from their grasp. Halifax had already taken the Yorkshire League Championship, Hunslet finally finishing a distant fourth, while the League Championship was destined for Wigan with Hunslet ending up an even more distant 12th in the table. If 1907–08 had been all about Hunslet and Oldham, 1908–09 was all about Wigan and Halifax, who finished first and second in the league. Each won both of their county competitions, both were knocked out of the Challenge Cup in the semi-finals, and Wigan's victory over Oldham in the Championship Final brought them three of the major trophies. Wakefield Trinity had gone on to win the Challenge Cup, beating Hull 17–0 in the final at Headingley.

Hunslet's season petered out and Albert was obliged to play in the forwards in the penultimate fixture away to Bradford Northern on 10 April, when he kicked a solitary goal in an 8–5 win. Even though he was well past his 37th birthday, Albert had taken part in 33 of Hunslet's fixtures, kicking 41 goals and claiming three tries.

On 16 June 1909 the *Yorkshire Evening Post* reported that Albert had decided to retire – again. This time he apparently meant it. Hunslet would finally have to do without their talisman. Hunslet struggled throughout the 1909–10 season, eventually finishing 15th in the league, having won only half their fixtures. Albert, perhaps inevitably, was coaxed into helping out as the season closed and turned out at centre at St Helens on 29 March, 1910. He kicked two goals in a 28–15 defeat. His final farewell on 9 April saw him restored to half-back but again he finished on the losing side, as Hunslet went down 3–2 to Salford at Parkside. Albert did not even kick his side's goal, which went to Fred Farrar. Farrar and Billy Batten both landed 18 goals during the season – a reflection of how much Hunslet had relied for so long on Albert's golden boot.

When he walked off the Parkside pitch for the last time, Ahr Albert had kicked 695 goals and amassed 1,565 points in his first class career as a Northern Unionist. That was more than any other player in the Northern Union's history at that juncture. Hunslet finally bowed to the inevitable in September 1913 when they crossed Albert off their playing register.

Even then he was not quite done. On the occasion of the benefit match for two of his old colleagues, Billy Jukes and Fred Smith, on 7 April 1920, he was induced to turn out, along with a number of other geriatrics, for Billy Batten's XIII against the current Hunslet team. By then he was 48. A match report ran, "Those who thought the game would be one-sided and farcical were soon disillusioned. Indeed, throughout, it was a serious contest. The old players entered into the fray with real zest and earnestness, and at one time, so evenly matched were the sides, the score was 10-all. Albert Goldthorpe, after a lapse of many years, again donned the jersey, and he played an uncommonly good game. He repeated his former triumphs by dropping a beautiful goal, and, in conjunction with Fred Smith, at half-back, he gave an ideal exhibition of the passing game." In the end Batten's XIII lost 18–10 in front of 7,000 spectators.

Among all the goals Albert kicked, all the match-winning scores, from improbable angles and distances, he picked out his most memorable in a *Sports Post* article (circa 1924), which ran: "Albert Goldthorpe, now comfortably settled in the secretarial chair at Parkside, has a story to tell of a drop kick that sent the ball a lot further than he calculated. If I remember it rightly, the match was at Widnes – one of the Lancashire grounds anyway. The ball came to the Hunslet men, and was duly swung to Albert. He was inside his own half. He 'dropped' the ball into the air, and set off to follow it up, intending to get possession and make play for his backs. 'But the wind was a strong un that day', he says, 'and the faster I ran, the faster the ball seemed to go through the air. I went on after it, and then to my absolute astonishment I found I had dropped a goal, for the wind took the ball right among the spectators. I was so surprised I started laughing. It was a grand goal'."

After retiring from playing Albert looked around for other work to do at Parkside and was vice-president, vice-chairman, trustee and member of the team committee. In October 1924 he took over the post of club secretary, following the departure of Charles L Reynard to Huddersfield. He also became the first team coach. Albert remained Hunslet's secretary until 1931, by which time he had served the club in various guises for 43 years.

The year 1931 also saw Albert and his wife Jane ('Ginny', née Holmes) leaving Urn Farm. They moved to 12, Grimthorpe Terrace, a rented house close to the Headingley ground. Albert bought a milk round, which he worked until he retired. In the 1939 Register Albert, then aged 68, was described as a retired farmer. Jane, born 8 September 1872, was described as performing "unpaid domestic duties", in other words, a house-wife. The Second World War pitched Albert into a new career as a full-time Civil Defence worker. Albert and Jane had married in 1897 and had two children, Edward and Gladys.

Albert Goldthorpe died on Friday 8 January 1943, aged 71. On 11 January The *Yorkshire Post* ran an obituary, topped by his portrait and, below it, the heading "HUNSLET RUGBY STALWART". It reported, "Albert Goldthorpe, one of the most famous of Yorkshire Rugby footballers, has died at his home at Headingley, Leeds, after a long illness. The funeral service will take place this afternoon, at 2pm, at Hunslet Cemetery." Under a sub-heading, "A Great Team Leader", it continued, "Albert Goldthorpe was one of the greatest of club footballers – a man with the ability to inspire his colleagues and a man who had the skill to make the most of those who played with him."

Albert's obituary, including his portrait, covered a mere 12 column inches. However, that was not so bad – there was a war on, after all. Sadly, his wife Jane died a couple of weeks after Albert. The two rest together in Hunslet Cemetery.

A drawing of Albert.

3. Cobblers & Kangaroos – a tarnished reputation

On 21 April 1988 the author of this book wrote the following letter to the greatly esteemed Australian magazine *Rugby League Week*:

"The events you are about to see actually happened" – "Well sort of", it should have said.

It is the introduction to *The First Kangaroos* which is being shown on Channel 4. We have been waiting with bated breath for this since Christmas, but somehow it could not be fitted into the schedule until now. It could be worse – we are still waiting for the telecast of the 1987 Sydney Grand Final but never mind. After all, Channel 4 is for minority interests and over here that means rugby league.

Bearing in mind that *The First Kangaroos* is supposed to be light entertainment and that all film-makers are entitled to restructure the truth – for art's sake, of course – what follows can be taken either as a typical Pom doing what Poms are best known for – whingeing – or an attempt to enlighten you Aussies as to a few of the real historical truths surrounding those first Kangaroos of 1908–09.

As the film was produced from the Australian point of view it was only to be expected that the Aussies should be portrayed as honest, larrikin, open, friendly, salt of the earth types and the Brits were bound to be conniving, arrogant, condescending coves, who considered all Australians criminal or simple, or both. Fair enough, at least rugby league in Australia is regarded highly enough to actually make films about. We should be so lucky.

All films need a plot and a climax and to that end the clash between Australia's golden boy, Dally Messenger, and Hunslet's renowned captain and half-back, Albert Goldthorpe, becomes the central theme. It is to be league's cinematographic answer to *High Noon*, the gun-fight at the *OK Corral*, the chariot race in *Ben Hur* – and, like them, it is pure make-believe.

The most dishonest aspect of *The First Kangaroos* is the gross misrepresentation of Albert Goldthorpe. What would Australian league followers think of a film, which portrayed the sublime Dally Messenger in the same light as *The First Kangaroos* portrays Goldthorpe? What would they say if Dally was depicted as paranoid as to his own pre-eminence in the game, as arrogant, devious, fond of his beer and whiskey and a thug on the field? They would soon let everyone know it was so much garbage, as accurate as a chocolate watch. Of course, Dally was none of those things and neither was Albert Goldthorpe.

Nor was Goldthorpe, or "Ahr Albert", as he was known to the Hunslet fans who adored him, some sort of official big wheel in the Northern Union hierarchy, which is what the film asserts. It is hardly conceivable that he lived in a mansion in palatial splendour surrounded on all sides by the game's major trophies and pandered to by a house-keeper like Mrs Oaks. Goldthorpe was in fact a farmer, a teetotaller and, according to all contemporary evidence, one of the fairest of players. There was no [known] blemish on his disciplinary record in a career which stretched from 1888 until 1910 and he was universally regarded as 'The Gentleman of Yorkshire Football'. In 1906 *The Pilgrim* was moved to write of Albert, 'You play such a sporting game. You are respected by your opponents, who would think it shame to mis-handle a man who is so courteous, a man who never loses his temper, and who, I believe has never done a discreditable act on the football field'. This rather makes one wonder about those lingering, slow motion shots of Albert pummelling Dally's bloodied head with fist and elbow. Were I Albert's relative I would sue for family defamation.

Nor was Albert ever 'the fastest thing in the game', as one character describes him. Speed was one thing Albert was never noted for. He was an organiser, a schemer, one of the best captains of his era and probably the most prolific kicker of drop-goals in history, but fast – never.

The First Kangaroos made Goldthorpe a more interesting character than Messenger – baddies are always more interesting. One character said of Dally, 'He's pure as the driven snow. He doesn't drink, smoke or hang about with loose women and he's not interested in money'. We all knew that Dally was a god when it came to footy but we never knew he was a saint. He also loved and honoured his mother. In fact, he came across as a real 'mummy's boy' – clearly as much of a misrepresentation as the nonsensical caricature of Goldthorpe.

It was quite amazing that Dally was represented as the wide-eyed, innocent, all-Australian sporting hero abroad in a strange land when history shows that just the previous year he had been a member of the All Gold (New Zealand) touring party to Britain. He had in fact played against Albert Goldthorpe on Boxing Day, 1907, when Hunslet and the New Zealanders drew 11–11. Strange to relate, it was Albert who defied injury to play and landed four crucial goals.

It would be churlish to bore the readers with the many other historical inaccuracies of the film, and there were some real lulus, believe me. It is just such a shame that the film should use one of Australia's great rugby league heroes to counterpoint one of English rugby league's greatest champions in such an untruthful manner.

One thing the film was right about – it is bloody cold in Halifax! Poms always have something to whinge about."

Needless to say, the letter was never published. No doubt *Rugby League Week* had moved on by the time the letter arrived. After all, the film had gone out on Channel 10 on Wednesday 23 September 1987, which was seven months before the letter was posted. Old news from a cantankerous Pom was probably not high on their wish list, especially if it was critical of anything Australian.

The First Kangaroos struck some raw nerves in England, or at least it did in Rugby-league-land. That was a shame as it had cost a reputed $3,000,000 and *The Sun* (Australia) had gone so far as to produce "a special pictorial souvenir lift-out to celebrate the world premiere of *The First Kangaroos*". The tele-movie was a joint production between Network TEN (Australia) and Channel 4 (UK). A Canadian, Frank Cvitanovich directed the film, which starred Dennis Waterman as Albert Goldthorpe and Dominic Sweeney as Dally Messenger. Other members of the cast included Chris Haywood, who played the Australian tour promoter James Giltinan, Philip Quast, Clarissa Kaye Mason and Neil Schofield. The English script-writer Nigel Williams "knew very little about rugby league before the project", according to *The Sun*. Williams said, "I didn't find it difficult writing about Australians as I've worked with many of them and I have an affinity with them. I think it's time to finish with the ocker stereotype."

The Sun reported, "You may not find stereotypes [sic] but you will find some real footballers among all the actors." Balmain's Wayne Pearce and Cronulla's Andrew Ettingshausen, both real RL Kangaroos, had acting parts, while Russell Fairfax (Easts, Souths and New South Wales) played a referee and Ron Coote, the great Souths and Australian back-rower, was a technical advisor on the film. *The Sun* asserted, "It's a film that the British like so much, it is being held back from television for theatrical release and is now due to open in London in December."

The producer told *The Sun*, "Unlike some other productions, we do not portray the Australians as ockers. The end result shows a strong contrast between the English and the Australians and it shows the Australians' ability to have a go, their lack of pomp, ceremony and diplomacy. Their warmth, spirit and courage. It also shows the Englishmen's initial reluctance to accept anything and the barriers they put up. As they respond on the level of achievement of sport, these barriers are broken down. It's a film that entertains people on an emotional level."

English commentators begged to differ. Trevor Delaney, editor of the much-lamented *Code 13* quarterly, in June 1988 wrote: "This badly researched film, which is so full of historical and personal inaccuracies, has angered many rugby league people. Those who have felt the hurt most are those relatives of Albert Goldthorpe who are still alive today, and who can vouch for his character ... If only to correct the slander which has been perpetrated by the film, it is necessary to attempt to put the historical record straight. One is loath, however, to spend too much time on what was pure fiction disguised as an historical documentary. For the record the film was not too well received either by television critics. Hugh Herbert in the *Guardian* said, 'Directed by Frank Cvitanovich who made his name with horses, and possibly should have stayed with them ... It is played entirely in slow motion, like most of the acting, with a lot of grunts, and moans. Like most of the acting.'

The game on which the film was based ... was clearly a keenly fought affair with a hostile crowd, but, as the report says, 'it was not a dirty game'. Although the great Dally Messenger was injured and had to leave the field, there is no mention of any one player being responsible or a player being sent off. The film unfortunately played down the collective reputation and tactics of the 'Terrible Six' to satisfy the whim of the script-writer. I doubt, however, if even their methods would have resulted in the great man looking as if he had been run over by a Leeds tram! As a half-back, Albert Goldthorpe was opposed, in fact, by Sid Deane, whilst Billy Batten scored the try credited to Albert Goldthorpe in the film. Messenger, who had toured, of course, a year earlier with the New Zealand All Golds, failed to inform his mother about this in the film!

The comedy aspects were not confined to the characterisations. It was the little points, such as the heraldic backdrop to the Parkside ground looking like a set from *Ivanhoe*, the reference to the soccer city of Sheffield being 'a stronghold of the Northern Union', as the train weaved its way between Hull and Halifax, and Albert, as a player, doubling up as the secretary of the Northern Union with his headquarters presumably at the Anchor Hotel prior to renovation. There have been many myths perpetuated about the game of rugby league, and it seems we are now faced with a few dozen more."

A FAMOUS AUSTRALIAN.

H. H. Messenger, the brilliant Australian three-quarter back, whose play has been one of the features of the New Zealand team now touring the Northern Union area of influence.

John Callaghan joined in, writing in the *Yorkshire Evening Post* on 22 April 1988: "Television has a bad habit of sneering at everything but itself, and sport has proved particularly vulnerable to the efforts of the pretentious, self-congratulating artistic cliques who make so many programmes. *The First Kangaroos*, an alleged account of the first Australian tour to this country, which filled Channel 4's share of the output for two embarrassing hours last night, provided a classic example of the disgraceful standards which prevail. As with that other flight of confused fancy *Bodyline*, in which a gaggle of indifferent actors added another dimension to the expression 'flannelled fools', this production hardly raised itself above the village hall level of entertainment ... Every member of the cast turned out to be no more than a caricature. All those associated with English rugby league were directly related to Andy Capp and all Australians were simple, upstanding country boys ... The actual sporting content dragged the whole shoddy business unbelievably to an even lower level. As a matter of record Albert Goldthorpe, a genuine all-time great, enjoyed an unchallenged reputation as a polished footballer, who never became involved in breaking the laws by resorting to violence, and his influence over the code was restricted to the field ... The whole sad saga, therefore, gets none out of ten for content."

Somewhat perversely, the British screening of *The First Kangaroos,* on 21 April 1988, coincided with the 100th anniversary of Albert Goldthorpe's first team debut for Hunslet in 1888. It also coincided to within four days of the 80th anniversary of Hunslet's winning of the Challenge Cup Final, a 14–0 beating of Hull at Fartown on 25 April 1908. A fortnight later Albert's men won the Northern Union Championship to complete the historic annexation of All Four Cups. No doubt Albert would have been mortified to have known that his own and his team's achievements and characteristics had merited such odium at a time when they deserved quite the opposite – praise, honour and fond remembrance. Whilst it was true that the name Albert Goldthorpe had been raised again into public awareness, several generations after his halcyon days, *The First Kangaroos* had tarnished rather than enhanced the reputation of one of rugby league's great standard bearers.

A 1900 studio photo of James Archer ('Archie') Rigg

4. Archie Rigg – the most gentlemanly player

It was 10 November 1900 and Halifax were playing Bradford at Thrum Hall. It was a clash of the season's two leading Yorkshire sides, which were both unbeaten. Halifax were top of the Yorkshire Senior Competition and Bradford were three points behind them, having suffered a two-point deduction for breaching by-laws 22 and 23 of the professional regulations. Despite the fact that it had teemed down with rain between one and two o'clock, with snow thrown in for good measure, a huge crowd was expected. In fact, there were 13,342 paying spectators, who contributed £341/15/4 at the turnstiles. Including season ticket-holders the attendance was 15,300 and they witnessed a real sensation.

The visitors were leading 3–0 in a gripping encounter. At that point, according to the local press, "An unlooked for and sensational incident happened. Rigg had put in a long kick and afterwards was obstructed by a Bradford player. A conference took place between the players and the referee. We were all expecting that the Bradfordians would be penalised for obstruction. Instead of that, the referee ordered Rigg off the field! What a verdict! What a roar of disapproval! A football crowd was never more surprised! Here Rigg had been playing all these years, and this was the first time he had been ordered off the field. The press representatives were at a loss to know as to what grounds the referee had based his decision, and were informed that it was alleged that Rigg had kicked an opponent. The Halifax players were indignant and conferred together. We should not have been surprised if the game had come to an abrupt conclusion. However, hostilities were continued."

Unfortunately, Halifax no longer had any stomach for the game and folded up under the pressure. They lost 18–0 and conceded as many tries as in their previous 10 games put together. The man who had the effrontery to dismiss "the most gentlemanly player in Yorkshire" was Mr TF Wilkinson. Rigg himself had expected the Bradford forward John Hutt to be dismissed, but remained sufficiently gentlemanly to merely say, "Thank you", to the referee, before walking from the field. Needless to say, the crowd was angry and at the final whistle the police escorted the official from the field and later from the ground.

The final editions of that day's *Halifax Evening Courier* thundered with the headline "RIGG ORDERED OFF THE FIELD!" on its sports page. Under a sub-heading, "NOTES BY ROCKET", specifically timed at 5.30 pm, *Rocket* fulminated: "Mr TF Wilkinson, of Leeds, who was the referee, has achieved a notoriety which I wouldn't possess for a few bright sovereigns. Just when the game had got well going he ordered Rigg off the field! That decision threw everything out of joint and completely spoilt the game.

I wouldn't be so completely disgusted with everything in general if the referee's decision had been just. It came about this way, so far as I can make out. Rigg was illegally fouled when he had taken his kick. His body swerved on one side, and up went one leg. The referee gained the impression that Rigg was attempting to kick his opponent, and without any caution, ordered the most gentlemanly player in Yorkshire off the field!

The spectators were simply astounded. Rigg had played in first class football for eight years or so, and I believe I am right in saying that he had an absolutely clean record when the game commenced ... For Halifax to suffer through referee highhandedness is aggravating beyond measure. After the match the referee had a rough passage. If the crowd had had their way he would have presented a sorry sight in a minute or two. This would have been very unfortunate and might have ended in the Halifax club being smartly penalised."

The Halifax players and officials did their best to protect the referee and, aided by a numerous police presence, got him to the pavilion "without disaster". *Rocket* concluded by writing, "The decision of the referee ... was roundly condemned in all quarters, and there is no doubt that it will be the talk of Yorkshire to-night."

It transpired that Hutt had already been cautioned and the referee had told him, "The next man I catch will have to go off." In the event Hutt obviously got lucky and Archie was the proverbial sacrificial lamb, despite the fact that he had done nothing wrong. The dismissal must have been exponentially galling for him. Bradford had originally objected to the appointed referee. The Northern Union had offered four or five alternatives to the clubs and it was Archie Rigg who had suggested that Mr Wilkinson should be appointed.

Once he had been ordered off, Archie dressed and was back at his business premises long before the game ended. He was afraid that his presence on the ground would inflame the feeling against Mr Wilkinson even more. The newspapers were predictably full of letters deploring the referee's decision and, among many, the *Leeds Mercury*, *Yorkshire Post* and *Athletic News* all vigorously proclaimed Rigg's innocence and integrity. The Northern Union disciplinary committee could do nothing other than offer a sending-off sufficient verdict.

Seventy-three years later, another half-back of impeccable character, Alan Hardisty, was sent off for a high tackle in Leeds's shock defeat by Dewsbury in the Championship Final at Odsal. Hardisty did the deed, but it was neither premeditated nor malicious, merely an unfortunate reflex action. Such was the shock that the *Yorkshire Post's* venerable rugby league correspondent Alfred Drewry was famously moved to write, "Such is the esteem in which Hardisty is held that it was difficult to believe that he had done so. It was as though the churchwarden had been caught with his hand in the collection bag." If those who were present at the 1900 game could offer comparisons, they may have said that Archie attacked the vicar as he made his escape with the collection money!

The reaction to Archie Rigg's dismissal, a potent mixture of disbelief and outrage, was eloquent testimony to his high stature in the sport. This was arguably the biggest star of the early Northern Union game, the darling of Halifax, one of its leading clubs, and for the last five years captain of Yorkshire, the greatest force in English rugby. It was simply inconceivable that such a clean and sporting player could have committed such a foul. James Archer Rigg was a name synonymous with good sportsmanship, a truly brilliant practitioner of the art of half-back play and was that treasured rarity – a genuine match-winner.

Unlike Albert Goldthorpe on the family farm, Archie Rigg was brought up a townie in Halifax, one of those heavily industrial West Riding towns, which in the nineteenth century well merited William Blake's sonorous description as being "builded here among those dark satanic mills". Although noted for its importance in the wool trade, Halifax also rejoiced in its title "the town of a hundred trades". Archie's father, John Rigg, was a joiner, a native of Halifax, who was born in 1837, according to the 1871 census. His wife Sarah, three years his junior, was also a local. The couple had set up home at 6, Southowram Bank, Southowram and by 1871 had three children, Atkinson (born 1864), Mary (1867) and George (1869). By the time of the following census in 1881 two more children had appeared in James Archer, who was nine, and William, who was six.

Tragically, however, John Rigg had died in 1876, while his daughter Mary no longer figured in the census return, possibly having died in infancy, a not unusual occurrence in Victorian Britain. Sarah was thus left with four sons to rear. In that respect she shared something with Albert Goldthorpe's mother Grace, similarly widowed early with five sons. Archie's mother, however, did not enjoy the security of Urn Farm, Grace's inheritance of 186 acres with its own work force of six men. The 1881 census described Sarah as a charwoman, aged 40. Her eldest son, 17-year-old Atkinson, worked at a mechanics' shop, while 12-year-old George was employed in a mill as a worsted doffer. Archie and William were still schoolboys attending Halifax Parish Church School. The Rigg family suffered a third grievous blow in 1889 when Sarah died. Archie was then 17 and was working as a dyer's labourer.

Two years later, Archie was living at Holly Mount in Southowram, the Rigg household now reduced to three, his 21-year-old brother George, now a mechanic fitter, being the head of the household, while 16-year-old William was a mill hand at a worsted company. Archie's eldest brother Atkinson, following in his father's footsteps as a joiner-carpenter, had married in 1890 and became something of an itinerant, living in Stoke and then Oldham.

Archie, born on 14 February 1872, had clearly experienced a disrupted childhood and early manhood but had something special going for him – his athleticism and passion for sport. He first took up rugby playing at Caddy Field Tip, then joined Ovenden St George's, aged about 15. After a couple of years, he graduated to the Halifax Gymnasium Club, one of the more prominent junior sides in Halifax. In later years it was reported that Archie had captained the Gymnasium Club for three years. Certainly, he developed leadership powers that were to stand him in good stead in his subsequent stellar career. Apart from his prowess as a 'footballer', as rugby players tended to be called, Archie was a gifted boxer, gymnast and cricketer.

By the age of 19 Archie had caught the attention of Halifax club officials. At the start of the 1891–92 season, he swapped the chocolate and white colours of the Gymnasium for the famous blue and white hoops of Halifax, one of the most powerful and successful clubs in British rugby. Founded in 1873, Halifax had already won the Yorkshire Cup, the game's biggest tournament, in three of the four finals they had contested, including the inaugural final of 1877. Their ground at Thrum Hall had been their home for only five years and was consequently considered extremely up to date, attracting big crowds and hosting major matches, including the 1887 and 1890 Yorkshire Cup Finals, while Yorkshire had played Cheshire, Middlesex and the Rest of England on the ground, the latter, in 1889, being the first occasion that the fixture between England and the season's champion county had been staged. Archie must have been acutely aware that he had joined a big club with big ambitions.

He was treading in famous footsteps as Halifax had produced England internationals in George Thomson, Harry Wilkinson and Albert Wood and many Yorkshire caps, three of whom, Thomson, Edmund Buckley and Jimmy Dodd, had captained the county.

On Saturday 5 September 1891, the *Halifax Daily Guardian*, in previewing the coming season, noted that "Nash and Rigg, the latter a very smart youngster from the Gymnasium club, will be available as backs." The following Saturday, 12 September, Archie made his debut in the 'A' team away to Rochdale Hornets, where they completely outmatched the home side. The *Halifax Daily Guardian* reported, "Rigg played a splendid game at half-back, scoring three tries in irresistible style, and with W Copley's assistance finding Quinn, Lawton and Jenkinson [the three-quarters] plenty to do." As debuts went Archie Rigg's was sensational and he was drafted into the first team when Halifax visited Bradford on 19 September.

The occasion was a huge one – games did not come any bigger than Bradford-Halifax derbies in those days and there were 10,000 at Park Avenue. It was a baptism of fire for Archie, the opposing half-backs being Arthur East and Arthur Briggs, both exceptional players. Briggs would in fact go onto win three England caps later that season. Halifax lost 6–5 and the *Daily Guardian* observed, "Rigg got nicely away from the scrummages".

The following Saturday, Pontefract, who had caused a sensation by winning the Yorkshire Cup a few months earlier, came to Thrum Hall and were defeated 7–5. It was reported, "Rigg was a good deal more in evidence than at Bradford, and on a few occasions he got nicely away with the ball, and effected a neat transfer. He is a very active, plucky and cool-headed young player, but against men of the calibre he has to meet with the first team, he ought to give more attention to passing, and rely less upon his efforts to get away with the ball."

Halifax decided that for the time being Archie should learn his trade in the 'A' team, although he did make a further four first team appearances later in the season. In the meantime, he played in his first final when Halifax 'A' met Sowerby Bridge in the Halifax Charity Cup at Thrum Hall on 19 December, 1891. Sowerby Bridge had knocked Archie's former team Halifax Gymnasium out 17–0 in an earlier round. Around 4,000 spectators paid £58 at the gate, which all went to Halifax Infirmary. The competition, which was open to local clubs, but not Halifax's first team, had so far contributed over £200 to the Infirmary over its six-year existence. The ground had been protected from frost by a covering of husks and a good, keen game ended in a 7–2 victory for Sowerby Bridge and doubtless some disappointment for Archie Rigg.

During Archie's first season at Thrum Hall, Halifax won 25 and drew five of their 40 fixtures. Among their victims were Durham City, Durham University, Welsh Wanderers (twice), Wigan (twice) and most of their big Yorkshire rivals, apart from Wakefield Trinity. Their biggest disappointment, however, came on 2 April 1892 at Leeds in the third round of the Yorkshire Cup. Despite scoring three tries (worth two points each), Halifax went down controversially 9–6 before a crowd of 27,654, possibly a record for a rugby match anywhere to that date. Leeds went on to reach the final but were crushed by Hunslet, Albert Goldthorpe playing a leading part in their demise.

It is worth noting that Archie Rigg's first season in senior rugby was also the first season that games were decided by a majority of points. That first points system comprised five points for a goal (that is, a converted try), two points for a try, four points for a drop goal and three points for a penalty goal. Unlike in modern rugby union, penalty goals were as rare as hen's teeth. Halifax, for example, did not kick a solitary penalty goal in the entire 1891–92 season.

Archie found himself in the Halifax first team from the start of the 1892–93 season as half-back partner to Arthur East, who was a member of the military based at Wellesley Barracks, close to Thrum Hall. A major innovation was the forming of the Yorkshire Senior Competition, which comprised the county's top 10 clubs – Batley, Bradford, Brighouse Rangers, Dewsbury, Halifax, Huddersfield, Hunslet, Liversedge, Manningham and Wakefield Trinity. A similar competition was inaugurated in Lancashire. The establishment of league rugby in Yorkshire and Lancashire was frowned on by many in the game, but was to have profound effects in the near future. Halifax, captained by full-back Harry Bromwich, and Bradford were installed as favourites to win the YSC.

Halifax began the season in cracking form and Archie was quickly making his name as a dashing, try-scoring half-back. It should be noted that the half-back positions were indistinguishable at this period. Either half-back could put the ball into the scrum. Some pairs obviously developed specialisms, but often the only differentiation appeared to be standing on opposite sides of the scrum. Archie's style of play indicated that he would be the outside-half (stand-off) rather than an inside-half (scrum-half). Reports, however, indicate that he often did feed the scrummages.

The blue and whites began the season with six wins and a draw. In their seventh match Halifax beat Liversedge 10–0 at Thrum Hall on 8 October and *The Yorkshireman* reported, "The Liversedge men could do nothing with Rigg and East, the Halifax halves, who simply played with the opposition, and afforded the Halifax trio of three-quarters fine scope for displaying their powers ... Rigg scored a try, and was very near getting over on other occasions. It is now a moot point which is the better, he or East, and as the soldier is better than ever he was – well, you may guess the rest."

Bradford attracted a crowd of at least 16,000 to Thrum Hall on 22 October, but found Halifax in irresistible form, losing 14–0. The Bradford half-backs managed to contain Rigg and East up to half-time, largely by playing off-side, but after the break the Halifax pair changed their tactics "with the result that Rigg gave some long raking passes that gave the Bradfordians fits". *The Yorkshireman* gushed, "Rigg was the best back on the field, and Charley Marsden, the referee, avowed that he was the best half since Bonsor, whilst the Rev. Fieldmarshal, in proclaiming the game as the best he had seen for many a long day, avowed that he could not tell what the county committee were doing to leave Rigg out of the trial matches."

This was high praise as Bradford's recently retired Fred Bonsor had been the Yorkshire captain in the late 1880s, was widely regarded as the best half-back in England and had captained England against the New Zealand Native XV in 1889. The "Rev Fieldmarshal" was

The Yorkshireman's snide referral to the Reverend Frank Marshall, headmaster of Almondbury School and the leading anti-professional member of the Yorkshire RFU committee. Whatever else he might have been, Marshall knew a good player when he saw one. On this occasion, at least, the followers of Halifax would have agreed with the troublesome priest, for none of the Halifax players had been selected for the early season Yorkshire trials.

Archie's performances were, however, rewarded when he was belatedly selected for the Whites versus Stripes and subsequently for the Possibles against the Probables. The latter match was probably the first time that Archie and Albert Goldthorpe had appeared on the same pitch. Albert was selected for the game against Durham at Hartlepool on 12 November and played in all five of Yorkshire's pre-Christmas fixtures as centre-three-quarter, three of which were won and the other two drawn. Archie failed to make the team. *The Yorkshireman* observed, "Rigg was also strong in the running for the [half-back] post, but it was thought he played a little too much for his own hand."

There was to be no denying Archie's rise, however. On 7 January 1893, Halifax travelled to Swinton, arguably the best of all the Lancashire sides. The pitch was so hard that all the Halifax first team backs, bar Archie, refused to play. Even so, Halifax earned a draw and the *Halifax Daily Guardian* reported, "Rigg was undoubtedly the best man on the field, and the admiration of his supporters knew no bounds, whilst his opponents were amazed at his play." He scored his team's only try "after several exciting scrimmages close to the Swinton goal-line". *The Yorkshireman* more graphically described his effort as "that fearful plunge which scored the try and [left] sore bones".

A week later at Bradford, Archie was in the Yorkshire XV which faced Somerset. Dickie Lockwood, Yorkshire's most famous player, was his captain and Arthur 'Spafty' Briggs was his half-back partner. The Yorkshire team for Archie's county debut was: Lorimer (Manningham); Lockwood (Heckmondwike), Summersgill (Leeds), Dyson (Huddersfield); Rigg (Halifax), Briggs (Bradford); Bradshaw (Bramley), Broadley (Bingley), Fletcher (Leeds), Jowett (Heckmondwike), Lorriman (Leeds), Redman (Manningham), Richardson (Leeds Parish Church), Speed (Castleford) and Toothill (Bradford).

A notable absentee was Albert Goldthorpe, who had paid the penalty of being "too selfish" in his role as centre-three-quarter and not getting the ball to his wings. His place had gone to Tommy Summersgill, Albert's deadly local rival. The controversy as to who was the best centre in Leeds – Albert or Tommy – was to rage for several years and for now, at least, the Yorkshire selectors had come down in favour of Summersgill. It was ironic that Archie's county career should coincide with Albert's displacement from the game's premier XV. Yorkshire played 23 more games before the advent of the Northern Union. Albert figured in none of them while Archie missed only four, usually through injury.

Yorkshire made light work of Somerset, winning 29–0. It would have been a bigger score if Lockwood had not retired hurt at half-time, having converted two of Yorkshire's three tries. Thereafter Jowett, Broadley and Briggs missed a series of conversion attempts, some of which were sitters. Summersgill did, however, manage a drop goal. Archie made his mark with a second half try and the *Halifax Evening Courier* was pleased to report, "Rigg, though nervous and at fault in the first quarter of an hour, shone conspicuously on attack, some of the best runs of the day being contributed by him. After his performance he is almost sure to have another trial for Yorkshire this season, and if his defence proves as good as his attack, he should get a permanent place in the team next season. Rigg showed great tenacity and much skill in securing the ball and utilising his fine turn of speed, the only blemish in his display being a desire to run too far before feeding his wings. With more experience he ought to make a really high class player; at present he lacks judgement and this lost him a certain try."

The Yorkshireman concurred: "Rigg made a very creditable show, playing most unselfishly. He has a good turn of speed, which he could, however, have several times turned to better purpose had he doubled into the field of play instead of making tracks for touch. That he will be played again with the county is beyond doubt, and his blooming into an international would surprise no one."

The following Wednesday, 18 January, Yorkshire met Devonshire at Dewsbury, and made six changes. Archie and Dickie Lockwood were among the absentees, but Yorkshire won comfortably by four tries and a conversion to nil. Yorkshire played their third game in seven days at Halifax on the following Saturday, when 10,000 braved the elements to watch Cheshire receive a 19–5 drubbing. Halifax were represented by Archie, forward Ben Mellor and flying wingman Fred Firth. Archie scored a try in each half and he and Firth won high praise. The *Halifax Evening Courier* trilled, "It was certainly delightful to see the manner in which both of them worked. Rigg was undoubtedly as good as anyone on the field. He came away from the scrummages grandly, and many a bout of capital passing amongst the three-quarters was initiated by him. The fact that two tries were credited to him shows also that he knew what to do when he got hold of the ball." Firth never made a mistake and kicked three goals.

At Thrum Hall for the Cheshire game were Rowland Hill, Honorary Secretary of the RFU, Temple Gurdon, past President of the RFU, and several of the International Selection Committee. *The Yorkshireman* noted, "The half-back play was highly spoken of, but Summersgill, from whom much had been expected, was voted disappointing." The RFU bigwigs would undoubtedly have been present at Yorkshire's next game on Monday, 30 January, 1893, at Richmond where Middlesex were the opposition. Victory was crucial, if Yorkshire were to retain their grip on the County Championship. Middlesex were tough nuts to beat, being able to call on international players from all four home nations. This game was particularly notable because Yorkshire decided to play four three-quarters for the first time – Dyson, Lockwood, Keepings and Firth. Dickie Lockwood was said to be much in favour of the system and the inclusion of Halifax centre Bill Keepings, who had played many times in Cardiff's four three-quarter line prior to moving north in 1891, was undoubtedly a form of insurance. Middlesex were already used to playing four three-quarters.

Yorkshire proved far too good for the Middlesex men. After their gargantuan forward Donald Jowett kicked a monster of a penalty goal to give Yorkshire the lead, Archie skipped over for two tries before half-time to give his side a 7–0 lead. Arthur Gould, Wales's captain and national hero, then claimed a try after a wonderful three-quarter line movement, which was converted by England captain Andrew Stoddart. However, Yorkshire's forward power killed off the Middlesex challenge as Jack Toothill and Harry Bradshaw scored further tries, one converted by Lockwood, to triumph 14–5. It was reported in the *Halifax Evening Courier,* "The forwards were admirably seconded by the half-backs. Both men were quick at snapping up the ball from the heels of the scrummagers, and bold in picking up before the opposing forwards. Rigg thoroughly deserved the glory of getting his tries, for he worked hard and well from first to last, though Duckett was hardly inferior." The *Halifax Daily Guardian* reported that the streets around the Upper George Hotel, the Halifax club's HQ, were thronged with people waiting for telegrams announcing the half-time and full-time scores and "when it became known that Rigg had scored the first two tries for Yorkshire the greatest satisfaction was felt. The final result was greeted with cheers." It also related that about 30 Halifax enthusiasts had accompanied the Yorkshire team to London, while there were also strong contingents from other West Riding towns.

Archie's half-back partner, Horace Duckett (Bradford), did enough to win his England cap against Ireland the following Saturday. *The Yorkshireman* commented, "There was some disappointment at Halifax in consequence of Rigg not being selected for the Irish match. We all know his worth, and that his turn will come is beyond doubt." Sadly, time and football politics proved *The Yorkshireman* wrong.

Yorkshire's final game, on Thursday 16 February, would decide the 1892–93 County Championship. Their opponents were Cumberland, who had not had their line crossed in any of their matches. The venue was Lismore Place, Carlisle. Archie and Fred Firth, "the two Halifax Trojans", left by the 9.25 am train to Bradford, where they boarded a saloon attached to the Carlisle train and scheduled to arrive at 1 pm. Lunch at the Red Lion Hotel preceded the kick-off at 3 pm. A crowd of 8,000 filled the ground with "a fair sprinkling from Yorkshire" despite heavy rain. The referee was William Cail, President of the RFU.

Cumberland resisted heroically, but the result was never in doubt. By half-time Yorkshire had scored three tries – two from the Leeds forward Mark Fletcher and another from winger Jack Dyson (Huddersfield) – and a conversion by Lockwood to lead 9–0. In the second half "Rigg, feigning a pass, ran and gained a try" and a final try from Donald Jowett secured a 17–2 victory and Yorkshire's fourth title in five years. The *Leeds Mercury* wrote, "Rigg was especially brilliant considering the difficulties he laboured under, and in saving, passing and running stood out as one of the best men on the field."

The *Yorkshire Post* reported, "The Yorkshire half-backs were a long way better than their opponents. In fact both Duckett and Rigg got through a marvellous amount of work." The *Bradford Observer* noted, "The winners were immensely superior behind the scrummage ... Eagland [the Huddersfield full-back], Rigg and Duckett were in rare form, and the forwards were a great deal too clever for their rivals." Archie and his team-mates were rewarded with 18 carat gold medals which were about the size of a half-crown and bore the arms of England and of Yorkshire in enamel. *The Yorkshireman* declared, "They are exceedingly handsome, and are naturally very much valued." For Archie it was the first of three such medals he would win in consecutive seasons.

Archie still had one more match to play for Yorkshire. On 25 February the Tykes, as champion county, faced England at Fartown, in what was becoming an annual ritual. There was a very heavy, snow-covered ground and as more snow threatened, it was agreed to play two 35-minute halves.

1892 Halifax reserves at Thrum Hall. Archie Rigg is sitting on the ground, extreme left.

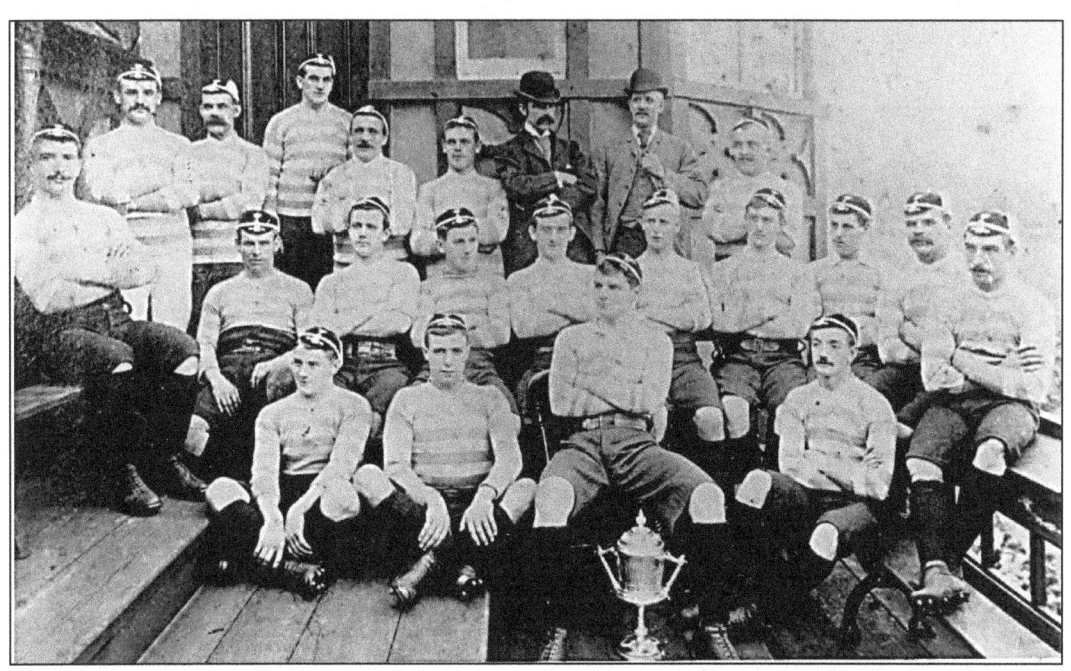

In 1893 and 1894, Halifax won the Yorkshire Cup. Captain Otis Fletcher straddles the trophy. Archie Rigg sits next to him on the ground, second left front row.

Left: Archie Rigg (on ground) and Joey Arnold playing for Yorkshire versus Lancashire at Manchester on 24 November 1894.
Right: Fred Firth. A flying winger, he played for Yorkshire in the Rugby Union and Northern Union eras, and for England at rugby union. He captained Halifax in 1894–95. Archie succeeded him in the first season of the Northern Union.

The Yorkshire XV which defeated England 2–0 at Huddersfield in 1893. Standing: Knaggs (Secretary), Bradshaw, Lodge, Jowett, JA Miller (President), Redman, Bromet; Seated: Fletcher, Dyson, Toothill, Lockwood (captain), Speed, Broadley, Eagland; Front: Firth, Brooke, Rigg.

Under the circumstances the game was excellent. The *Yorkshire Post* described it as "an exhibition of football which will rank as the finest and most stirring ever seen on any similar occasion in the county ... the football was very clever and delightfully exciting."

Yorkshire fully expected to win handsomely but their anticipated superior power in the forwards failed to materialise and they emerged undeserving winners by the skin of their teeth. The only score of the match was a try to Yorkshire, which began with a tremendous burst by Harry Bradshaw, followed by excellent passing and ending in Fred Firth diving over at the corner. It was sufficient to give Yorkshire a 2–0 victory. The England XV to meet Scotland the following Saturday at Headingley was selected at the George Hotel after the match and six Yorkshire men were included but not Archie Rigg or Fred Firth. The *Athletic News* wrote, "Halifax ... expected Rigg as a certainty and Firth as a probable winner of International honours. On his play on Saturday Firth was worth his cap. Rigg certainly was not, and this player is apparently not seen to advantage behind beaten forwards."

So for Archie it was back to club rugby for the remainder of the season. On the afternoon that England lost 8–0 to Scotland at Leeds before a crowd estimated at 21,000, Archie was in the Halifax team at Park Avenue for a game which was likely to decide who lifted the inaugural Yorkshire Senior Competition Shield. Halifax led the competition, a point ahead of Bradford, who, however, had a game in hand. Such was the interest in the clash that a crowd of 22,000 to 23,000 assembled, despite the counter-attraction at Headingley. This time Archie was on the losing team as Bradford won 3–2 and, after drawing at Liversedge the following week, Halifax had to concede that Bradford would indeed take the title.

There was, however, the little matter of the Yorkshire Cup to be decided, still the highlight of the season for most followers of the game. Archie's half-back partner Arthur East had suffered a broken leg in a 2–0 victory at Hunslet on Boxing Day, an injury which ended his career with Halifax. At first Halifax had employed Bob Winskill, normally a forward, albeit a fast and versatile one, as Archie's half-back partner, but by the time the cup-ties arrived another young player, Joey Arnold, had established himself alongside Archie. The pairing might have been made in heaven.

Halifax met Elland at Thrum Hall in the first round on 18 March, drawing a crowd of 10,000 for the first game to be played between those near neighbours. Halifax had thus far rejected any request for a fixture from their aspiring rivals from Old Earth. Tries by Archie and Bill Keepings, who also converted one of them, gave Halifax a 7–0 victory. Elland had tried to get Halifax disqualified before the match kicked off by objecting to the *bona fides* of Ben Mellor, who they claimed was a Sowerby Bridge player. This was quite a novel move, as although the Yorkshire Cup organisers were used to objections, they were invariably lodged after clubs had lost, not before! Four days after the Elland tie Archie and Keepings represented The Rest against Bradford, in the first challenge match to be staged between the winners of the Yorkshire Senior Competition and the rest of the YSC.

Wakefield Trinity, experiencing an uncharacteristically woeful season, were crushed 29–6 at Belle Vue in the second round. Archie kicked a goal but winger Abe Toothill, with a hat-trick of tries, and Keepings, with four conversions and a try, did most of the damage. The third round, on April Fools' Day, took Halifax back to the Wakefield area and a tie at Ossett. Archie was lucky to miss that encounter with a leg injury. Halifax won 5–4 and then reported

Ossett to the County Committee. The *Yorkshire Post* reported, "Ossett vowed either to kill or win, and they very nearly did both ... It was surprising to see how Ossett's supporters cheered each new piece of roughness indulged in by their favourites. When the match was finished the Halifax team could hardly have been worse damaged had they been engaged in a hand-to-hand tussle with some uncivilised tribe from Darkest Africa. They were likened in fact to walking hospitals." Ossett had acquired notoriety throughout Yorkshire for their ferocity and on this occasion six Halifax players were reported to have been laid out. They were lucky as in the first round Greetland fared even worse at Ossett, allegedly losing eight men injured for their next fixture.

The fourth round – the quarter finals – threw up another Bradford versus Halifax clash at Park Avenue, presenting Halifax with an opportunity of exacting quick revenge for their loss in the crucial YSC game five weeks earlier. Bradford were favourites, but history was never on their side when cup-ties against Halifax beckoned. They had lost all five previous Yorkshire Cup-ties with the men from Thrum Hall and they lost this one 11–2. Despite increased admission charges, 12,000 saw Archie outplay Horace Duckett to give a sharp nudge to the international selectors. Halifax progressed serenely to the semi-final against Bradford's 'other' team, Manningham. The game was played at Fartown on 15 April, attracting a crowd of 15,000. Archie's leg injury kept him out of the semi-final, but Halifax gained a comfortable 12–4 victory, tries coming from Bob Winskill, filling Archie's boots, Otis Fletcher and Joey Arnold, plus a couple of goals from Keepings.

The final against Batley at Headingley on 22 April attracted 17,288 spectators, 3,000 of whom had travelled from Halifax on special excursions. Halifax were short of their captain and full-back Harry Bromwich, who had been one of Ossett's victims. In his place at full-back was 39-year-old Jimmy Dodd, who had begun his Halifax career in 1876 and played in all Halifax's previous Yorkshire Cup Finals. Yorkshire forward Otis Fletcher captained the side. Archie Rigg was "still palpably lame" but took his place in the halves. The day was described as "too hot for football", but the game was open and intensely exciting, even if it never reached the highest standard. Dominant in the forwards, Halifax took the Cup with an 8–2 win, to equal Wakefield Trinity's record of winning the cup four times. They led 5–2 at half-time, thanks to a try by forward JW Mellor, converted by Bill Keepings. A touch-line penalty goal from Bob Winskill in the second half sealed the victory.

The *Halifax Evening Courier* noted, "Both Rigg and Arnold got through a vast amount of work. The former's run to the verge of the line was one of the best individual efforts of the day. At the commencement of the game, however, he twice made the mistake of passing too soon after he had got clear of the scrimmage. This is not Rigg's usual style, and probably his weak leg had caused him to doubt whether it would be safe for him to race towards the line or give the ball to someone who was all right."

Archie's first full season in first class rugby had yielded far more than he could have reasonably expected. He had established himself as a key member of one of the nation's top club sides, earned a winners' medal in the sport's most prestigious competition and become one of the fulcrums of the pre-eminent county XV in England. He had only just passed his 21st birthday. How much more was there to come from Archie? *Rocket* evidently believed the answer was plenty. His season summary in the *Halifax Evening Courier* on 24 April 1893 ran: "Rigg has played so consistently and splendidly that really he is almost indispensable. A better man for getting away from the scrimmage there is not, whilst at opening out play and giving the three-quarters plenty of chances he is A1. ... His really brilliant style was seen to perfection in all the county matches in which he took part."

The 1893–94 season saw another change in the scoring system. A try was upgraded from two points to three, while a conversion was reduced from three to two. This was also the season in which the four three-quarter system was universally adopted. Halifax had toyed with it for several years but, like most teams, had generally employed three three-quarters, while sticking to the nine-forward pack. Wakefield Trinity, Hunslet, Bradford and Manningham held to the old system for a time but by the end of the season had all fallen into line. Halifax had enlisted a new centre in Walter Jackson from Gloucester and could now field a brilliant three-quarter line in Toothill, Jackson, Keepings and Firth. Archie and Joey Arnold merely had to supply them with the right ammunition.

Another newcomer was Alf Chorley from Kendal, who became an outstanding full-back and was amazingly capped by New Zealand against the first Northern Union Lions in 1910 having emigrated. The Halifax backs were so talented that Ernest Faber Fookes, a young three-quarter from New Zealand, who had attended Heath Grammar School in Halifax and Owen's College (later Manchester University) had to be content with occasional first team outings. He would go on to captain Yorkshire and win ten England caps. Otis Fletcher captained the side, which played such entertaining rugby that it was dubbed "the Newport of the north".

Put simply, Archie and Halifax repeated the previous season's exploits, albeit with a little more *élan*. Their performance in the YSC was excellent until the later stages which saw them fall back to third. Manningham and Brighouse Rangers tied at the top before Manningham took the title after a replayed play-off. Archie continued his Yorkshire career, missing just one of their eight games. His half-back partner was Liversedge's Bob Wood and the pair proved a rare handful for opponents. They were first paired together against Durham at Headingley on 11 November, 1893, an 18–0 victory before a crowd of 10,000. The following Saturday Yorkshire won 9–0 against Northumberland at Newcastle in atrocious conditions. Archie scored the opening try from a loose scrummage wide out and Harry Speed (Castleford) claimed a second try just before half-time. A blinding sleet storm restricted the second half scoring to "a really clever try" by Bob Wood very late in the proceedings.

Almost equally wretched weather afflicted Archie's first appearance in a Roses Match on 25 November at Bradford. Park Avenue was a quagmire and continuous rain fell. Yorkshire won 11–3 before a crowd of about 8,000 soddened onlookers. Normanton winger A Davey scored a spectacular interception try but Lancashire equalised just before half-time with a try from Oldham's Welsh International three-quarter Bill McCutcheon. Bob Wood won the match with two second half tries, one of which was converted by Dickie Lockwood. In a forward dominated tussle, the Yorkshire half-backs proved the decisive element. The *Leeds Mercury* described Wood as "brilliant on attack" and Archie as "wonderful in defence ... a department in which some critics used to think him deficient". *Old Ebor* in the *Yorkshire Post* remarked, "Though Wood scored two clever tries, I should feel inclined to give the palm to Rigg, who defended splendidly, and really did the lion's share of the work."

The county matches resumed on 13 January 1894. Yorkshire crushed Somerset 27–0 at Weston. Archie scored one of Yorkshire's seven tries, while Fred Firth bagged two. The *Athletic News* reported, "The Yorkshire backs gave a splendid exhibition of the running and passing game, Rigg, Firth and Lockwood being constantly on the aggressive." The *Leeds Mercury* noted, "At half, Rigg and Wood overplayed the opposing couple with consummate ease ... Of the two, Rigg was, perhaps, the more conspicuous." Two days later in a non-Championship game Glamorgan proved much sterner opposition at Swansea; Yorkshire scraped home 3–0. On 27 January Cheshire were overcome 16–6 at Birkenhead; Archie bagged one of Yorkshire's four tries. Injury kept him out of the final County Championship match on 7 February, a 9–0 victory over the Midlands at Fartown, which clinched the title for the Tykes.

Archie's form for Halifax and Yorkshire led many to believe that England would this time award him his international cap. England did cap two Halifax players. Fred Firth played in all three games on the wing and Walter Jackson played in the final game against Scotland on 17 March at Raeburn Place, Edinburgh. Jackson came in for Dickie Lockwood, who had figured in England's victory over Wales at Birkenhead on 6 January and their loss to Ireland at Blackheath on 3 February. Archie's county partner Bob Wood had won his only England cap in the Irish match. England seemed to want to stick to a half-back pairing of Cyril Mowbray Wells (Cambridge University and Harlequins) and Ernest William 'Little Billy' Taylor (Rockliff and Northumberland).

Archie's continued exclusion from England selection became a serious bone of contention in Yorkshire. When he was overlooked for the Irish match, *The Yorkshireman* facetiously reported, "The county president [James Miller] suggested him to the Rugby Union, and the great [Rowland] Hill replied that they had not seen him play down south. Indeed! Who was the main instrument in beating the conglomerate lot of Internationals, English, Irish and Scotch, who last year represented Middlesex? I guess Rigg scored two brilliant tries there, and Hill & Co. went to see that."

On 3 March 1894, Archie, along with Fred Firth, was in the Yorkshire XV which met England at Headingley, while their Halifax and Yorkshire colleague Walter Jackson was in the England three-quarters. A crowd of 14,324 saw a good game on a glorious afternoon and Archie had the opportunity to prove the selectors wrong. He and Bob Wood were opposed to the England captain EW Taylor and the former Bradford half-back W Hall (Ulverston and Westmorland), who had come in for the indisposed CM Wells.

Unusually, the Yorkshire forwards came off second best and England won 15–9, but the defeat did not prevent Archie from illuminating the proceedings. He scored two of Yorkshire's tries and made the other for Bob Wood. Wood acted as scrum-half but had an indifferent game there, the *Leeds Mercury* observing, "Rigg was undoubtedly very clever, but as his confrere worked the scrimmages, he naturally suffered from Wood's inability to get the ball out to him."

The *Bradford Observer* wrote, "Rigg performed splendidly, and will prove a capital substitute for Wells in case the latter should be unable to turn out at Edinburgh. Rigg's two tries were cleverly obtained and ought to have been converted but the Yorkshire kicking was weak all round." After the game the Halifax pair Fred Firth and Walter Jackson were selected for the England side to meet the Scots, but the *Halifax Evening Courier* still complained, "Why Rigg was not chosen after the performance he gave is hard to tell."

Archie did get as far as being travelling reserve for the Scotland match, which England lost 6–0. The English half-backs were distinctly outplayed. *The Yorkshireman* moaned, "The 'great' Wells of whom so much was expected was a conspicuous failure and Taylor, although a little better, was not so useful as he ought to have been. Wood of Liversedge would have been an acquisition to the English team, and so would Rigg of Halifax." The *Halifax Evening Courier* was even more miffed, declaring, "After reading what the papers say of Wells, the southern half-back, we can only say, 'If they had only tried Rigg'."

Three decades later, Archie Rigg's treatment by the England selectors still rankled with some people. In the Halifax versus Hunslet match programme for 30 January 1926, the following was written: "Notwithstanding his great achievements Rigg never gained international honours, but he certainly deserved them, if only for his play in one game in which Yorkshire were to be beaten at any cost. It was Middlesex who were entertaining Yorkshire, and they got together a team of Internationals, Welsh, Irish, Scotch and English, including AJ Gould, Stoddart, Orr, etc. The White Rose prevailed, however, and created a rout, Rigg adding to his quota by scoring two tries, afterwards to be told he lacked experience for an international. Still, he was selected as reserve against Scotland on March 17th, 1894, and was in attendance at Edinburgh ready for playing, but HC Wells foiled him by chartering a special train from Cambridge and arriving just in time. A few Thrum Hall supporters of the present day were at that match – almost 32 years ago."

As Archie was kicking his heels in Edinburgh, Halifax opened their defence of the Yorkshire Cup with a 13–0 success at Idle. Archie returned to the team for the second round, when Halifax salvaged a scoreless draw before 10,000 at Batley. The replay, on 27 March, saw Halifax rout the Gallant Youths 35–0; 12,000 attended. Four days later, highly fancied Liversedge came an even bigger cropper in the third round, going down 43–6 at Thrum Hall.

The tie pitted Archie directly against Bob Wood and *The Yorkshireman* saw a battle royal: "The Yorkshire county men, particularly the halves, must have been studying new fakes, for both Wood and Rigg got all sorts of side, screw and bottom on, possibly with the intention of avoiding each other. Wood was particularly dodgy in his own sweet way, and Rigg more so, and with the additional advantage of a brace of tries, the result of unique dodging, the opposition catching thin air and leaving Archie to take a walk beneath the posts."

On 7 April the quarter-finals took Halifax to Manningham, who had just won the Yorkshire Senior Competition Shield. Halifax upset the tipsters, edging through 5–3. Archie's try, converted by Fred Firth, decided the issue. George Lorimer, the celebrated Manningham and Yorkshire full-back, was unhappy to have missed a couple of goals which he would normally have kicked and was even more disconsolate at taking Archie's dummy. *The Yorkshireman* asked, "How much satisfaction did Lorimer get out of Rigg when he told Archie, 'Dash thee Rigg. We should ha' won but for thee'. 'Nay', said Rigg, 'It's thy fault; tha should ha' tackled me'. 'I should ha' done, but aw thought tha wor gooin' ta pass'."

The semi-final paired Halifax with Bradford at Fartown and the game remained scoreless until the closing minutes, although Halifax had been the better side by far. A crowd approaching 15,000 witnessed a stirring encounter in which Rigg was the star turn, combining brilliantly with Joey Arnold, making several long dashes and providing the three-quarters with plenty of chances. Tries by Alf Chorley and Ben Mellor, both converted by Bill Keepings, gave Halifax their 10–0 triumph. Archie believed he had won the game earlier, but his claim for a try was disallowed. He told the press, "I got as fair a try as ever I did in my life; he seized me low down and swung me over the line."

The Final at Headingley on 21 April attracted a crowd of 16,093. Castleford were Halifax's opponents and were expected to give Otis Fletcher's blue and whites' pack a mighty contest, even if everyone knew that Halifax's backs would be much superior. The latter supposition was decidedly correct, but Castleford's vaunted forwards were overwhelmed by the Halifax eight and the game was practically 'no contest'.

Halifax ran up a record score for a final of 38–6. Keepings scored 13 points from five goals and a try, while Firth equalled the record of Wakefield Trinity's Herbert Hutchinson, who had scored three tries in the 1880 Yorkshire Cup Final.

Archie was too hot for Castleford to handle and his orchestration of the backs was sublime. Two tries were credited to him and *The Yorkshire Owl* eulogised, "No one could possibly have desired to see better football than Halifax exhibited, and when the ball once got loose, they played like a book ... As soon as a pack was broken up, away glided the ball from one pair of hands to another, and with such alacrity too, that the Castleford men fairly broke their hearts over it at times, and gazed in simple wonderment and ten-fold jealousy. Once among the Halifax backs, and no power on earth could pull it down. Clockwork is not a good enough word for the accuracy with which all the Halifax backs manipulated that leather."

Archie's personal performance caused the *Halifax Evening Courier* to report, "Rigg was in fine form, and he plagued his opponents dreadfully by his dodging. It was very amusing to see him making apparently for an opponent's arms, and then to glance off as clean as possible, and be yards away whilst his opponent was grasping at a shadow. Both his tries were fine examples of his prowess in this direction."

Halifax had created a record by taking the Yorkshire Cup for the fifth time, one more than Wakefield Trinity. A second Yorkshire Cup winners' medal was thus added to a second County Championship winners' medal in Archie's growing collection. He had set new standards for himself in a record-breaking season for Halifax. He had broken Tom Scarborough's club record (18 tries in 1881–82) by piling up 21 tries in 30 appearances, as well as claiming another five for Yorkshire.

That was a phenomenal scoring rate for a half-back in first class rugby in Victorian times. Bill Keepings had also broken Halifax club records in amassing 58 goals and 154 points. Fred Firth (17 tries) and Walter Jackson (16 tries) provided evidence enough that Halifax had benefited from the four three-quarter system, while skipper Otis Fletcher had bagged 14 tries, despite being tied to the scrums, mauls and line-outs.

The Halifax captaincy passed from Fletcher to Fred Firth for the 1894–95 season, but the campaign was not as successful as anticipated. Halifax won 19 matches, lost 15 and drew four. They dropped to fifth in the Yorkshire Senior Competition, behind Liversedge (champions), Manningham, Bradford and Leeds. Of that quartet only Manningham took a point in visits to Thrum Hall, but Halifax failed to gain a solitary point in the return fixtures.

Despite Halifax falling a little from grace, Archie Rigg continued to captivate the club's followers. His form was as good as ever and he played a major role in Yorkshire's successful defence of the County Championship. He played in seven of the county's nine fixtures. The only blemish on their record was a desperately fought 3–3 draw at Leicester against the Midlands on 11 February 1895, when 10 minutes from time "Wood equalised the score from a pass by Rigg". Otherwise it was victories all the way – Glamorgan 31–0, Durham 16–5, Northumberland 19–5, Lancashire 26–10, Cheshire 28–0, Devon 12–5 and Cumberland 5–3. Archie missed the Cheshire and Cumberland fixtures. His partnership with Bob Wood had developed famously. Of the game against Durham at Hartlepool on 10 November the *Yorkshire Post* observed, "Rigg and Wood played splendidly together, adapting their tactics to the circumstances throughout, and they played with the more confidence knowing how well they could rely on the assistance of the men behind them."

For the Roses Match, in Manchester on 24 November, Archie had a temporary new half-back partner, his club colleague Joey Arnold, who was understandably nervous on his county debut. Joey, a genuine crowd-pleaser, could be an entertainment on his own, often somersaulting around the pitch after his side scored a try. Yorkshire won easily and Rigg was acknowledged as the best half-back on the field. *Rocket* wrote in the *Halifax Evening Courier*, "I am very sorry that Rigg has not been selected for the North team, and the papers this morning mostly condole with him.

The *Leeds Mercury* said, 'We cannot but condole with Rigg at the hard fortune which prevents him securing the legitimate reward of his brilliant abilities'." *Rocket* followed by musing, "Is it going to be a repetition of last year, I wonder?" Well, essentially it was. England selected very few Yorkshire players in their three fixtures and amazingly only one forward, WE Bromet, late of Tadcaster, but now playing in the south with Richmond. Bromet was an Oxford Blue, who thus did not fit into the category of "yer average Yorksher forrad". As far as Archie was concerned he was overlooked entirely, the England half-backs for all their games were 'Little Billy' Taylor and another Oxford Blue, RHB Cattell (Moseley), who would soon become a clergyman.

The 1894–95 season was notable for the many suspensions of northern clubs and players by the RFU on charges of professionalism. It was clear that big changes loomed ahead. For many in Yorkshire the RFU's hostility was reflected in the glaring omission of the county's players in the international XV. For Archie, this would have been a personal disappointment and history would ensure that he would never again have the opportunity to win an England cap. He and his Yorkshire team-mates did, however, have an opportunity to prove the RFU mandarins wrong, when Yorkshire met England at Headingley on Monday 8 April 1895, a month after England had lost their last match to Scotland 6–3 at Richmond. Yorkshire swamped the Rest of England 21–3.

Bob Wood and Archie Rigg took on Cattell and Taylor, outshining them completely. Wood made Yorkshire's first two tries for three-quarters Fred Cooper (Bradford) and Hainstock (Leeds). Archie made the third for Osbert Mackie (Wakefield Trinity) and with two conversions from George Lorimer (Manningham) Yorkshire's lead was 13–3. Cooper then ran three-quarters of the length of the field for a magnificent try before Archie completed the rout with a try from a scrum, which Cooper converted.

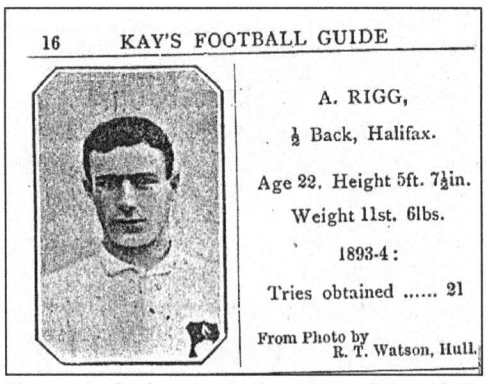

Above: Archie's entry in the 1895 edition of *Kay's Football Guide*.

Right: A 1900 picture of Archie.

Apparently, England got off lightly, as the referee turned down seven appeals for further tries by Yorkshire. Rowland Hill was at the game, but was conspicuous by his absence at the post-match dinner.

Rocket wrote of Rigg, "As usual he right worthily filled the post of honour. It is simply sickening to see the way in which Leeds football papers puff up Bob Wood and neglect Rigg. I am well aware that Wood is a fine half-back, and I greatly admire his play, but when it is remembered that Rigg gives him the ball or takes it after Wood has got it out of the scrummage, it is plain that one ought to have just as much credit for the 'donkey work' as the other. Without overstepping the truth I can safely say that for downright useful work the game through Rigg was second to no man, his run through which led to Mackie dropping over the line being quite equal to Wood's similar run in the first half whilst his strong, sharp burst in the last minute or two of play, which found him behind the England posts before anyone knew where the ball was, quite delighted the spectators."

There was less joy for Archie when Halifax entered the battle to retain the Yorkshire Cup for a third successive season. Shipley were despatched 26–0 in the first round at Thrum Hall on 16 March 1895; Archie scored a try and a goal. The following week Halifax lost 3–0 to Batley at Mount Pleasant in the second round. It would be another decade before Halifax would contest a Yorkshire Cup-tie, albeit under different auspices.

Archie's last game for Halifax as a rugby unionist was against Rochdale Hornets at Thrum Hall on Monday 15 April 1895. Despite fielding a scratch side Halifax won 8–0. The *Evening Courier* noted, "Rigg scored a splendid try after some clever play by Arnold, and Jackson kicked the goal, besides scoring the other try with one of his speedy bursts." He missed a scoreless draw against Wigan at Thrum Hall the following Saturday, which proved to be the final game Halifax ever played under the tyranny of the RFU.

5. Archie and the Northern Union

Archie Rigg was awarded the Halifax captaincy for the historic 1895–96 season, which marked the birth of the Northern Rugby Football Union. Two vice-captains, Bob Winskill and George Dickenson, were also appointed. Nearly all the Halifax players who had turned out for the club in the previous season joined Archie in the ranks of the Northern Union. Among the exceptions were Sam Ripley, Ike Webster and Ernest Faber Fookes. Ripley and former skipper Webster, forwards who had won Yorkshire status in the late 1880s, may simply have retired because of age and weariness, but the 21-year-old Fookes was clearly mindful of the taint of professionalism.

He was studying to be a doctor. Socially and professionally, he would hardly be swayed by the prospect of earning six shillings for the loss of broken time. Instead, he chose to join the Sowerby Bridge club, a couple of miles down the hill from Thrum Hall. Sowerby Bridge remained true to the RFU and for several years reaped the benefits of the removal of the most powerful clubs in the county. From being a third class team – they finished fourth in the Yorkshire No. 3 Competition in 1894–95 behind Pudsey, West Riding and Hull Kingston Rovers – they rose to being one of the top clubs in the county, winning the Yorkshire Cup in 1899 with Fookes as captain. Near neighbours Mytholmroyd won the trophy in 1900, while further up the valley, Hebden Bridge were runners-up in 1898. Despite playing in a backwater with Sowerby Bridge, Fookes, a brilliant three-quarter, attained the captaincy of Yorkshire RU from 1896 to 1899 and played 10 times for England. One wonders just how the England selectors' minds operated – doubtless so did Archie Rigg and his admirers.

Archie's chances of international honours disappeared when he threw in his lot with the brave new world of Northern Unionism. The new organisation did not stage its first international match until 1904, by which time Archie was 32 and a year away from retiring. Instead, he would find challenges enough in the competitive atmosphere of the new rugby. The Northern Union comprised 22 clubs in 1895 – 11 from Yorkshire and 11 from Lancashire and Cheshire. They were all to play each other home and away – a massive 42 matches to decide the inaugural Northern Rugby League Championship (sometimes referred to as the Combination). Within the NRL Championship were the Yorkshire Senior and Lancashire Senior Competitions, a continuation of the competitions which had operated for the last three years in the old game.

Halifax were among the favourites to lift the trophy, along with Liversedge (current YSC holders), Tyldesley (LSC holders), Runcorn, Oldham, Manningham, Bradford, Hunslet and Brighouse Rangers (Yorkshire Cup holders). The forecasters were largely correct, as of that group of nine only Bradford (11th) and Liversedge (15th) finished outside the top seven.

Under Archie Rigg, Halifax had a team well capable of challenging for the title. Sixteen of his men had won or would soon win county caps and Fred Firth and Walter Jackson were England men, who had now burnt their boats. The season kicked off on 7 September, Halifax travelling to Liversedge – a tough opener, especially as Halifax had had no match practice. Halifax returned triumphant after winning 5–0, although the *Evening Courier's* headline screamed "Halifax lick the Shield-Holders". It reported, "Rigg and Arnold got fairly into swing and some of their play was very clever and tricky." After a scoreless first half Jackson scored Halifax's first try in the Northern Union "following a brilliant dash by Rigg" and Bob Winskill added the conversion. The *Courier* also noted, "For the first time in his career Rigg was compelled to leave the field owing to an injury to his proboscis, which 'ran like a tap' … Winskill became half, and Liversedge now put in a dying kick and looked like business, but Rigg returned and all was well."

Halifax won their first four games, Broughton Rangers (11–8, away), Widnes (6–3, home) and Oldham (10–0, home) falling to them on successive Saturdays. Against Widnes on 21 September, nearly 6,000 turned up for a 3.30pm kick-off only to have to wait until 4.25pm for play to begin, owing to problems over a colour clash. Widnes led 3–0 until "at last Archie Rigg nipped through their defence and scored a try" – Halifax's first at Thrum Hall under Northern Union laws. A late penalty goal by Winskill sealed the victory.

Within a month of the season's start, no team remained unbeaten. Halifax were the last team to surrender their unbeaten record, when they went down 3–0 at Hull on 5 October. Three weeks later a second defeat was incurred when Brighouse Rangers won 5–0 at Thrum Hall before 12,000 spectators. The New Year dawned with Halifax having won 16 and lost just four games – the others being at Manningham (16–4) and Huddersfield (3–0). After the New Year's Day fixtures Halifax and Manningham, led by Alf Barraclough, were tied at the top of the table with 32 points, although Manningham had played 21 matches to Halifax's 20. Brighouse Rangers stood third (29 points from 21 games), followed by Runcorn (28 from 20) and Oldham (28 from 21).

Very soon after the Northern Union was inaugurated, there was agitation for changes to the laws of the game, which remained, of course, those of rugby union. Within a fortnight of the season's start, Halifax proposed that 13 a-side should be tried and a game against Manningham was arranged for Thursday, 1 October, 1895 at Valley Parade. It was also agreed to play the game with a round ball and with no line-outs. It was, as one newspaper put it, literally "a test match". Archie turned out at centre, alongside Bill Keepings, for this most novel of matches.

All the big wigs of the Northern Union attended and the press and spectators were agog with curiosity. In the event nature vented its spleen. There was thunder, lightning and heavy rain and at one point the ball burst. Manningham lost two forwards through injury and the game ended in a 3–3 draw. The use of a round ball did not find favour. The *Halifax Guardian* declared, "It is objectionable because it will remove one of the greatest characteristics of the Rugby game." It was admitted that there was some merit in reducing the sides to 13s, but doubt was expressed whether players could cope with the pace if line-outs and scrums were much reduced. Some feared it might become too much like soccer! The lack of the line-out was, however, considered a relative success.

Halifax 1895–96
Top row: J Knowles, H Bottomley, J L Garside, Greenwood;
Second row: R Winskill, W Jackson, J Arnold, Whiteley, Riley;
Third row: H Wilson, Mellor, A Rigg, Robertshaw, Barnes;
Fourth row: Firth, Wilson, Dickenson
Bottom row: Toothill, Chorley, Keepings, Dawson.

There was much interest in the experimental game from the newspapers in Wales, where many of the same concerns about the spectacle and governance of the sport had hit similar raw nerves as in the north of England. Cardiff's *Evening Express* carried the head-line "AN INTERESTING EXPERIMENT" on its front page of 2 October 1895. The match was staged, according to its writer, "with a view of providing ocular demonstration of the effect of reducing the number of forwards and abolishing the line-out and substituting a round ball for the oval one customarily used. The game was somewhat disappointing. Two half hours were played. The game was commenced with a round ball, but after 15 minutes play it burst, and an oval ball was substituted. A round ball was used in the second half. The weather was dull at the commencement, and at half-time a thunder shower came on. Manningham lost two men by accidents, and altogether the circumstances were not favourable to forming a judgement on the value of the proposed changes. On the whole, the abolition of the line-out was considered a very advisable change, and the bouncing of the round ball was truer, while the leather travelled further in the round than in the oval shape. The men bore the strain of the faster and more open game very well."

The *Evening Express* commented in its next edition (3 October 1895), "Line-outs are no earthly good, and nine times out of every 10, end in a scrimmage five yards outside. Occasionally a forward gets the ball away to his backs, and, yet again, a forward breaks away with it 'on his own', and starts a round of passing, but these are the exceptions rather than the rule, and the time occupied by a line-out is time practically wasted". As to the alternative, the *Evening Express* journalist thought a five-yard scrum would be best "or throw the ball in to one of your own men, not necessarily in a straight line but after the style of the Association throw-in."

When it came to the crunch at a Northern Union meeting on 9 December, there was no appetite for radical change. Halifax's Joe Nicholl, the Honorary Treasurer of the Northern Union, proposed a change to 13 a-side, but the motion was defeated 18–9. Leeds's proposal to abolish the line-out was also defeated. The only substantive changes were the introduction of a penalty for a deliberate knock-on (passed by 22–4) and the resolution that the ball should be put into scrummages on the side where the referee stood (passed unanimously).

Another change the Northern Union was loath to make was the abandonment of county matches. A championship was arranged between Cheshire, Lancashire and Yorkshire. It was good news for Archie, who was selected for the Yorkshire County Trial at Bradford Park Avenue on 13 November and scored a try in the Probables' 15–6 victory over the Possibles. When the XV for Yorkshire's game against Cheshire at Headingley on 25 November was announced, Archie was its captain. If there was to be no longer any chance of an international cap, the captaincy of Yorkshire NU might be considered the next best thing. His Halifax colleagues Fred Firth, Bill Keepings and Jack Riley were also selected, but there was disappointment at a 5–9 loss to the Cestrians.

Archie retained the captaincy for the Roses Match on 7 December at Oldham, where the pitch was covered by two inches of freshly fallen snow. This time Yorkshire won 8–0, all the points coming in the first half. Archie scored Yorkshire's second try, which effectively settled the issue. The *Yorkshire Post* reported, "A scrummage was ordered and Bob Wood passing to Rigg, the latter with a short sprint got easily through the defence and scored near the posts for Sharpe to kick a goal."

As each of the three counties had won one and lost one match, the Northern Union decided to have them play each other again to decide the champions. Archie missed Yorkshire's 16–6 win over Cheshire at Runcorn on 12 February 1896, having suffered an ankle injury. Fred Firth scored two of the Tykes' four tries and Bob Wood took over the captaincy. However, Archie was back in charge for the return Roses Match at Fartown on 29 February, which would decide the County Championship. A foul afternoon and a sodden field were not conducive to an open game and Yorkshire went down 8–3 to the Lancastrians, who thereby took the county title. The game was notable as for the first time Archie and Albert Goldthorpe played together in the county team. Albert was drafted in to the centre in the absence through injury of Bradford's Fred Cooper. Albert and Archie only played together for Yorkshire five times, the remaining four occasions all resulting in Yorkshire victories.

Meanwhile in the Northern Rugby League, Halifax and Manningham had begun to pull away from the rest in the fight for the top of the table. Halifax had wobbled alarmingly in the period between 4 January and 8 February, losing at St Helens, Oldham and Leeds and drawing at Stockport. Their only wins in this period were away to Rochdale Hornets (6–0) and crucially at Thrum Hall against Manningham (5–0). However, with 16 games left, Halifax pulled themselves together, winning 12 and drawing four of those fixtures.

On Monday 16 March, Archie took his team to Tyldesley, Halifax having agreed to a 5.30pm kick-off "to please the natives", according to the local paper. Barely 3,000 turned up, but were well pleased with a 3–3 draw. They were even more pleased with the referee, Mr Underwood from Wigan, who awarded just one free kick to Halifax and 20 to Tyldesley. The Halifax press described him as "biased and worse" and declared that he "took the bun, biscuits and the factory". Halifax got so frustrated that "Rigg gave up putting the ball into the scrum". Tyldesley had taken a 3–0 first half lead with a penalty goal kicked by Billy Berry and it was not until the final minutes that Halifax salvaged a point, when Fred Firth fielded an uncharacteristically misdirected kick from Berry's more famous brother, "Buff". Picking up the ball at breakneck speed, Firth zoomed 50 yards for a try, which levelled the score. Crucially Fred fluffed the conversion from under the posts. The point Archie's team surrendered was the last they lost that season. No one yet realised how vital its loss would prove.

Manningham lost three games at Bradford, Runcorn and Stockport in their last 13 fixtures, as they ran neck-and-neck with Halifax. Archie's men won all seven of their final games after the draw at Tyldesley and the captain did his bit, scoring tries in the victories against Wakefield Trinity (10–3, away), Leigh (17–3, home, two tries) and Runcorn (5–4, away), the latter winning the penultimate match and keeping Halifax in the title race. He also booted three conversions in an 18–0 home success against Stockport.

The decisive games took place on Saturday 25 April, when Manningham went to Parkside to play Hunslet and Halifax travelled to Warrington. Manningham had already secured the Yorkshire Senior Competition Shield, finishing six points clear of Halifax, whose more successful cross-Pennine forays proved scant consolation. Manningham entered the final

Saturday one point ahead of Halifax, so defeat at Hunslet for them and victory at Warrington for Archie's men would present the title to Halifax.

Never could Halifax folk have prayed so ardently that Albert Goldthorpe would drop a few goals. Halifax achieved their part of the equation with an 8–0 win, which included a penalty goal from Archie. Hunslet gave Manningham a scare and there was indeed a crucial drop goal. However, it did not come from the boot of Ahr Albert. As the game entered its death throes, the telegraph wires between Hunslet and Warrington sizzled with the latest scores. The game at Parkside remained scoreless until the closing minutes, which would have meant that a play-off would have been necessary. However, the prospect of such a finale was obliterated when Goldthorpe's direct opposite centre, Jack Brown, launched a drop at goal which agonisingly hit the post before dropping over the cross-bar to give Manningham a last gasp 4–0 victory and the first Northern Rugby League Championship.

The top of the Northern Rugby League Championship had finished thus:

	P	W	L	D	F	A	PTS
1 Manningham	42	33	9	0	371	158	66
2 Halifax	42	30	7	5	302	139	65
3 Runcorn	42	24	10	8	313	144	56
4 Oldham	42	27	13	2	374	194	56

Archie's team had lost the title by a hair's breadth. They had lost fewer games than Manningham, but lived to regret those five draws. Defensively Halifax had been supremely efficient. Only Leeds (18), Manningham (16) and Oldham (14) had managed to reach double figures against the blue and whites and no team had managed such a feat at Thrum Hall. On no fewer than 19 occasions, Halifax had nilled opponents. Fred Firth headed the Halifax scoring list with 63 points (8 tries, 18 conversions and a penalty goal), but Archie Rigg was the leading try-scorer with 16, adding three conversions, a penalty goal and a drop goal to total 61 points. In all games Archie finished third in the Northern Union leading try-scorers' list with 18, behind wingers Jack Hurst of Oldham on 28 and Arthur Boothroyd of Huddersfield on 20. As an attacking force no half-back could rival Archie.

At least Archie had the opportunity for another crack at Manningham. On the Tuesday following Manningham's annexation of the NRL Championship, Valley Parade hosted a game between the Yorkshire Senior Competition Champions and The Rest – another example of the unwillingness to dispose of one of the traditions of former days. Archie was captain of The Rest XV, which included three other Halifax men in Fred Firth, Jack Riley and George Kitson. The latter was a rising forward, but on this occasion partnered Archie at half-back. The Halifax quartet had the satisfaction of being on the winning side as Manningham were beaten 16–12.

Halifax players, officials and supporters were understandably disappointed to have been pipped so close to glory. The *Halifax Guardian* of 2 May 1896 did not hold back. Rather ungraciously, it commented, "The Manningham players have certainly been very consistent all through the season and if they have been blessed with a more than ordinary share of luck, they have proved themselves to be a sturdy, determined and capable set of men. As exponents of the best class of football, however, Halifax, Oldham and Runcorn are admittedly superior to the Champions, who are indebted more to physique than science for their present position."

The Northern Union made changes to the fixture format for the 1896–97 season. The gargantuan Northern Rugby League competition was abandoned and a reversion to Yorkshire and Lancashire Senior Competitions was made. The Yorkshire Senior Competition admitted five extra clubs – Bramley, Castleford, Heckmondwike, Holbeck and Leeds Parish Church, which meant a programme of 30 fixtures. In Lancashire the addition of Morecambe, Salford and Swinton provided for a 26-match programme. Extra spice was introduced with the creation of a Challenge Cup Competition to be played at the conclusion of the league fixtures.

Archie was again given the Halifax captaincy and, although never a front-line goal kicker, he was pressed into service for that duty for most of the season. Halifax were embroiled in a three-cornered fight for the YSC Shield with Manningham and Brighouse Rangers. With only three matches remaining, any of that trio could have taken the title but Halifax buckled and, after winning 4–3 at Manningham on 2 March 1897, secured only one point from the remaining six available. Archie's team finished third on 40 points behind the winners Brighouse Rangers (48 points) and Manningham (46 points). The fact that they had done the double over both Rangers and the Valley Paraders only made the failure harder to fathom.

At representative level Archie captained Yorkshire in both their games – a 17–10 victory over Cheshire at Hull on 7 November and a 7–3 loss in the Roses Match at Oldham a fortnight later. He also captained The Rest who beat Brighouse Rangers 8–5 at Lane Head in the annual YSC Champions challenge match on 20 April, kicking a conversion.

The highlight of the season, however, was the introduction of the Challenge Cup, which it was hoped would restore the excitement generated in the old game by the Yorkshire Cup, not to mention large amounts of gate money. Halifax's Cup fighting record in that competition was so well-known that very few pundits would have wagered that Archie's men would not make a good show in the new-fangled Challenge Cup. The first round took place on 20 March and Halifax made light work of the junior club Stockport Rangers at Thrum Hall. There was no stopping Archie, who repeatedly ripped through the defence as Halifax amassed 15 tries in a 55–5 rout.

The *Evening Courier* observed, "Rigg ran in his '94 style, and we all know what that means". Archie dribbled clean through to open the scoring, claimed the ninth try and walked over for the 12th. He did, however, miss four conversions and passed the kicking duties over to others, four players managing just five conversions between them. Doubtless some of the onlookers were more interested in George Kitson, who was on the side-lines nursing a splintered big toe and showing everyone his "Roentgen Rays" image – that is, an x-ray of the injury – quite a novelty in 1897.

The second round on 27 February saw Halifax victorious by 11–0 at Leeds Parish Church, one of Halifax's best performances of the season, Archie claiming one of his side's three tries. The following week Halifax entertained another junior club, Crompton. The Lancastrians, who had been drawn at home, had asked for £100 to switch the game to Thrum Hall, but settled for £60. Again, it was hardly a contest as Halifax cruised to a 50–0 win. Fred Firth bagged three tries, but was upstaged by Archie who re-wrote the record books. He scored 20 points (two tries, two drop goals and three conversions) – a club record for a match and a new Northern Union record.

Halifax were now in the quarter finals and probably regarded as favourites for the trophy. Brighouse, Manningham, Oldham and Broughton Rangers had all been eliminated and on 10 April Halifax were faced with a trip to Warrington, who finished seventh in the LSC. It was certainly a winnable fixture, but the Wire proved just too good for Halifax, winning 10–8. Both sides scored two tries, but Warrington centre Cross's drop goal was worth twice as much as Archie's conversion.

Archie's season had been a successful one as far as scoring was concerned. In all first class matches he had scored 18 tries, second only to Hunslet's winger Billy Hannah who claimed 19. He landed 24 goals to finish third in the NU chart, just two behind joint leaders Albert Goldthorpe and Ben Sharpe of Liversedge. His 112 points placed him at the top of the points scoring lists, 27 ahead of Ahr Albert, who was the runner-up. Archie broke the NU record set the previous season by Fred Cooper (Bradford) and George Lorimer (Manningham), who had both tallied 106 points. Among the more bizarre of Archie's achievements were two goals he kicked from marks – i.e. following fair catches – in easy victories against Holbeck on 10 October and against Heckmondwike on 5 December, both at Thrum Hall. They were the last four-point goals from marks ever scored by a Halifax player. Archie also had the distinction of scoring Halifax's last four-point drop goal in a 7–4 defeat in a friendly at Runcorn on 11 April, 1897.

On 1 May 1897, the *Halifax Evening Courier* eulogised Archie thus, "The one prominent feature [of the season] … is undoubtedly the splendid service rendered to the club by the ever-popular captain – James Archie Rigg – than whom a better half-back or a more gentlemanly player never donned a jersey. Last season he was at the top of the scoring account with 16 tries, one dropped goal and four placed goals. In this, his second year as captain, he tops not only his own but all previous individual records of Halifax players by scoring 20 tries, dropping three goals, and placing 21 from tries or penalties. When one remembers he has been kept out of five club matches through an accident, and when playing for his county, it is a really marvellous season's work and will take some beating. His kindly unassuming nature and sportsmanlike behaviour both on and off the field make him endeared by all, and his team are all cut up in that they have failed to cause Rigg's name to be the first engraved on the Northern Union Cup." It should be noted that the *Courier's* scoring figures included some friendly fixtures.

The 1897–98 season saw the Northern Union abandon the line-out, which was replaced with a punt in from touch. It was also decided that all goals should now be valued at two points. Halifax made a change in the captaincy, which passed from Archie to winger Abe Toothill and, when Abe lost his place, Jack Riley took over. Whoever was captain, Archie Rigg was still Halifax's main man in a campaign which never hit the heights of former times. A poor start – three defeats in four games – was a bad omen. Early season leaders Leeds Parish Church were then defeated 2–0 at Thrum Hall, thanks to a goal from Archie, on 2 October. That began a sequence of nine games in which only one point was dropped – a draw at Bramley. It was a false dawn as three defeats in a row around Christmas virtually ended Halifax's hopes of the YSC title. Halifax finished the season in fourth place with 35 points, well behind Hunslet and Bradford who tied at the top on 48 points, while Batley finished third on 37. Hunslet eventually took the YSC Shield by beating Bradford 5–2 at Headingley in a play-off.

The Challenge Cup brought its usual excitement. Halifax beat St Helens Recs 17–0 in the first round at Thrum Hall on 26 February 1898. A week later, in the plum tie of the second round, 15,000 piled into Thrum Hall to watch Oldham, the eventual LSC winners, snatch an 8–3 victory, after trailing to a Fred Firth try. The club had a consolation in record ground receipts of £349 and 12 shillings.

Archie played 24 games for Halifax in 1897–98 and topped both the try-scoring list with 16 and the goal-kicking one with 9 for the club. Eight of his games were in the three-quarters, where he was increasingly employed over the next few seasons. On 22 February, Archie had scored a hat-trick of tries from the wing in a 16–6 win over Liversedge at Thrum Hall. Halifax had already beaten Liversedge 8–0 at Thrum Hall on 20 November. The game in February had been played at Thrum Hall because Liversedge, winners of the YSC just three years earlier, had fallen on desperately hard times and agreed to the arrangement in order to alleviate their financial problems. Halifax had agreed to give them the gate money. However, the YSC had not sanctioned the arrangement and ordered the game to be replayed at Liversedge on 16 April. Halifax had a problem because they were scheduled to play at Castleford in the last league fixture at the same time.

In what may be a unique occurrence, Halifax played at Castleford and Liversedge at the same time! Most of the first team journeyed to Castleford, where they lost 29–3. Meanwhile four first-teamers - Archie, Abe Toothill, Alf Chorley and Harry Eastwood - went to Liversedge with a rag-bag team and won 3–0. For a club of Halifax's standing, the season had been uninspiring and the fact that 50 players had been used in the first team spoke volumes. At least they were better off than Liversedge.

Archie rose above his side's mediocrity. He captained the Probables against the Possibles in the major Yorkshire County trial at Clarence Field, Leeds on 27 October. The game, along with other county trials at Broughton on 6 October and at Thrum Hall on 20 October had been used to experiment with two referees. It is not recorded what Archie thought of the idea, but the experiment, tried again in the Yorkshire trials the following season, was not repeated for over a century, when the Australians decided to adopt it. Archie skippered Yorkshire to the County Championship, scoring two tries at Stockport on 6 November, when Cheshire were hammered 22–3. The title was secured when he led Yorkshire to a 7–6 victory over Lancashire at Bradford Park Avenue a fortnight later. Cumberland played their inaugural county match against Yorkshire at Hunslet on 5 February, 1898, when Archie led his team to an 8–0 success, although this was a non-Championship affair.

On 18 December 1897, the *Halifax Evening Courier* commented on Archie Rigg's good judgement in displaying in his shop window the match ball which had been used in the Roses Match at Bradford, when Archie had led Yorkshire to the County Championship. Archie had recently become a tobacconist at 1, Swine Market, at the bottom of Gibbet Lane, a thoroughfare that ran upwards from town all the way to Thrum Hall and was therefore on the route of many spectators winding their way to and from the ground. The *Courier* noted that Walter B Walton had transformed the ball into "a pleasing ornament ... gilded with gold leaf and painted with a red and white rose". It bore the legend "1897, Lancashire versus Yorkshire" and was "well worth seeing".

Two days later, *Wanderer* wrote in the *Courier*, "The new game doesn't suit Halifax so well as the old one, not that they did not always like an open game, but it proved too open for them since this new rule came into vogue. To my mind, the secret of their former success lies in the fact that Halifax were always smart in parting with the ball immediately it left the forwards' feet and the three-quarters were to be seen handling the ball one to another before the forwards had time to get out of one another's fond embrace. By this means they seldom had other than the opposing backs to encounter, whereas today, with not half the scrummages occasioned by the abolition of the line-out, they are materially hampered as regards passing the ball, and they have very little better chances of running in tries than the forwards."

Wanderer may well have had a point, but Archie still managed to score 18 tries in first class rugby in 1897–98 to finish fifth in the leading scorers. No Yorkshire club player scored more tries than Rigg.

The 1898–99 season proved even less successful as Halifax continued to rebuild, using 41 men in their 31 fixtures. Starting with only four wins from their first 11 YSC games, they were never in the hunt for honours, finishing eighth with 15 wins and 15 defeats, miles behind Batley on 48 points and Hull on 47. Ironically, they did beat both of those teams at Thrum Hall, but such performances were few and far between. Archie missed a lot of matches through injury, the worst coming in a 3–0 defeat at Bramley on 3 December, causing him to be absent for nine games until the start of February.

Fortunately, Archie was healthy for the period in which the County Championship was staged. He captained the Probables against the Possibles in the county trial at Wakefield, scoring a try, as did Albert Goldthorpe, who was in the Possibles' three-quarter line. Albert joined Archie in the Yorkshire team for all three of their matches. Archie was in rare form in those games, leading as a captain should and scored two tries in a 14–2 win over Cheshire at Valley Parade on 29 October, another against Lancashire, who were vanquished 20–9 at Salford on 5 November, and a third when Yorkshire clinched the Championship by beating Cumberland 8–5 at Clarence Field, Leeds on 28 January. His value to Yorkshire was underlined by his selection for that game, which was his first since his injury at Bramley.

Four years after the formation of the Northern Union there were still rugby enthusiasts who yearned for reconciliation with the Rugby Football Union. The England international side had suffered significantly from the loss of so many top class northern players and in the 1898–99 season lost all three of their matches for the first time. On 16 January 1899, the *Leeds Mercury* discussed reunification and the make-up of the England XV after a particularly gruesome 26–3 loss to Wales at Swansea, remarking, "Nor would we barter Rigg for any other English half-back, even with EW Taylor at his best thrown in". Ernest William Taylor, or 'Little Billy', as he was popularly known, had been the darling of the England XV, winning 14 caps between 1892 and 1899, in six of which he was captain. It must have been hard for Archie and his supporters to accept what he had sacrificed in terms of possible international fame and status when he became a Northern Unionist.

Halifax 1898–99: Back row: Councillor Tyson (President), G F Dickenson, Morton, Riley, Dewhirst, A Dickenson, Mallinson, Kitson, Skinner (Secretary) Midgeley (Trainer); seated: Ambler, Arnold, Winskill (Captain), Rigg, Stoyle, Nettleton, Nicholl; front: Helliwell, Langhorn.

Halifax won eight out of their last 10 YSC fixtures, which coincided with Archie's return. On 11 March 1899, Halifax's last league engagement yielded an 11–3 win at Holbeck after a scoreless first half. Archie was magnificent in attack and defence. *Clito* noted a wonderful effort in the latter department: "The sprinter, Goodfellow, got absolutely clear, Firth failing in his final dive to get at him, but Rigg came with a wet sail and grabbed his prey just in time. What price Archie's even time after this!" He contributed a stunning try too: "Halifax were badly pinned, but amid this the Yorkshire captain supplied the tit bit of the match. Archie commenced with a dribble well within his own 25, and, unaided, got to the centre, where he picked up, and after a dashing run, in which he handed off half-a-dozen stalwarts, one of whom was knocked down, got up again, and had the dose repeated, he wound up a capital piece of play by scoring between the posts."

Halifax's season ended catastrophically, however, the following week when they crashed out of the Challenge Cup in the first round at Castleford. The score was only 8–0, but the defeat was dismayingly comprehensive. If nothing else, Halifax defended heroically, *Clito* declaring in the *Halifax Daily Guardian*, "Rigg [did] the lion's share of the tackling and clearing, the old hand working desperately hard". The *Leeds Mercury* noted, "Rigg played throughout with an energy and dash and daring, which is characteristic of the man."

Archie's status in the game was well illustrated in the *Halifax Daily Guardian*, which reported, "On April 22nd Rigg captained The Rest v Batley after which there was a reception at the Victoria Hotel, Bradford at which the winning County Champions, Yorkshire, received their championship medals. A special presentation was made to Rigg. A medal made by Fattorini's of Bradford 'of exceptional value and beauty about the size of a florin and of 18 carat gold with enamelled centre. The county rose is at the head of the medal and is formed of six diamonds with two gold leaves as companions'."

The 1899–1900 season was memorable in many ways for Archie Rigg. When he was available, his continuing brilliance helped Halifax, with 43 points, shoot up the YSC to third place behind eventual Shield winners Bradford who finished on 50 points and runners-up Batley on 48 points. Unfortunately, injuries saw him miss half of Halifax's 32 fixtures. The season began well enough with six wins and two draws in the first nine games. Included in those successes was a 14–6 victory at Hull on 9 September, which many Halifax followers deemed to be one of the club's finest performances ever seen. Archie kicked his side's only goal, but probably had other things on his mind. He would be a married man before he played again. His bride was Josephine McGovern, a cotton spinner, who had been born in Ireland, but brought up in Halifax. She was the daughter of Colour Sergeant John McGovern, who had been stationed with the West Riding Regiment at Halifax Barracks, near Thrum Hall. Archie's wedding was registered at Portsea Island, Portsmouth, presumably because the McGovern family had moved to Hampshire.

By the following Saturday, Archie and his bride were back in Halifax and Archie turned out in a home game against Manningham. It was reported that there were 8,000 in the ground at kick-off, but more were constantly streaming in. The game was drawn 7–7 and Archie was the star turn. The *Halifax Evening Courier* of 16 September 1899 exclaimed, "Here's health to Rigg! He has come home from his brief honeymoon to win new laurels. Thrum Hall resounded with his praises today, for he certainly did magnificent work. He got the first and only [Halifax] try, and the spectators recognised his success with a wave of enthusiasm seldom equalled in volume on a football field. But apart from this, his play throughout was manly."

Archie pulled Halifax back from 5–0 down with his try, the *Courier* noting, "Rigg gained possession just beyond the centre and dodging man after man in fine style, eluded the full-back, and put on three points for Halifax." Halifax trailed 7–3 at the break, but a penalty from Archie and a drop goal from winger Reggie Mallinson snatched a point for the Thrum Hallers. *Rocket*, in the Monday edition of the *Halifax Evening Courier*, was even more effusive, writing, "Rigg was the best man on the field once more. He got through the work of two or three men, and whenever there was any especially good work on the Halifax side he seemed to have a finger in the pie. It was Rigg who scored the only try secured by Halifax, it was Rigg who later kicked the penalty goal, it was Rigg who passed the leather to Mallinson when 'Reggie' dropped that goal and it was Rigg who knocked the corner flag down when almost again a scorer. Well played, Archer!"

Archie's form in the opening weeks was fine and on 30 September he ran rings around Liversedge in a 14–0 home win and scored two tries. For the first time his half-back partner was Johnny Morley, formerly of Sowerby Bridge RU Club, with whom he won the Yorkshire Cup in 1899. A smaller version of Archie, Morley would eventually become Halifax club captain and play for the England NU team. One observer described him as "slippery in the tackle, alert, resourceful, determined and gentlemanly and, like Archie Rigg, never does anything foul or shabby."

CHATS WITH
Celebrated Yorkshire Footballers.

No. 7—JAMES ARCHER RIGG.

Some men are born great, and others have greatness thrust upon them, but James Archer Rigg, of Halifax, claims neither.

When I ran him to earth at his place of business in the "Beacon Town," he was quite good-humoured and beaming, as usual, but when he found out my errand he seemed to shrink within that retiring nature of his all at once.

It is useless to attempt to thrust greatness upon the Halifax pet, and it was with great difficulty I got him to say anything about himself further than the last census did.

The tall, athletic, and well-developed figure of Archer Rigg, as most of us know him, carries the weight of twenty-six years and some months, besides bone and muscle. He entered this world via Southowram Bank, near Beacon Hill, on the fourteenth day of February, 1873.

Halifax has reason to be proud of him, especially when it is remembered that the whole of his football career has flourished there.

He commenced manipulating the leather, and making a name for himself, when about fifteen years of age, his first services being rendered to Ovenden St. George's, a junior team of some note in those days.

As a centre three-quarter he soon shewed what kind of stuff was necessary for that particular position.

After two seasons with the St. George's team, he went over to the Halifax Gymnasium, with whom he stayed three seasons.

He was nineteen when he was given the position of half-back in the premier team of the town.

James Archer Rigg.

"My first match with Halifax," says Rigg, "was against Bradford. It being the end of the season, I only played in two or three matches. The following season I turned out with the blue and white once more. That was in the season 1892-3, the same year I got into the County team."

Since then Rigg has played continuously for Halifax, and many a fine exhibition have the Hanson Laners been treated to by their favourite up to this. It seems very likely too, that they are in for a lot more, for Rigg never played better in his life than he is doing at the present time.

Since entering the County team he has never been "shelved" for a better man, and has played in almost every match; only missing when sickness has interfered. This is his fourth season of captaincy of the White Roses.

He has led the Halifax boys for two years in a style we are all familiar with.

I think readers of "Y.C." will agree with me in saying that we have yet to see the half-back who can get the upper hand of James Archer Rigg.

Curious experiences have been very rare in Rigg's case. "Indeed," said he, "I can only mention one. Previous to the County match against Cheshire, on October 28th, I had, in all my career, only been damaged twice sufficiently to necessitate my having to leave the field. It is a curious coincidence that in both these earlier cases it was on the Bramley ground, and on each occasion in almost the identical spot."

The following story, of which the popular Yorkshire Captain is the hero, may or may not be exactly correct, but that such a thing happened at some time or another there is no doubt.

"One very foggy day the team were playing away from home, and it was found, upon entering the field that one member of the team—popular opinion says Rigg—was missing. After waiting some time it was decided to proceed without him. The fog increased in density as the game progressed, and it was not until the second half of the game was fairly started that the missing one turned up. He entered the field unobserved by the opposing team, which had so far been very cocksure of winning. The hero of the day got the ball from a 'scrum' and romped over his adversaries' goal line in fine style. The surprise of the home team may be better imagined than described when they saw the man they thought lost, sitting contentedly on the ball directly behind the posts. This was the winning point in that never-to-be-forgotten game."

It is only fair to state that Rigg emphatically denies the truth of the yarn. How the story got abroad with his name attached to it is one of those mysteries outside the range of solution.

Rigg's opinions on the new rules have been or will shortly be published, so that I will not trouble you with anything second-hand.

The Yorkshire Captain is one of the most gentlemanly players who ever went on to a field, and, by example alone, has done a vast service to Rugby football in the broad acres. May he have health and strength to continue to do so.

Next Week:
ERNEST NEEDHAM.
Captain of Sheffield United.

"A scientist named Mivart will soon issue a work on the cat," says a literary paper. We have done that already. It was a heavy copy of Shakespeare's plays, and we issued it from a third-storey window, and it took her right between the shoulders, and we hope it broke her back.

"My friend, if you don't want whisky to get the best of you, you must get the best of whisky."

"I do when I can; but it's difficult when feller's only got three 'apence."

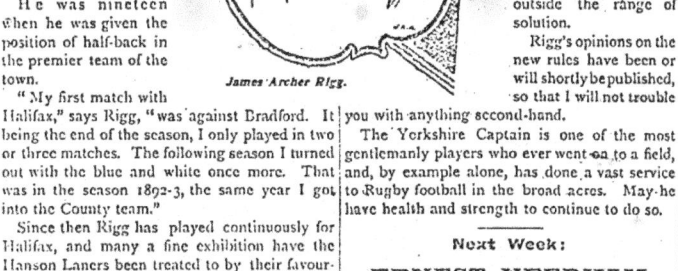

Article from *Yorkshire Chat* 1899. Rigg's birth is given as 1873. In fact, it was 1872.

As usual, Archie captained the Probables against the Possibles, scoring a try in a 17–12 win at Clarence Field, Leeds, and was duly selected to lead Yorkshire against Cheshire at Birkenhead on 28 October. Tries by Archie and Huddersfield forward Milford Sutcliffe, one converted by Fred Cooper, gave Yorkshire a lead of 8–0 at half-time. Unfortunately, Archie broke his collar-bone 10 minutes before the interval and took no further part in the game, which Cheshire finally won 9–8.

He was unable to play in any further county matches in 1899 and did not return to the Halifax XV until 23 December, when Hull were beaten 8–6 at Thrum Hall. In his absence Halifax lost four of their five games, effectively forfeiting their chances of taking the YSC Shield. The Hull game marked the start of a period that brought Halifax 13 wins and a draw from their last 16 YSC fixtures. It also brought an end to the season for skipper Bob Winskill. Archie took over the captaincy and moved to centre. However, he lasted only eight games in those roles before a bad shoulder injury at Bramley on 24 January ended his season and Jack Riley became Halifax's third captain of the campaign. Rigg's injury was so troublesome that the club arranged for him to travel to London on 19 February to start a week's course of treatment "with a bone specialist of much repute".

The new millennium had begun inauspiciously for Halifax's favourite son, but Archie was to receive an extraordinary accolade from an unexpected source, which indicated just how highly he was regarded in Northern Union circles. The celebrated *Boy's Own Paper*, known and loved by boys throughout Britain and the Empire, carried an article by a 'B.O.P. Special Correspondent' in its edition of 3 February, 1900. It was titled "A CHAT WITH THE NORTHERN UNION FOOTBALL CHAMPION – MR. ARCHIE RIGG, OF HALIFAX". The contents are very much like any bland, politically correct press release that the sport's leading body might issue today, giving the NU's justifications for its procedures and laws, but revealing very little about Archie as a player or person.

However, the very fact that *The Boy's Own Paper* considered an article about the Northern Union was appropriate for and significant to its massive readership was a compliment to the fledgling sport. Archie's star status and his position as Yorkshire's captain for the last five years marked him out as a genuinely exceptional figure within the game. *The Boy's Own Paper* had chosen Archie, when they might just have easily featured icons such as Jim Valentine (Swinton), Dickie Lockwood (Wakefield Trinity), Tom Broadley (Bradford), all former England RU caps, or even Ahr Albert, to name just a few luminaries of the Northern Union.

The summer of 1900 was momentous for Archie and the town in which he lived. Josephine presented him with a son, John Edward, while the Thrum Hall cricket and rugby grounds staged the "Halifax Universal Exhibition, World's Fair and Carnival". This was a massive undertaking, opening on 23 July and running for three weeks. All manner of trade stands and all manner of machinery were exhibited. There were daily amusements and concerts, and military bands including the Royal Horse Guards, the Coldstream Guards and the York and Lancaster Regiment played on the cricket green during the afternoons and evenings. Among the variety of entertainments were *Permane's Troupe of Educated Bears*, the *Great Achmed Ibrahim Troupe* of Bedouin Arabs, one of whom could hold eight people on his shoulders, and Alethea, "the most graceful and accomplished Contortionist in the Universe".

Halifax 1901: Top: T Nicholl, J A Rigg, G Kitson, W Knowles;
Middle: J Bartle, J E Jones, A Brown, J Arnold, E Helliwell, G H Langhorn;
Bottom: Jack Riley, R E Winskill, J Swinbank, W Morton, Joe Riley.

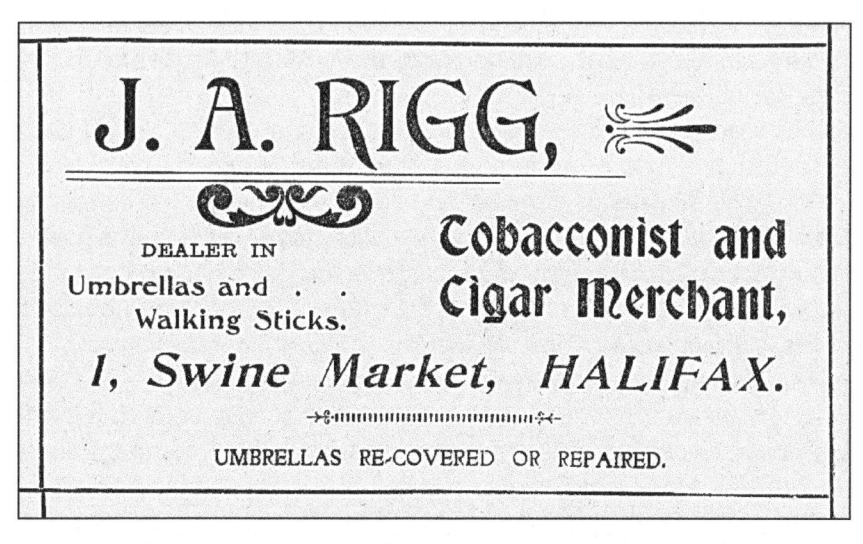

Advert for Archie Rigg's tobacconist shop, which appeared in the souvenir catalogue for the 1900 "Halifax Universal Exhibition"

Among the minor attractions was Messrs Haydon and Urry's Eragraph, "as used in several of the large London theatres, showing the latest Anglo-Boer War pictures, the Northern Union Cup-tie (Halifax versus Oldham), the Operatives of Dean Clough Mills leaving the Mills, etc". The cup-tie referred to was the second round Challenge Cup game at Thrum Hall on 24 March, which Halifax lost 10–5 before a crowd of 13,657, who paid a ground record £573. Probably Archie was present at that game, even if his injury prevented him playing and perhaps, he took a look at the Eragraph with some of his team-mates. What is certain is that he took out an advert in the 200-page Exhibition programme promoting his tobacconist business, which reveals that he was also a dealer in umbrellas and walking sticks. Unfortunately, the extravaganza ended in a catastrophic loss of over £2,500, largely because of terrible weather.

George Dickenson, who had been a first-teamer as far back as 1890, took over the Halifax captaincy for 1900–1901 and led Halifax to runners-up spot in the Yorkshire Senior Competition. Halifax won 22 and drew three of their 30 YSC fixtures, but Bradford finished the season with 51 points to Halifax's 47 to take the Shield. In any other season Halifax may well have been champions. Archie missed seven of the first eight games, but then missed only two of the remaining games. However, Johnny Morley and Arnold Nettleton formed the half-back pairing and Archie only played four times in his usual position. Now he was employed in the three-quarters, often on the wing and a couple of times he figured at full-back. It did not seem to make much difference to his effectiveness and at the season's end he and the other winger, Tommy Nicholl, topped the try-scorers with 15 each, which gave them a place in the top 10 of the NU's leading try-scorers.

By the time Archie had begun to play regularly again, the County Championship had started and George Marsden (Bradford and an England RU cap) and Welshman Dimmy Franks (Hull) formed Yorkshire's half-back pairing for all their fixtures. Archie's county career was not quite over yet, however.

The matches which effectively decided the destination of the YSC Shield were Halifax's two encounters with Bradford. As we have seen, the first at Thrum Hall on 10 November was the occasion of Archie's infamous dismissal and culminated in an 18–0 defeat. By the time of the return at Park Avenue on 16 February, an epoch had ended with the death of Queen Victoria three weeks earlier. The clash was a must-win match for Halifax, but Archie's try was their only score in a 9–3 defeat. Halifax won their remaining six games, but Bradford only faltered against Hunslet in their last six matches to finish worthy champions. Hopes of progress in the Challenge Cup came to an unexpected early conclusion in the first round on 2 March, when Halifax went down 10–2 at York in a sea of mud before a crowd of 7,000. York was a Second Competition club, which made the result the shock of the season. It was beginning to look as if Archie would never emulate his feats as a winner in the old Yorkshire Cup in this new fangled Challenge Cup.

Archie Rigg, now approaching 30, was awarded the Halifax captaincy for 1901–02 after a gap of several years. The Northern Union had decided to create a 14-club super league, a new Northern Rugby League. Below it the Yorkshire (14 clubs) and Lancashire (13 clubs) Senior Competitions continued. Halifax, along with six other Yorkshire teams, six Lancashire teams and one from Cheshire (Runcorn) comprised the NRL. Although a superlative

Broughton Rangers team ran away with the league and won the Challenge Cup, it was a tough competition. After losing their first four games Halifax showed they were still amongst the best teams in the land. They finished fifth on 28 points from their 26 games, behind Broughton Rangers (43), Salford (31), Runcorn (30) and Swinton (28), the Thrum Hallers being the highest placed Yorkshire side.

Archie played in 23 of the NRL fixtures, predominantly at centre. He was leading a group of players that was blending into a formidable force. Among the newcomers to the club in the 1901–02 season were Joe Riley, from Sowerby Bridge, who would go on the first Lions tour in 1910 as a centre, Billy Little, a Cumbrian full-back with a howitzer kick and a contrary personality, who would play for England, and Billy Bulmer, a local who would also gravitate to international status as a forward. They joined established players of renown in Johnny Morley, Jack Riley, Ike Bartle, Walter Morton and George Langhorn, who would all represent England in the near future.

Despite a creditable performance in the NRL, Halifax once again failed in the Challenge Cup, going out in the first round, albeit against formidable opponents. Swinton did the trick at Thrum Hall on 15 March, winning 2–0, thanks to a first half penalty goal landed by forward Jack Preston. Halifax's only consolation was a crowd of 15,970 and record receipts of £595, which would not be surpassed until 1913. The game was also notable as Fred Firth's final game for Halifax. Thrice an England RU International, Fred had played 20 times for Yorkshire as a RU man and six times under the Northern Union, often as a colleague of Archie. Between 1890 and 1902 he had scored 502 points for Halifax, a club record, but Archie had that record firmly in his sights. Fred would have set a bigger target had he not left Halifax for Wakefield Trinity in 1899, spending the next season and a half at Belle Vue, having taken a pub in Westgate. He returned to play for Halifax in January 1901.

There was a return to county rugby for Archie. He played, along with Ike Bartle, for Whites against Stripes in the county trial at Bradford on 23 October 1901, while Tommy Nicholl was on the opposite side. On 30 November Archie was in the Yorkshire centres for the game against Cheshire at Edgeley Park, Stockport but the Tykes went down 13–3.

Archie leads Halifax to the Cup and League Double

Seven years after the formation of the Northern Union many Halifax fans, officials and players were probably wondering what had happened to the good old days when their team had regularly won trophies or at least challenged for them. The brilliant double-winning Broughton Rangers team of 1901–02 had set new standards. Their nearest rivals, Salford finished a massive 12 points adrift as league runners-up and were routed 25–0 by the Rangers in the Challenge Cup Final.

Broughton fielded a coruscating back-line, which included the game's leading try-scorer, captain and centre Bob Wilson who bagged 38 tries, and half-back Willie James who topped the goal-kickers with 75 successes. In 26 league games they conceded a mere 112 points, while in attack they amassed 285 points, twice as many as Halifax (142) had managed.

To some observers, Broughton Rangers appeared to be in a different league. In 1902–03 they were – and so were 35 other clubs. It had been decided to run a two division Northern

Rugby League with 18 clubs in each division. Four clubs – Hull KR, St Helens, Widnes and Wigan joined the 14 existing members of the NRL's top table to form the First Division. The winning of the league would now necessitate successfully negotiating a daunting fixture list of 34 games – eight more than the previous season.

For the 1902–03 season the Northern Union abolished the punt-in from touch and replaced it with a 10-yard scrum, a major change which curbed much of the scrambling play which often followed a ball being kicked off the field. The new law certainly suited Halifax, who began the campaign in fine style under the captaincy of George Kitson, leader of an exceptionally potent pack. Halifax had strengthened their backs too, bringing in three men from far afield. Herbert Hadwen, formerly of Morecambe and Salford and a Lancashire cap, added pace on the wing, while 'Wax' (WW) Williams, a stylish centre from Cardiff, and Bill (WR) Wedgwood, a 19-year-old goal-kicking winger from Seaton, Billy Little's old club, considerably bolstered Halifax's armoury. Williams and Archie Rigg would get along famously in the Halifax centres, although Archie would periodically be used on the wing.

Halifax displayed astonishing form from the off. Hull KR, Hunslet, Wigan and Widnes were vanquished in September and on 4 October they faced another unbeaten side in Bradford at Thrum Hall. A crowd of 18,000 (14,708 paying £400/5/10) saw Archie score a late try as Halifax won 9–0 to maintain their place at the top of the league. The following Saturday Halifax won 5–0 at Huddersfield in a rough affair scarred by too much keenness. *Rocket* complained bitterly, "It is a keenness of the wrong order, the keenness which reminds me of Castleford in its roughest days, when the glassblowers walked to victory over the maimed forms of their opponents." It must have been a heck of a struggle. Two days later, on Monday 13 October, Archie turned out at centre for the Probables against the Possibles at the Boulevard, Hull in a Yorkshire County trial, his side winning 10–3. Halifax's Arnold Nettleton partnered George Marsden in the Probables' half-backs, while Billy Little was full-back for the Possibles.

On 18 October, Halifax still topped the table, followed by Runcorn and Swinton, but dropped their first point of the season when a dropped goal by Warrington half-back Arthur Burgess on the stroke of time earned the Wires a 2–2 draw at Thrum Hall. Home victories over Brighouse Rangers (5–2) and St Helens (8–0) followed. Archie missed the latter on 1 November, along with Ike Bartle and Jack Riley, because they were otherwise engaged with Yorkshire at Headingley. Cumberland were dispatched 29–2 and the game marked the close of Archie's wonderful career as a county player. That career stretched back almost a decade to January 1893 and yielded 32 caps and 22 tries. However, Archie's Yorkshire finale was stained by tragedy. Cumberland half-back, 21-year-old John Hill Richardson, a Whitehaven Rec player, received a fatal injury – his bowel was ruptured. The young man died in Leeds Infirmary on the Monday following the match. The Leeds City Coroner returned a verdict of accidental death.

On 8 November, Halifax visited fourth-placed Runcorn who had only lost one match. The Linnets' centre, Jim Butterworth, had the distinction of scoring the first try of the season against Halifax, the previous nine teams having failed to cross the blue and white line. However, Halifax had the last laugh, winning 5–3 with a late goal from Billy Little. During the match Runcorn spectators mobbed the referee and the ground was later suspended for 18 days. Huddersfield suffered a similar suspension later that season and chose to use Thrum Hall for their game against Oldham on 28 February 1903.

Halifax finally surrendered their unbeaten record on 22 November, crashing 12–0 at Salford, for whom James Lomas booted three goals. The following Saturday third-placed Swinton shared "a marvellous game" and the spoils in a 3–3 draw at Chorley Road. After trailing 3–0 at half-time, Archie saved Halifax with a characteristically brilliant try following a tremendous burst down the wing from Herbert Hadwen.

Suddenly Halifax's fortunes dipped alarmingly. Five defeats in seven games between 20 December and 31 January was definitely not championship form, even allowing for bad luck with injuries. Even so, only Swinton had risen above Halifax in the table, although Broughton Rangers and Salford were also pressing hard. With the Challenge Cup just around the corner, Halifax's floundering ship began to steady itself. A last-minute penalty goal by Billy Little was the only score in a tense victory at Wigan on 4 February. A 7–0 home success against Huddersfield followed in a nine-match period when Archie Rigg was pushed out from centre to the wing. Thereafter, Halifax contested 18 matches between 14 February and 27 April, a 10 week battle of endurance, which involved eight cup-ties and a number of vital league games. Only two were lost and Halifax's cast-iron defence conceded only 27 points.

The first round of the Challenge Cup, on 14 February, threw up a local derby with Salterhebble, a Yorkshire Combination team, in the same league but a considerable distance behind Halifax's 'A' Team. However, Halifax fans with long memories recalled catastrophic defeats by Salterhebble back in 1883 and 1886. On this occasion they need not have worried as Halifax won 34–0 at Thrum Hall, where the crowd was returned at 5,500 (4,256 paying £81), including 1,000 boys.

Archie Rigg claimed one of Halifax's eight tries, but as the game drew to its close it was apparent that they were deliberately throwing away scoring chances in an effort to allow full-back Billy Little to get a try. Full-backs were not really expected to score tries and Little had not scored one all season. It transpired that the Halifax president, Alderman Tyson, had promised Billy a sovereign if he got a try. Billy got the try and the sovereign, thanks to his solicitous team-mates. *Rocket* noted, "Plenty of useful work was accomplished by Joe Riley and Rigg", while "For a junior lot, the Salterhebble forwards proved a lusty set, but, of course, were outclassed by the Halifax eight."

Halifax were drawn away to lowly Second Division side Castleford in the second round on 21 February. Castleford had beaten Halifax's near neighbours, Thrum Hall FC, 2–0 in the previous round before a very small crowd. Consequently, Halifax tried to persuade Castleford to switch the venue to Halifax – to no avail. *Rocket* observed, "It was like trying to get water to remain on a duck's back persuading the Castleford managers to agree to the proposed change." Ironically the day of the match was ideal for ducks, if not for rugby. The rain fell in torrents and *Rocket* reported, "There wasn't any football worth speaking about. It was mud-larking pure and simple." The players were consulted before the kick-off about proceeding with the match. Halifax wanted to play and Castleford did not. The referee decided to proceed despite the ankle-deep slush. *Rocket* moaned, "It was more like a polo match than anything else – a lot dirtier, of course ... I believe Rigg never touched the ball in the second half." The game finished scoreless and the drenched crowd of 3,000 yielded a meagre gate of £44/10/6, leaving each club with about £10 after expenses. Not a good day for anyone.

On the following Tuesday, 24 February, Halifax beat Broughton Rangers 7–0 at Thrum Hall in a crucial league fixture, played in a gale before 7,000 spectators. Twenty-four hours later the Halifax versus Castleford Challenge Cup replay took place at Thrum Hall in conditions similar to the first game. Rain delayed the kick-off and "downpour was followed by tornado", according to one observer, while the pitch was "a perfect puddle". Castleford took a disputed 3–0 lead, but a try by Walter Morton levelled the scores. As half-time approached Castleford forward Sherwood was sent off and Halifax went on to win 10–3. Archie and Joe Riley engineered the match-clinching try for Johnny Morley. Conditions were so vile that only 2,000 spectators turned up but the gate was up by two shillings and sixpence at £44/13/-.

A fourth game within seven days, on 28 February, proved too much for Halifax, who embarrassingly lost 7–3 at bottom of the league St Helens. Matters did not improve much the following Saturday, 7 March, when Halifax were held to another 0–0 draw against Brighouse Rangers at Thrum Hall in the Challenge Cup third round. Halifax were still top of the league and Rangers were next to the bottom.

Still, it was a typical derby cup-tie, even if Brighouse never looked like scoring. The Halifax backs squandered numerous chances in "a stiff tussle under unpleasant conditions", as it rained on and off throughout. The consolation for both clubs was a share of the gate of £249/12/11, the crowd consisting of 9,864 paying customers plus about 800 members. The replay at Lane Head took place on the Tuesday following and produced a gate of £230 from a crowd estimated at 8 to 10,000. This time Halifax controlled the match, tries from Langhorn and Wedgwood making the difference in an 8–2 win. Billy Bulmer and Rangers' forward Walton were sent off in the last minute.

Halifax's next engagement was a league fixture at Batley. General Redvers Buller, one of Britain's conquering heroes of the recent Boer War, performed the kick-off, with 10,000 looking on. It was a significant game for Archie Rigg, who was to take over the captaincy until the season's end as George Kitson's own campaign ground to a halt through injury sustained in the match. Archie had already stood in for George on eight occasions earlier in the season and, after his spell as a winger, he was now back at centre. Halifax won 11–3 and Archie landed the only goal of the game. It was the 51st and last goal he ever kicked as a Northern Union player for Halifax. More importantly, although it was not known at the time, that goal took Archie's points total for the club to 503, breaking the previous club record of 502 by Fred Firth.

Thus far Halifax had made heavy weather of their Challenge Cup campaign, winning scratchily against teams they should have had little trouble defeating. The quarter-finals, on 21 March, presented them with a formidable obstacle – Runcorn away, first versus second in the league, the undoubted tie of the round. Archie's men were photographed before leaving on the 10.45 train via Liverpool, a long trip. Five hundred supporters followed on a special excursion. Their team was 6–4 against, according to the bookies. The Canal Street ground was reckoned to be able to hold about 4,000 spectators, but there were already an estimated 7,000 packed in at kick-off time. However many were actually there, they saw a titanic struggle, largely contested by the packs. After a scoreless first half, Halifax played into a strong wind in the second. With five minutes left there was still no score. At that juncture Sammy Houghton, Runcorn's former England Rugby Union full-back, kicked to clear his line. Herbert Hadwen caught the ball cleanly despite the fierce crosswind and claimed a mark. Archie instructed Billy Little to attempt a shot at goal, as was allowable from a mark. Under the conditions it was literally a long shot and few expected a goal to ensue. However, Little judged the wind perfectly and *Rocket* reported, "The ball went to a lofty height, seemed to hesitate in its course, tacked in and dropped. The touch-judge raised his flag. A goal! What a cheer!" 2–0 was enough to see the Thrum Hallers into their first Challenge Cup semi-final.

Victory over Runcorn suddenly opened up the possibility that Halifax could emulate Broughton Rangers' double-winning performance of the previous season. The next three games would certainly test Archie Rigg's team's mettle. First up were Runcorn at Thrum Hall on the Thursday following the Cup-tie – half-day closing in Halifax. Another scoreless first half set the nerves jangling but tries by Archie and Ike Bartle and a Little goal brought a priceless 8–0 victory and went some way to killing off Runcorn's challenge for the First Division title. Two days later, 28 March, third-placed Swinton went down 13–0 at Thrum Hall.

It was not all good news, however. Archie had badly wrenched his knee against Swinton and it was touch-and-go whether he would be fit for the Challenge Cup semi-final against Hull at Fartown on 4 April. The decision was made for him by the Professional Sub-committee of the Northern Union, which refused him permission to play because he had not worked three days since the injury occurred.

He had fallen foul of the notorious working clauses enforced by the Northern Union. The decision was announced on the evening before the semi-final. A bad mistake had been made - the Sub-committee had misread a date. Halifax secretary Arthur Ricketts at once informed the NU secretary and in return received a wire on the morning of the match expressing regret at the mistake, but deciding it was too late to rectify it! *Rocket* was probably as unhappy as Archie, declaring, "There is no player in the Northern Union who is more anxious to comply with the working clauses than is Rigg."

Halifax thus faced Hull without their captain George Kitson, without his deputy Archie and without star forward Billy Bulmer. Jack Riley captained Halifax, whose train turned up 25 minutes late and consequently caused the kick-off to be delayed by 15 minutes. Both teams were new to Challenge Cup semi-finals and although Hull were only 12th in the league table, they had yet to concede any points in the Challenge Cup. A crowd of 17,500 saw Hull take an early lead with a try from winger Moxon. Joe Riley levelled the scores and by half-time Halifax led 8–3 following another try by Ike Bartle, converted by Bill Wedgwood. The only score of the second half was a penalty for Hull and so Halifax progressed to the final via an 8–5 victory. Five minutes from time Halifax forward George Langhorn, his head bleeding from a wound, was ordered off, much to the annoyance of his team's supporters, bearing in mind that several Hull players had previously been cautioned without sanction.

Another incident often recalled from the semi-final involved Hull's Welsh winger Jim Parry, who leapt clean over Billy Little's head but was prevented from scoring by a splendid tackle by Johnny Morley.

Rocket was able to celebrate Halifax's triumph but noted, "One thing which encouraged the men from the East was the fact that Rigg was unable to play. Invariably when opposed to Hull, Archie plays in accomplished style, and he has earned their respect. Rigg is also popular with Hull spectators. His absence did not at all bode well for Halifax, for it not only fired the Hull men with greater determination but also to a certain degree affected the combination of the Halifax back division. Of course, his absence could not be helped."

Archie missed the next two league matches, protecting his injured knee. The first, on 10 April, produced a 2–0 defeat at Warrington, leaving Salford and Swinton breathing down their necks in the struggle to finish top of the league. The following afternoon Halifax met Hull again at Thrum Hall. Halifax were short of five key men, but by half-time were 8–0 ahead. An amazing second half saw no change to the score but Hull had three players sent off.

Crunch time had now arrived, but at least Archie Rigg was fit enough to lead the blue and white assault on the double. With three league matches remaining Salford, Halifax's opponents in the approaching Challenge Cup Final, were top of the league on points average over Halifax, both teams having earned 44 points. Oldham were third. On 16 April Salford were the visitors to Thrum Hall and anticipation was high, reflected in a crowd of 14,064 ((£379/9/6). At the final whistle no one was any wiser. Herbert Hadwen had given Halifax a 5–0 interval lead with a try he converted himself against his former team-mates. Fourteen minutes from time the great star of the period, James Lomas, saved the game for Salford with a try and conversion and the match was drawn 5–5. Two days later, 18 April, Oldham arrived at Thrum Hall desperate for victory. However, tries from Archie and Wedgwood, a drop goal from Joe Riley and a goal from Wedgwood gave Halifax a precious 10–0 victory. That result looked even better two days later when Salford lost 12–5 at Hull. Halifax were now two points clear of Salford, both teams having one league fixture to play.

1903 Challenge Cup Final: Archie Rigg and James Lomas toss up before the game.

Before that, however, they faced each other at Headingley on Saturday, 25 April, in the Challenge Cup Final. It was Halifax's first appearance in the final, but Salford had already figured in it twice, losing in 1900 to Swinton and in 1902 to Broughton Rangers. Interest in the 1903 Challenge Cup Final was intense, attracting a crowd of 32,507, a record for a Northern Union game in Britain which stood until 1922. The gate of £1,834/8/6 was also a new high for the sport.

Salford were slight favourites to lift the Cup, primarily because they had James Lomas in their ranks, a centre with matchless match-winning qualities, a man who scored tries for fun and was a prodigious kicker of goals. He could be skilful, artful and artistic one minute and the next aggressive and abrasive. He was not tall, but he was bullock strong. He was also Salford's captain and a natural leader. In other words, he had it all. If Archie Rigg had indeed been the leading light in Yorkshire rugby in the late Victorian period, then James 'Jumbo' Lomas was assuredly the most luminous player in the entire Northern Union in the Edwardian era. If Lomas was allowed any space or time, it was odds on that his team would win. No one who knew about these things thought any other way. The Halifax plan had to be simple – stop Lomas. The best way to accomplish that was to overpower Salford's pack, thereby denying space or time to the Salford backs and particularly Lomas.

So, Archie Rigg had a lot on his plate. He was Lomas's rival captain – leadership counted for much in crucial matches. Even more pertinent was the fact that it was Archie's and 'Wax' Williams's specific task as centre three-quarters to shackle Lomas, if and when the heavier Halifax pack could not prevent the ball going to the Salford centres. Unlike for most of Halifax's cup-ties, the sun shone and the ground was so hard that it was proposed that a water cart be employed to soften the turf, but the Challenge Cup Committee vetoed the idea. The final kicked off at 3.30pm, but after a few minutes, according to *The Bradford Observer*, "The game was suspended for a few minutes owing to the crowd breaking in at the entrance side to the ground, then pouring into the field like a flood."

When order was restored the match kept the crowd on tenterhooks through its intensity and closeness, but there was precious little entertaining rugby. Half-time arrived scoreless, the Halifax forwards having smothered nearly all Salford's attempts to open out play for their backs. Three minutes into the second half the Halifax forwards made a pell mell rush to the Salford goal line, the ball at their feet and Ike Bartle dropped on it near the posts. Hadwen, the first player to represent two different clubs in Challenge Cup finals, improved Ike's try and Halifax led 5–0. Twelve or so minutes later Hadwen potted a simple penalty against his old club and the scoring ended. The Halifax pack kept up their relentless suffocation of the Salford eight, and, apart from a monumental surge beating off five defenders, James Lomas hardly got a sniff of a chance.

Halifax's hard-won 7–0 victory enabled Archie Rigg to become the first Halifax captain to lift the Challenge Cup aloft, a distinction no man better deserved. The first leg of Halifax's quest for the double had successfully been accomplished. Two days later, on Monday 27 April, Halifax had a tough match at Leigh to negotiate while Salford had what appeared to be a somewhat easier task at Hull KR. A Salford victory and a Halifax defeat would mean a play-off for the Championship between the two at Rochdale on the Thursday. Halifax were to kick-off at 5.30pm, while the game at Hull KR started earlier. The *Halifax Evening Courier* expected to hear the result from Leigh within seconds of the final whistle. A flag would be raised over the *Courier* building immediately the result was known and within a few minutes of that the public would be able to buy the *Courier's* special match edition.

Around 500 Halifax fans found enough time and money to take a special excursion to Leigh, even though it was a working day, and the route was apparently labyrinthine. They were well rewarded. Archie Rigg's men were 6–0 up by half-time and at full-time the score had grown to 11–0. Winger Billy Wedgwood was the hero, scoring all the points – three tries and a goal. Meanwhile Salford had given up the ghost at Hull Kingston, where the Rovers won 16–0. The Championship and the double were Halifax's. The top of the league table read:

	P	W	D	L	F	A	Pts
1 Halifax	34	23	3	8	199	85	49
2 Salford	34	20	5	9	244	130	45
3 Swinton	34	18	7	9	254	119	43
4 Runcorn	34	19	4	11	239	139	42

Archie's triumphant team was certainly not on a level with the Broughton Rangers double-winning side of the previous season as far as attacking play was concerned. It would, however, be difficult to find a meaner defence than that of the Thrum Hallers. One over-awed critic wrote that the whitewash on the Halifax goal-line might as well have been the Great Wall of China as far as most of their opponents were concerned. They simply could not get over it.

In 42 league and cup games Halifax conceded a mere 95 points and their try-line was crossed only 19 times. Tries were conceded in only 13 games and opponents were nilled 21 times. The highest scores recorded against Halifax were at Salford (12), Oldham (11) and St Helens (7). Opposing teams found it almost impossible to even score at Thrum Hall, where the biggest concession was six points to Batley – 2 tries – in November. Only two other teams managed to score a try at Thrum Hall – Castleford in a cup-tie in February and Salford in April.

Another Challenge Cup (minus Archie), a testimonial and on into retirement

The annexation of the double in 1902–03 was, without doubt, the crowning glory of Archie Rigg's rugby career. He had captained the team at the business end of the season and once again proved himself as a leader of men. Yet it is George Kitson's name which is engraved on the bases of the Challenge Cup and Championship trophies. Kitson's injury problems had come at the worst possible time for the elected captain and no one begrudged George's name being inscribed on the trophies, least of all Archie Rigg. It had been suggested that both Kitson and Rigg could have been inscribed, but the engraver was clearly not so instructed.

Rigg was 31 when the 1903–04 season kicked off. He was past his best, undoubtedly. He was certainly not the try-poacher he had been and the speed in his legs had slowed, but he was not a spent force. In contrast, George Kitson's injuries had persuaded him to retire, although he returned briefly to action for Halifax in 1904–05. Halifax's new captain for 1903–04 was Johnny Morley, a smaller half-back version of Archie Rigg, but 10 years younger and a real bobby dazzler. Halifax's defence remained almost as obstinate as the double winners', conceding just 161 points (31 tries) in 39 league and cup games. On the debit side Halifax only mustered 36 tries and 174 points themselves.

Consequently, there was never much chance that the First Division Championship would return to Thrum Hall and Halifax's final position was ninth out of 18 clubs. Their away form was appalling, only the games at Huddersfield and Wigan being won, with draws at Broughton Rangers and Widnes – a mere six points out of the 34 available. Only 31 points were acquired from the 34 league fixtures – way behind joint leaders Bradford and Salford who each had 52. Oddly enough, Halifax beat both of them at Thrum Hall in October. Bradford won the title after beating perennial runners-up Salford 5–0 in a play-off at Thrum Hall on 28 April, 1904.

Archie Rigg played in 23 of the league fixtures, 17 of them at half-back and frequently in partnership with Johnny Morley. His try tally, however, was a meagre two. Even so, Archie had some highlights to look back upon. Not least was his benefit match on 23 January 1904. Benefit matches were a novelty at this point in the game's history. Gradually benefits/testimonials were granted to players who had given a club 10 years unbroken service. This remained a staple reward for loyal northern union and rugby league clubmen for almost a century, but since the Super League era criteria for benefits have become somewhat more elastic, decided by who knows who, who knows how. When Archie was granted a benefit, the Northern Union was only a tad more than eight years old but, as he had been playing for Halifax since 1891, and was held in such high esteem throughout the game, he appeared to qualify for a benefit beyond any quibbling.

Halifax's opponents for the occasion were arch local rivals Huddersfield. Despite the fact that the Fartowners were languishing near the foot of the First Division and would eventually finish bottom, the crowd was estimated at 10 to 12,000. A special illuminated programme was produced for the occasion – possibly the first proper programme ever produced for a Halifax match and the mayor of Halifax, Alderman J Wade, JP, kicked off. He was accompanied by the club president, Alderman Tyson. The *Halifax Evening Courier* commented, "Rigg has been one of the smartest half-backs going, and in the height of his form was one of the most dangerous men who ever stepped on to the field ... There was a pleasing incident when Archie led his men on to the field. The King Cross Band struck up *Auld Lang Syne* and there was general cheering. Meanwhile Rigg looked the bashful fellow he is. I quite sympathise with him."

At half-time former Halifax players took a collection for the beneficiary and sold souvenirs – Fred Firth was pleased to announce that he had sold three gross (432, for anyone who does not know what a gross is). Halifax won the match 12–3 and Archie Rigg was reported to have performed really well. A particularly telling compliment declared, "Rigg made another big effort á *la Lomas*".

A welcome by-product of Archie's benefit match was the introduction to the Halifax first team of two young men who would go on to great things. Ernest Ward was a local centre from Lee Mount, who would represent Yorkshire and England. He fathered two sons, Ernest junior, also a centre, and scrum-half Donald, who both later won huge acclaim with Bradford Northern's great team of the 1940s. Ernest Ward junior captained Yorkshire, England and Great Britain and is surely a prime candidate to join Albert Goldthorpe in the Rugby League Hall of Fame. The second debutant was Joe Brearley, a cousin of Joe Riley, who would play over 200 games for Halifax and was regarded as one of the fastest forwards to have worn the blue and white.

On 5 March there was a game with a difference at Thrum Hall. The rugby pitch was totally unplayable due to frost so the fixture with Leigh was staged on the cricket ground. About 6,000 freezing spectators ringed the ground and were warmed up as the result went Halifax's way, 8–5. The *Courier* reporter enjoyed the novelty of watching the game from one of the pavilion's turrets, declaring the experience, "like reporting football from a balloon". At the conclusion of the match 4 to 5,000 of the crowd stayed behind as the proceeds of Archie's benefit match were presented to their idol. A portion of the grandstand was reserved for the ceremony. Archie was given £224 and an illuminated address, outlining his achievements, while his wife Josephine also received a present of silverware. Sir Savile Brinton Crossley, MP did the honours. The dignitaries included the ubiquitous Mr J Wade (mayor of Halifax), Sir Alfred Arnold JP, Colonel WG Gray JP VD, and J Garside JP. Speeches were made and Archie responded before the shivering masses departed and the chosen few were treated to refreshments in the pavilion. Archie's celebrations finished with dinner at the White Swan Hotel in the evening.

Once Archie's benefit presentation had been completed Halifax began to focus on the defence of the Challenge Cup. Their form so far did not inspire confidence. Seven league matches remained and Halifax won only twice – 3–2 against Batley on 7 April and 10–2 against Widnes on 18 April, both at Thrum Hall. The latter game was notable in that Archie Rigg scored the 133rd and last try of his career for Halifax. From February to the season's end Halifax played 18 fixtures and Archie was used in only five of them – all league matches.

The Challenge Cup proved a different kettle of fish. The side's league form became a side issue as trainer Joe Midgley decided that retaining the Cup was what mattered. To that end he announced that a squad of 20 players would be entrusted with the job. Archie was one of them. History shows that Halifax dispatched St Helens, Barrow, Leeds and Hunslet and, unlike the previous season, no replays were necessary. The final, on 30 April, saw Warrington defeated 8–3 at Salford, Johnny Morley skippering his side to a convincing victory. The captain and Joe Riley scored Halifax's tries, while Herbert Hadwen kicked a goal.

Despite being in the squad Archie was not used in any of the five cup-ties, although he was down to play centre in the semi-final against Hunslet at Wakefield on 16 April. In the event Joe Riley, who had broken a finger in a 7–0 home loss to Hunslet in the league just 12 days earlier, was deemed fit and took the field instead of Rigg. Just why Archie never got a run in the Challenge Cup campaign is unknown, but Midgley and the club must have valued his influence and coaching nous.

A cartoon recording Halifax retaining the Challenge Cup in 1904. (From *The Athletic News*)

Evidence of that resides in the official photograph of the Challenge Cup-winning team taken on the Thrum Hall cricket field. Two of the Cup Final team, Jack Swinbank and 'Wax' Williams, are missing, but all 18 other players who played in the various rounds and consequently qualified for a winners' medal are present. Archie Rigg did not qualify for a medal, having not played in any of the rounds. He is, however, the central figure in the photograph, seated directly behind the Challenge Cup – a curious but eloquent testimony to his status within the Thrum Hall organisation.

Interestingly, Rigg played in the forwards for Halifax 'A' in the Halifax Charity Cup Final against Thrum Hall on Easter Monday, 4 April 1904. The Thrum Hall Football Club had no connection with the Halifax NU club, but was a successful junior club and at that juncture was in second place in the Yorkshire Senior Combination. The game was staged at Thrum Hall (the Halifax NU club's ground) in the morning because Halifax were hosting Hunslet in the afternoon, a game Archie's usual team-mates lost 7–0. Archie had better luck with the reserves. A crowd of around 2,000 turned up, the gate being donated to the Halifax Infirmary. Archie scored the only try of the match as Halifax 'A' took the trophy with a 5–2 victory. Archie had waited a long time to earn a winners' medal for the Charity Cup. His only previous opportunity back in 1891 had seen Sowerby Bridge beat Halifax 'A' 7–2.

The 1904–05 season, under the captaincy of Billy Bulmer, proved very disappointing after all the excitement of the preceding two campaigns. It proved to be the last season of two divisions, Halifax finishing in 10th place. Johnny Morley was sorely missed, not appearing until 2 January, when Halifax shocked the eventual champions Oldham at Thrum Hall, winning by 5–3. Billy Little scored the try and dropped the goal that won the match. Another famous victory was recorded on 11 February, when Bradford, league runners-up, were beaten 11–2 at Thrum Hall in a tough game watched by a crowd of 13,659. Unfortunately, Morley suffered another injury and missed the rest of the season, after playing just five games. Such highlights apart, Halifax had injuries and bad luck in many matches.

Archie Rigg was approaching his 33rd birthday, but had continued to answer the call to action as Halifax kept losing their half-backs to injury. Apart from Morley's woes, Arthur Gledhill, who Halifax had signed from Manningham the previous year, and Archie's fellow veteran Arnold Nettleton were also badly crocked. Needs must, so Archie played. The end was nearing, however. On Boxing Day, 1904 Halifax lost 4–3 at home to Hunslet. Archie played opposite Albert Goldthorpe, who kicked two penalties against a Herbert Hadwen try.

The *Courier* suggested Albert won the match on his own. It proved to be the last time Archie played for Halifax at Thrum Hall in his current incarnation. On New Year's Eve he figured in Halifax's 7–3 defeat at Salford, for whom James Lomas scored a try and a goal. On 14 January, Archie's career came to an apparent end with his appearance at Belle Vue against Wakefield Trinity. Halifax were third from bottom of the table and in a wretched run of form in which seven games out of eight were lost. Archie, who had not been down to play for either the first team or the reserves, formed a make-shift half-back pairing with Joe Riley but could do nothing to prevent another Halifax defeat, 9–3. By a strange quirk of fate George Kitson, Archie's co-captain in the glorious adventure of 1903–04, also played his last game for Halifax that afternoon. The two had been playing together since 1894 and George had put in a fair stint with well over 200 appearances in the Halifax pack. Within a year he had pulled on his boots again and was a Brighouse Ranger.

On the Tuesday following the Wakefield defeat, the *Courier* reported that Archie Rigg was injured and would not be considered for the next game at home to Leigh. There was no hoohah about retirement. Archie just slipped silently out of the public eye. His work was done and he had certainly done Halifax proud. He had scored 133 tries, a club record, 56 goals and 515 points – another club record – in 335 matches; almost certainly a club record. However, he was not quite done with rugby…

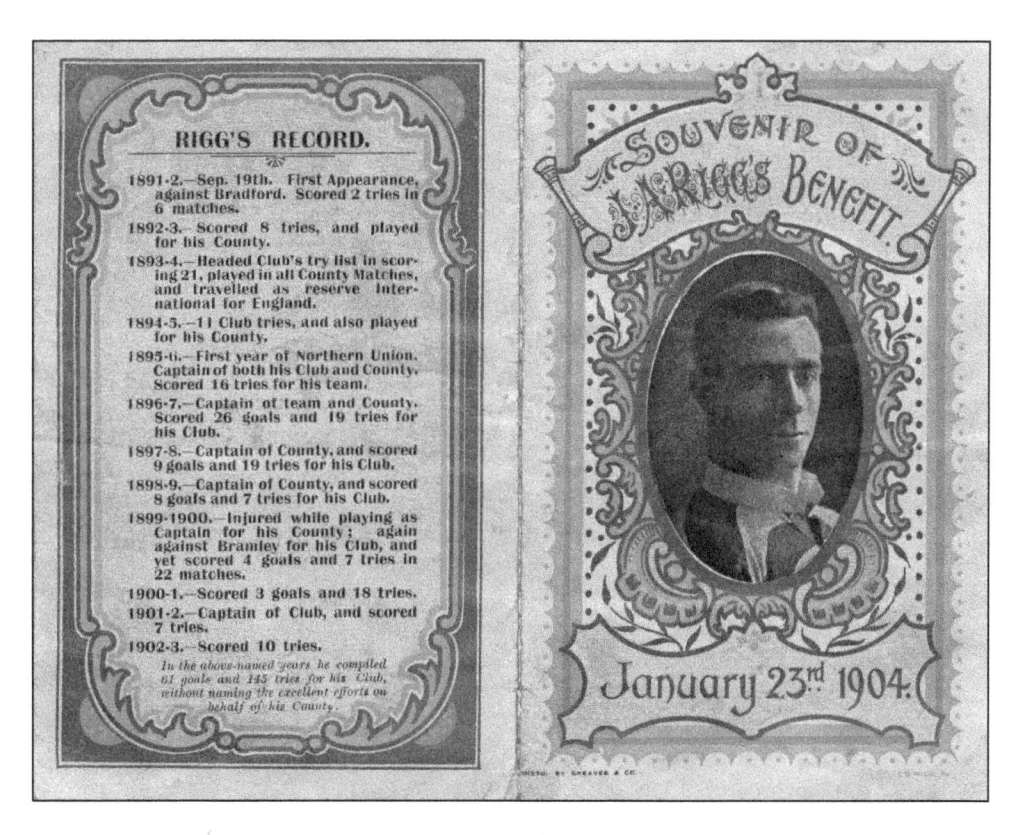

The programme for Archie Rigg's benefit match.

Left: The caption below reads:
Black Smut is the Queen of the Thrum Hall Thirteen
Who took care her paws well to butter
If they don't part with Smut and alter their luck
They'll come out at top with a flutter.

Right: An image commemorating the end of Halifax's 17-match unbeaten run, when Smut's and Fax's luck finally ran out with a 9–5 defeat at Salford on 23 February 1907.

These are post-card images of Smut, Halifax's lucky black cat (see pages 119–120), which became famous during Halifax's 1906–07 Championship winning season.

6. Bradford Northern – new club, new game

In the run-up to the 1906–07 season, *The Salford Reporter* ran a piece under the headline "J. Archer Rigg to be trainer at Salford". It announced, "Tall and slim, with a dark and piercing eye, J.A. Rigg is rather on the quiet side and seems a man of much determination. Quite recently he has filled the post of physical instructor at the Halifax Technical School ... Rigg did not come to the Borough [of Salford] at the first time of asking."

Strangely there is no evidence that Archie ever took up the role of trainer at Salford. Perhaps the *Salford Reporter's* correspondent was merely indulging in speculation, or Archie's domestic arrangements precluded such an appointment. Interestingly, however, the interview with Archie occurred on the very cusp of a revolution in the playing of the Northern Union game. The Northern Union had decided to change the game from 15-a-side into a 13-a-side contest, thereby breaking perhaps the most fundamental link with its rugby union origins. Additionally, the play-the-ball that came to truly characterise the game of rugby league was introduced for the start of the 1906–07 season. The result was that the game was radically transformed. It became quicker, more open and spectacular and the rate of scoring went through the roof. The *Salford Reporter* revealed Archie's views on how the new game should operate, noting that Archie favoured the formation of full-back, three three-quarters, two half-backs and seven forwards. History shows that the game went with the four three-quarter system and forward packs of six.

It is tempting to speculate how the new game would have suited Archie. For a man who scored so many tries under the old regime, the new style would surely have been a veritable paradise. He must have looked on with both pleasure and amazement as his old Thrum Hall colleagues ripped up the club record books in 1906–07 as Halifax topped the league and won the Championship under the new top four play-off system. By the time Halifax lifted the Championship trophy, Archie was 35 years old and long past thoughts of active service – or so it seemed.

In the late summer of 1908 tragedy visited Archie and Josephine Rigg. On 2 September their only child, John Edward, died aged eight. The death certificate gave the cause of death as "Nephritis. Convulsions." In other words, kidney disease. Interestingly, the death certificate described Archie as a tramway labourer. He appears to have given up his tobacconist shop around 1902 and the family were living at 18, Rose Terrace. That was just off Hanson Lane and below Queens Road – a very short walk from Thrum Hall. The fact that Archie had given up his own business and become a labourer would indicate that he had fallen on harder times. He would, however, presumably have had the cushion of the £200 testimonial he had received in 1904, or at least some of it. Shortly after his son's death,

Archie decided to play rugby again, almost four years after he had last turned out in Halifax's first team. In hindsight it would be easy to surmise that Archie was using a type of displacement therapy in the face of the loss of his son. Whatever the case may have been, Archie Rigg became a Bradford Northern player in November 1908, returning to a game that was far removed from the one he had formerly graced.

Just as the game had changed since Archie's 1905 retirement, so had rugby in Bradford. In Archie's heyday the city had supported two major clubs. The Bradford Football Club had been in rugby union days, at least in its own eyes, Yorkshire's most prestigious club. It supplied many players to the England team, enjoyed an enviable fixture list with major clubs throughout the British Isles, played before huge crowds at Park Avenue and made big profits.

Other Yorkshire clubs considered Bradford somewhat snooty, but they all wanted the opportunity to engage with them in (lucrative) combat on the field and to enjoy the post-match fare. For all their monetary power, prestige and influence, however, Bradford only managed to lift the Yorkshire Cup once, in 1884, and lost in the final to Halifax in 1886. Their neighbours Manningham, a much more working class club, lost to Batley in the 1885 final, but eclipsed Bradford in the first season of Northern Unionism by lifting the Championship and the Yorkshire Senior Competition Shield. Bradford had won the inaugural Yorkshire Senior Competition in 1892–93 but Manningham had wrested it from them in 1893–94. Post-1896 Bradford dominated the local rivalry, winning the Yorkshire Senior Competition in 1899–1900 and 1900–01, the NU Championship in 1903–04 and were runners-up the following season, as well as lifting the NU version of the Yorkshire Cup in 1906.

Despite such successes the game's fortunes and standing in Bradford had deteriorated alarmingly by the time Archie Rigg fetched up there. Manningham had been first to succumb, abandoning rugby for association football in 1903. Their ground at Valley Parade became and remains the home of Bradford City. Four years later "The Great Betrayal" saw rugby ousted from Park Avenue, as the soccerites took over and Bradford Park Avenue AFC was born. The Northern Union game at senior level was not completely obliterated, however. A new club, Bradford Northern, was formed, playing in reduced circumstances at the Greenfield Athletic ground in Dudley Hill in the 1907–08 season. By the time Archie arrived the club had taken up residence at Birch Lane, where they would remain like penurious and faded gentry until 1934, when they moved up in the world to the former council tip which became the cavernous, but problematic, Odsal Stadium.

Bradford Northern had finished 12th of the 27 teams in the league in 1907–08, which was better than most pundits expected. In 1908–09 they slumped to 23rd of 31 teams in the league and four of the teams below them were fledgling clubs in Wales – Mid-Rhondda, Treherbert, Barry and Aberdare. Archie Rigg was clearly not taking an easy option in joining Northern, whose only players of real note were test forward Alf Mann and Yorkshire half-back Tommy Surman. However, Mann and Surman got themselves into big trouble when they, together with Bradford's secretary Mr W Bayliss, were involved in a dodgy transfer deal with Hull KR. Mr Bayliss soon disappeared without trace. Alf Mann later failed to turn up for a game against Hunslet and was accused of speaking abusively to members of the Bradford committee. He was suspended and transfer listed. Bradford Northern was undoubtedly a club in crisis.

Left: Archie Rigg during his time with Bradford Northern. Right: A Baines card for the club.

Archie entered this maelstrom as he approached his 37th birthday. It was unlikely that even he would transform Northern's plummeting fortunes. His debut was set for Northern's home game against Wakefield Trinity on 21 November, 1908. Thus far Northern had won five and lost six of their league fixtures, but had gone out of the Yorkshire Cup in round one at York. However, their best performance had undoubtedly been against the touring Australians, who just salvaged a 12–11 victory on 7 October. Previewing the game against Trinity, the *Bradford Daily Telegraph* cheerfully observed, "This should prove one of the big events of the year, for Wakefield are making a plucky attempt to win the championship of the Northern Union ... If Bradford play up to their recent form they will beat Wakefield. That they 'mean business' is shown by their assiduous attention to training this week." *Discipulus*, in the rival *Bradford Daily Argus*, predicted of Archie, "His old head and skill will, I believe, be of considerable help to the side. Despite the fact that he is not in the heyday of a football career, he is in the pink of condition, and will doubtless show his confreres a thing or two."

Archie's debut ended in a 12–9 win for his new team. The *Bradford Daily Telegraph* ran with the headline "Bradford Northern's Brilliant Victory", praising the Birch Laners as "a side made up almost entirely of local players" and noting, "There was quite a respectable crowd [6,000, according to the *Yorkshire Observer*] and the greatest enthusiasm prevailed." Many hundreds dashed onto the field in delight at the final whistle, having enjoyed a fast, exciting spectacle in which only one Wakefield forward was cautioned "for being a little over-zealous".

The *Bradford Daily Argus* commented, "Rigg was good, making no mistakes, and doing a quantity of good solid work at centre. At the same time there is but little doubt that Ramsden would have been a better selection ... Rigg would have done better behind the pack ... Rigg played well and he opened out the game with great skill." The *Halifax Evening Courier* also covered the event under the headline "Archie Rigg's debut with Bradford". It commented, "Archie Rigg created nothing in the way of a sensation, although once or twice he gave glimpses of his old ability."

A couple of weeks later, Archie was joined at Birch Lane by his old friend George Kitson, late of Brighouse Rangers, who had decided to emulate his former Halifax co-captain in emerging from retirement. The pair must have wondered how long term the Bradford committee was looking! After the Wakefield victory Bradford lost four games in a row before beating Swinton 30–11 on Boxing Day, when Archie claimed his first try for Northern. The second half of the season was a severe trial for Bradford, who won only four of their last 15 league matches and saw Wakefield Trinity gain revenge by knocking Bradford out 13–3 at Birch Lane in the first round of the Challenge Cup, a tie Archie missed. On 15 March Archie faced Halifax for the first time and was on the losing side in a 10–3 home defeat. George Kitson had the pleasure of scoring Northern's only try but the following week suffered the ignominy of sharing in Bradford's lamentable 39–0 pasting at Batley. George promptly retired again, leaving Archie to soldier on.

His first season with Bradford Northern brought Archie 16 appearances, equally divided between centre and half-back, and three tries.

Despite throwing in his lot with a club in desperate straits, both financially and on the playing pitch, Archie Rigg's name still held a certain lustre. When a new publication, *The Yorkshire Weekly Record*, was launched in February 1909, Archie was commissioned to write a column – quite a tribute to a former star whose light was so apparently dimming. Two other Northern Union half-backs also provided columns. Billy Anderson, the Hull and England scrum-half, covered East Riding rugby, while Leeds's newly acquired Welsh stand-off Reg Jones dealt with the teams in the Leeds district. Archie's remit seemed wider and was headed "NORTHERN UNION" but he seemed to concentrate on the clubs in the West Riding, excluding Reg Jones's territory.

Interestingly, among the observations in Archie's first column for the *Yorkshire Weekly Record* was the comparative attraction between rugby and soccer. He wrote, "To my mind there is nothing which can arouse the enthusiasm of a crowd like a good, keen Rugby match. I do not profess to know much about Soccer, but I am bound to confess that the games I have witnessed under association rules were not calculated to arouse great enthusiasm, though, of course, everyone to his taste, as the man said who swallowed a spoonful of mustard. As an old Rugby player, I can testify to the great sympathy which exists between the crowd and a player. Provided the player has done his best, even though he makes a mistake, he receives a deal more encouragement than the Association player under similar circumstances. Then again, there is nothing in the world to equal the shout of a Rugby crowd, especially if the struggle they are witnessing is a cup-tie struggle, but in Soccer you've only a chance of shouting when a goal is scored, and then other incidents occur so soon afterwards that it is scarcely worth wasting your breath. No, they can talk about Association and its glories who like, but I'm Rugby through and through, and shall ever remain so."

The 1909–10 season opened with the news that Alf Mann and Tommy Surman had finally been transferred legally to Hull KR, further weakening Bradford's playing strength. Bill Eagers and Irvin Mosby, both former county and international three-quarters and both of whom had begun their first-class careers with the old Bradford club, rejoined the ranks. However, like Archie Rigg, their best days were behind them. Northern was definitely a selling rather than a buying club and when they did buy, the recruits tended to be veterans with good reputations but short-term playing futures.

Unsurprisingly, Northern struggled in another season when they finished 23rd in a 28 club competition. They won only nine of their 34 league fixtures and drew once – 5–5 at home against Hull KR on 27 November. Archie scored Bradford's try in that game. It came in purple patch for him, almost reminiscent of his early years as a master try-poacher. The Hull KR match was the first in a run of six games in which Bradford mustered nine tries, of which Archie scored seven. In that period he failed only to register a try in a 19–0 loss at Leeds.

They were the only tries he scored during the season but, amazingly, the seven were enough to make him Northern's leading try-scorer for 1909–10. The two other old hands, Billy Eagers (10 goals, and a couple of tries) and Irvin Mosby (nine goals), were the club's leading kickers. Archie played 24 games during the season – 21 in the halves and three at centre.

The 1910–11 season saw no real improvement in Bradford Northern's fortunes, as they finished 23rd for the third time in a row, above York, Ebbw Vale, Merthyr Tydfil, Coventry and bottom-of-the-table Bramley. Once again, their recruitment veered to the geriatric side. Alex Laidlaw, a 33-year-old forward, who had been capped in 1897, was the first Scottish International to sign for a Northern Union club when he joined Bradford in 1898. Now, after two years retired, he was persuaded to rejoin the ranks. Another returnee was George Marsden, a great half-back capped by England from the Morley Rugby Union club back in 1900. He had joined Bradford, captained England NU against Other Nationalities at Park Avenue in 1905 and led Bradford to victory in the Challenge Cup final in 1906, after which he had retired. He was now 30. Some younger blood was injected, however. Fred Littlewood, a forward who had played alongside Archie, arrived from Halifax. Another forward, Joe Winterburn, a Yorkshire cap, was signed from Keighley and proved a mainstay of the Northern team for the next decade.

Archie Rigg scored a try in the opening game of the season, an 8–3 win over Leeds at Birch Lane. Northern began the campaign with three wins and a draw from their first six league games but lost 9–5 at York in the first round of the Yorkshire Cup. Thereafter it was mostly downhill for Northern. Archie scored the side's only try in a 22–5 home defeat by Halifax, which would probably have been scant consolation. The *Courier* described it as "a soft try from a scrum just on half-time". It also noted that Rigg and Marsden were thoroughly outplayed by the Halifax halves, Squire Pemberton and John Medley, both very inexperienced players. The saving grace for Bradford was a crowd of 5,000, possibly the best of the season at Birch Lane. Archie Rigg was in and out of the team, making 17 appearances out of the 36 cup and league fixtures.

At the beginning of February 1911 Archie's old Halifax colleague Billy Little, the Cumberland and England full-back and siege-gun goalkicker, was signed by Northern for £50. Billy was heading for his 32nd birthday and was renowned for his ability to wring money from his rugby employers, so Northern probably stumped up somewhat more than the £50 transfer fee. Archie would have been sorry when he missed Billy's debut for Northern, who beat York

5–0 at Birch Lane on 4 February. He would have been relieved, however, the following Saturday to have missed Northern's dismal performance in losing 39–2 at Huddersfield.

There was, however, a small, welcome flourish towards the close of the season as the Challenge Cup-ties came round. A first round 12–4 win away to Wigan juniors Pemberton Rovers was safely negotiated. The second round then threw up a much tougher proposition – Halifax away on 4 March. For Archie Rigg, Billy Little and Fred Littlewood, this contest against their erstwhile playing colleagues, would be one to remember for the rest of their days. On the day of the match Halifax stood seventh in the league table, while Northern languished in 21st place. There was only one favourite and Archie Rigg no longer played for them. Halifax had annihilated York 63–0 in the first round and had despatched Warrington 44–0 in a home league fixture seven days before Bradford arrived at Thrum Hall for the Challenge Cup-tie.

On Friday 3 March, the *Halifax Evening Courier* previewed the match under the banner "Little and Rigg at Halifax". *White Rose* said the result was very uncertain to predict, adding, "Apart from the importance of the occasion, the appearance of WB Little and Archie Rigg at Thrum Hall as members of the opposition, be the day at all decent, is sure to draw the crowd of the season." Memories were evoked of the epic third round Challenge Cup-tie between the two fierce rivals in 1906, when 28,000 poured through the gates at Park Avenue, paying £761 – both record figures for the ground – and witnessed a scoreless draw for their money. The replay at Thrum Hall drew receipts of £521/11/9 from a paying attendance of 19,978. However, it was estimated that another 3,000 saw the game free when the gates in Springhall Lane were broken down. Bradford won 8–2.

White Rose continued, "It is quite a compliment to the stamina of Archie Rigg to be chosen in opposition to his old colleagues. What a player Rigg was for Halifax! The public are not likely to forget his heroic deeds, and he and Little are sure to 'bring the house down', when they step on the battle ground ... George Marsden too should come in for a deal of attention, for he and Rigg were probably the two finest half-backs the Northern union has produced ... Rigg had been an absolute god."

Unfortunately, when Saturday dawned the weather had been terrible overnight and continued throughout the morning. At 2pm the decision to play the game on the cricket ground was taken as the rugby field was a veritable swamp. Bradford made a formal objection to the pitch because it was not properly railed off, but the main problem appeared to be the lack of room behind the dead-ball line. The objection was over-ruled and the game was declared on. *White Rose* reported: "Climbing Gibbet Lane I heard one individual say he was 'baan to see Billy Little and Archie Rigg, if he deed' - i.e. even the dreadful weather wouldn't stop him ... Indeed this feeling was rampant." The attendance was certainly affected by the weather, but there were still 9,347 paying customers around the Thrum Hall cricket field. "Rigg was playing and the crowd were delighted", according to *White Rose*. He also noted, "Little looked remarkably reduced in weight" and it later transpired that he had an abscess on his thigh.

Billy's blighted thigh did not prevent him from kicking his team into the lead with a penalty goal "from an extremely difficult position" after five minutes. Bradford pressed hard for most of the first half. Archie, playing at centre, was almost over after good work from half-back

Jagger and Halifax missed a chance to equalise when Fred Longstaffe, a native of Bradford, missed with a penalty attempt. Little then astounded the crowd by missing an easy penalty goal after Archie had been obstructed. As half-time loomed, Archie was grassed within inches of scoring. Bradford did extend their lead on 37 minutes with a try from Town, their right winger, which Little converted. Even with a seven-point advantage, few believed Halifax would actually lose. Longstaffe finally landed a penalty to reduce the deficit to five points and when forward Horace Taylor scored a try it looked as if Halifax would at least earn a replay. However, Fred Longstaffe made a complete hash of the conversion and later admitted that he had lost his nerve at the vital moment.

Bradford Northern thus triumphed 7–5. The *Halifax Evening Courier's* match report was headed "Once more David has slain Goliath". It was a real turn-up. The Bradford forwards had been magnificent, as was Billy Little. Joe Winterburn had been the outstanding player, while "the old-fashionedness of Rigg and Marsden was a revelation to the younger players, for both set a delightful example in the campaign to adopt ... Before the home defence was beaten, I saw Rigg make a magnificent effort to get over. He was over the line almost six inches but in attempting to ground the ball was pushed back by three or four players. Archie looked crestfallen at his failure, but one remembers the day when the opposition would have experienced as much difficulty in preventing him from scoring as a youngster has in trapping a butterfly ... Rigg always did something tangible and was always able to get the ball away in the tackle."

In truth this was Archie Rigg's last hurrah. He played in Northern's third round tie, a gutsy 10–0 defeat away to Broughton Rangers, who went on to beat Wigan in the Challenge Cup Final. He figured in the following Saturday's 4–3 league win against Barrow at Birch Lane. The season ended anticlimactically, however, with four straight defeats. Ironically, the last of those was at Thrum Hall on 18 April, when Halifax extracted a small dollop of revenge with a 10–7 victory.

Almost ridiculously, Archie finished as Northern's joint leading try-scorer for 1910–11 with four. Playing for Bradford at Halifax would have probably been an appropriate way to finish his first-class career but it did not end there. Archie remained on Bradford's register and it is highly likely that he was paid to be on the training staff at Birch Lane, as his stated occupation on the 1911 census was "football trainer". The 1911 census also reveals that Archie and Josephine were then living at 59, Baird Street, West Bowling – just round the corner from Birch Lane.

Archie seemed to have retired from playing rugby following the close of the 1910–11 season, but was called upon by Bradford for one last game nine months later. On 13 January, 1912, a month before his 40th birthday, he lined up at centre for Northern at Huddersfield. This was the peerless Huddersfield "team of all the talents". In the opposite centre positions were Edgar Wrigley and Harold Wagstaff. Why Northern thought bringing back 40-year-old Archie would make any difference beggars belief. It would be nice to believe that Rigg, arguably the player of his generation, and Wagstaff, arguably the player of all generations, finished the match with respect for one another, even if it was no contest. Huddersfield won 56–5 with Albert Rosenfeld scoring five tries from the left wing for the Fartowners. He would end the season with a new Northern Union record of 78 tries, a feat bettered only by himself in 1913–14, when he bagged 80.

Bradford Northern and Archie Rigg finally parted company in August, 1912. He had made 58 first team appearances and scored 14 tries. On Saturday, 12 August, *The Halifax Evening Courier* reported that Archie Rigg had been appointed trainer to the Blue and Whites on an annual basis. He had been one of 36 applicants and would take up his appointment the following week. It also noted, "The appointment will be a popular one." On 24 September, 1912 Archie was added to Halifax's playing register, although no one seriously expected that he would ever be used. If he was expecting things to be better than they had been at Bradford Northern, he was soon disabused of that notion. Halifax had a nightmare season, winning only 10 of their 32 league fixtures, finishing 20th out of 26 clubs in the table, three places below Northern – out of the frying pan into the fire!

There was one stroke of luck for the Thrum Hallers – a bye in the first round of the Yorkshire Challenge Cup. However, by the time of the second round, a tie at Hull, on 26 October, Halifax had an injury crisis to add to a dismal opening record of one win and a draw from their first six league fixtures. *Argus*, in the *Halifax Evening Courier*, reported that the team for Hull contained several startling changes. Included among them were Archie at centre, partnered by a debutant winger, Joe Chadbourne, who had until recently been the captain of Halifax Town AFC. Halifax endured a fraught journey to the east coast with fog delaying their progress all the way to Wakefield and two hours in a saloon coach was not good preparation. There was no heating in the carriage and the players were "cribbed, cabined and confined and chilled to the bone". Unsurprisingly, when the team finally got onto the Boulevard pitch, "the blue and whites were weak and disorganised". A 15–0 defeat was the outcome from a rough game in which both teams had a man sent off, although *Argus* noted, "Rigg was often in the picture". There was one consolation – a £130 share of the gate from a 12,000 crowd, which paid £289/15/-.

The Hull cup-tie was Archie's 244th first class Northern Union game for Halifax and it came more than seven years after he entered his first retirement from playing. Surely he could now hang up his boots?

He continued as trainer at Halifax, overseeing a rise up the league ladder to 18th in 1913–14 and to 8th in 1914–15, after which the Northern Union abandoned competitive rugby for the duration of The Great War. By the 1915–16 season, the effects of the war had become catastrophic. Apart from vastly depleted playing resources with men in the fighting forces or doing essential war work, clubs struggled financially with small crowds. Travel was becoming increasingly difficult and matches were often played with teams one, two or even three men short. At the start of the season reimbursement of players and officials was set at a limit of travelling expenses and tea money (two shillings and sixpence) only. It was remarked in the *Courier* that players only seemed to want to turn out for home matches. Well, it was hardly worth the effort for players who were used to being paid. All competitive rugby was banned, but newspapers continued to compile league tables based on percentages. They were hardly credible, however, with massive discrepancies as teams played anything between 13 (Barrow) and 36 (Dewsbury) matches. Halifax played 31 games, but won only seven, finishing third from bottom of the 24-club unofficial league table.

The 1914 Halifax ground staff, including several players, near the Thrum Hall pavilion. Archie is in front of the cart shaft, towards the left foreground of the picture.

Matters were so grim that Archie was once more pressed into action. On 9 October 1915, Halifax lost 10–2 at Bramley and the *Halifax Evening Courier* reported, "The half-back line was depleted and Rigg partnered Herman Haigh. The veteran's hand has not lost its cunning, but the slowness was only too apparent." Two weeks later Halifax could only muster 10 players for the long trip to Hull, so Archie played alongside Jack Cottam at half-back. Cottam was the club's kit-man, whose only first team appearance for Halifax in November 1907 had also been in Hull, but against Hull KR. Hull loaned Halifax a winger named Greg to make up the numbers. The *Courier*, railed, "It was a farce, not a game of football... The forwards look all right but the backs? Where did they get 'em?" Hull won 69–2 – Halifax's worst defeat since the club's foundation.

A final appearance was forced on Archie at Oldham on 18 December 1915, when he filled in at centre. The game was described as "very keen but poor". At least this time Halifax were not humiliated, going down 7–3, although their winger Culpan was sent off near the final whistle. This time it really was the end of Archie's playing career. Aged 43 years and 306 days, Archie Rigg remains the oldest man to have represented Halifax at first team level.

In 1916 Archie gave up as Halifax's trainer, although his job specification also described him as "a cricket and football groundsman". It must have seemed decidedly pointless carrying on under ever worsening conditions. Apart from the misery provoked by The Great War, Archie mourned the death of his wife Josephine on 27 July 1916. Josephine died from heart disease, aged only 41. By 1916 the couple were living at 260, Hanson Lane, still hardly any distance from Thrum Hall. Possibly in response to Josephine's passing, Archie joined the army. Although conscription had been introduced through the Military Service Act, which was passed in January 1916 and came into effect on 25 May 1916, it applied only to men aged between 18 and 41. Archie was, of course, exempt but chose to volunteer. Interestingly, at the same time that Archie joined up so did his old-time half-back partner Arnold Nettleton.

In the early 1920s there was a revival of rugby union in the Halifax district. That game had practically died out in the area as the Northern Union expanded. The period 1920 to 1930 saw the birth of local clubs such as Old Crossleyans, Halifax Vandals, Heath Old Boys, Old Rishworthians and Old Brodleians, all of whom are still in existence. Others such as Caldene (Mytholmroyd), Copley and Elland were also established, but ultimately vanished. The town of Halifax did not, however, house a team bearing its name after Archie Rigg and his fellow Thrum Hallers joined the Northern Union in 1895. In 1919, however, a club known as West End Old Boys came into being, transmogrified into Savile Old Boys and then into Halifax Old Boys before taking the title of Halifax RUFC. In 1925 the club settled at Ovenden Park and was soon one of Yorkshire's most successful sides. Archie Rigg and Joe Riley became trainers at Halifax RUFC, despite everyone knowing that they were driving a coach and a herd of horses through the RFU's professional laws. A fine tradition of such goings-on at Yorkshire RU clubs developed down the years, blind eyes being the order of the day until someone too officious drew the attention of Twickenham and caused sanctions to be belatedly imposed.

There is no evidence that Archie took an active part in either code of rugby following his association with the Halifax rugby union club, but he was a frequent and welcome spectator at both senior Halifax rugby clubs.

After 14 years as a widower Archie remarried in 1930. His new wife, Florence May Horsfall – born 28 October 1898 – was 26 years younger than Archie. They remained together for 21 years. According to the 1939 Register, they lived at 4, Schoolcote Brow, Windy Bank, Holdsworth. Archie was described as a textile warehouseman, who was employed in heavy work, even though he was 67 years old. It was also noted that he was a special constable with Halifax Borough Police. For his age he remained remarkably active.

Archie Rigg died on 29 May 1951, aged 79 at his home at 35, Dickens Street, Highroad Well, which, as usual for his accommodation, was just a few good punts from Thrum Hall. Florence May survived him, living to a ripe old age before passing away in 1985. Archie's funeral took place at Christ Church, Mount Pellon on Saturday 2 June.

The day after his death, the *Halifax Daily Courier and Guardian* announced, "Death of Archer Rigg, greatest of half-backs." The reporter wrote, "Archie Rigg was one of the most brilliant players ever connected with the Halifax club. It has frequently been said of him that he was the finest player ever not to receive an English cap … He was an all-round athlete, a splendid gymnast, a good boxer and no mean cricketer."

Those words echoed the sentiments expressed by Sam Duckitt, a founder playing member of Halifax back in 1873–74. In an interview with *Old Ebor* (AW Pullin) in the *Yorkshire Evening Post* of 9 February, 1901, while Rigg was still in his pomp, Duckitt remarked, "There is no doubt in my mind that the best half-back that Halifax ever had is Archie Rigg. We have had several half-backs of exceptional ability, but they have been chiefly small in stature, and 'a good big 'un is better than a good little 'un any day', as the saying goes. Rigg's gymnastic training has served him well in his football. He is the most like [Bradford's Fred] Bonsor in style of all Yorkshire halves since that famous player's retirement. He had, perhaps, not the tackling powers of Bonsor, but, on the other hand, he could field a ball when going at a good speed in a way that the Bradford crack was unable to do. I entirely agree with local opinion that an injustice was done to Rigg by the English Union in passing him over for international honours. When Rigg was at his best he was passed over in favour of inferior men on several occasions."

A later eulogy was penned by Frank Williams in his 1954 history of Halifax RLFC, *Thrum Hall through six reigns and three wars*. Williams was a former Halifax and Wales winger, who was a member of the Northern Union side that played and won the most famous test in history – the "Rorke's Drift" test of 1914 against Australia. He arrived at Thrum Hall in 1913 when Archie Rigg was Halifax's trainer and knew him well for 38 years. Williams wrote, "Rigg was destined to become one of the most famous players in the North of England, and the old school of followers will assert that he was the greatest half-back the Halifax club ever possessed, and the most famous footballer in their eyes who never gained an international cap."

Some Thrum Hall Old-Timers

Archie Rigg with some former team mates: George F Dickinson, George Kitson, Archie Rigg, Walter Jackson, Ben Whiteley, Arthur Wilson.

OUR PORTRAIT GALLERY

J. ARCHER RIGG.

One of today's Touch Judges and one of the greatest half-backs Halifax have ever had, in both the Rugby Union and Rugby League games.

From the programme for Herbert ("Gillie") Hanson's benefit match on 4 May 1936.

7. James William Bulmer, Knight of the Realm

Billy Bulmer came from humble origins, enjoyed a comparatively brief but hugely successful career as a Northern Union forward, made a fortune and went on to be dubbed a Knight Bachelor at Buckingham Palace ... but eventually it all went wrong.

James William Bulmer was born on 8 August 1881 in Halifax. His father, William Bulmer, married Hannah Holdsworth, a 20-year-old dress-maker in 1881 (2nd quarter). The couple subsequently had three other children – Florence (born 1885), Clara Ellen (1886) and Arnold (1888). Hannah was the daughter of James Holdsworth, a master wool comb maker, and, according to the 1881 census, was the second oldest of the nine children in the household, James Holdsworth being a widower.

The family lived at 5, Horne Street, Halifax. Like their father, the three oldest boys of working age were employed as wool comb makers. The census, taken on 3 April 1881, was taken shortly before Hannah and James William Bulmer were married. The 1881 census placed William Bulmer as a boarder at 34, Horne Street. He was described as a yeast dealer, born in 1862 in Leeds. The head of the household was William Dickinson, who was also a yeast dealer, aged 54.

By the time of the 1891 census, Hannah Bulmer was living just down the road at 34, Horne Street, her husband's former lodgings. However, the head of that household was neither Hannah's father nor her husband, but her brother, 25-year-old James Holdsworth junior. Two of Hannah's sisters and another brother were living in the household. Hannah's four children were also present and Hannah, aged 30, was described as a dried yeast dealer, in the brewing trade.

It is not clear what had happened to William Bulmer. What is clear, however, is that life must have been difficult for Hannah and her children, living and working in the teeming streets in the shadows of the dark satanic mills of industrial Halifax in the late Victorian period. It is equally clear that the Bulmer-Holdsworth family stuck together over the coming years. James William Bulmer – Billy – left Pellon Lane Board School on 15 July 1892, three weeks before his 11th birthday. He found employment at Smith's brush works, in Parliament Street, Halifax. Three months into his employment, he was thrashed for climbing up the crane rope, which the *Halifax Daily Courier & Guardian* later described as "an early evidence of his spirit of adventure". He soon abandoned that career to become an errand boy for a tailor, Timewell Brothers, in Hanson Lane.

By the time he was 14 he had joined Scott Brothers to learn the engineering trade, but found that it did not agree with his health. Billy then spent a couple of years working for Norvell and Mitchell Joiners in Lister Lane and seemed to have found his vocation. The 1901 census shows that Billy was employed as a joiner and builder and was living at 13, Thomas

Street South, Halifax – less than half a mile from Thrum Hall. His mother Hannah was named as the head of the household, while Billy's sisters, Florence (aged 16) and Clara Ellen (15), were both employed as damask fringers. Billy's 13-year-old brother Arnold was a stationer's errand boy and the youngest child Horace (7) was at school. On 6 July 1901, Billy was admitted to the Halifax Branch of the Amalgamated Society of Carpenters and Joiners Trades Union, having had five years experience in the trade. However, by 1903 the Union's register had excluded him from membership on account of his "arrears".

When he had time and when he was not swapping jobs, Billy had certainly found a sporting vocation – rugby. Various sources say he played for Square Church, All Souls, Luddendenfoot, Halifax Gymnasium, Halifax Free Wanderers, Stainland and Sowerby Bridge before signing for Halifax in the Northern Union on 28 September 1901. After a few games for the reserves, he made his first team debut in the Halifax pack at Hull on 5 October 1901. Halifax lost 6–3, a disappointment, no doubt, to Billy, who was then just a couple of months past his 20th birthday. He was described as a "big, strapping fellow", standing at 5 feet 11 inches and weighing 12 stone 12 pounds. Nowadays, that would seem miniscule for a forward but in the death throes of Victorian England Billy was a decent size for the job. By all accounts he never got much heavier in his playing days. He was always noted for his speed about the field. Indeed, he was well-known locally as a track sprinter, who had won many prizes. Billy Bulmer's first class debut ended in defeat, but he would go on to prove that he was anything but a loser in whatever he undertook.

Billy was fortunate to join Halifax at a time when the team was building up to the great period discussed earlier in the review of Archie Rigg's career. Archie had been reinstated as captain for the 1901–02 season and was in charge of a group of players which could boast 16 past, present or future Yorkshire county caps. Billy could count on the help of eight men who figured in Yorkshire county packs – George Kitson, Fred Mallinson, Jack Swinbank, Bob Winskill, Ike Bartle, George Langhorn, Walter Morton and Jack Riley. The latter four also represented England. The backs also boasted eight Yorkshire county players – Billy Little, who also represented Cumberland, Archie Rigg, Fred Firth, Joey Arnold, Joe Riley, J Ernest Jones (despite being Welsh), Tommy Nicholl and Johnny Morley. Again, four represented England – Riley, Little, Firth and Morley.

Johnny Morley and Billy Bulmer were life-long friends. Apart from their rugby association, which included shared experiences with the Square Church, All Souls and Sowerby Bridge clubs, both were accomplished singers and performed together in choirs and various secular musical events. Billy was noted as a fine baritone, especially good in oratorios. He attended Trinity Road Baptist Church until he was 25 and later became a member of the choir at Park Road Congregational Church. Johnny's place of worship was Salem New Connexion Church in Halifax. The two committed choristers must have seemed an unlikely pair of rugby stars to many whose paths crossed theirs.

Halifax won only one of their first eight league fixtures and earned a 5–5 draw at Batley. In the solitary victory, 19–2 over Huddersfield at Thrum Hall on 19 October 1901, a young three-quarter, Arthur Devitt, scored two tries on his second appearance for the first team. Two weeks later Bradford inflicted a crushing 23–8 defeat on Halifax, when Devitt was the victim of "the nastiest piece of play seen for years" at Thrum Hall. A Bradford forward picked

Devitt up and threw him over his shoulder, dropping him on his head, much to the fury of the Halifax crowd. Devitt was very shaken and played only one more match for the Thrum Hallers. Billy Bulmer must have briefly wondered what he had let himself in for. Billy proved, however, that he was made of stern stuff. Halifax's form improved and they went on to finish fifth in the league, ending the campaign as Yorkshire's leading club. Billy appeared in 21 of Halifax's 27 first-class fixtures and was clearly a star in the making.

As we have seen, the 1902–03 season was a spectacular success for Halifax, who completed the Cup and League double. Billy Bulmer celebrated his 21st birthday a month before the season began and by the end of it he had two gold medals to cherish. He played in 35 of Halifax's 42 games and was a leading light in the pack that strangled the life out of Salford in the Challenge Cup Final at Headingley.

The only try of the final came from a forward rush near the Salford goal-line and in the confusion of bodies various members of the press credited Jack Riley, Ike Bartle and Billy Bulmer with the touchdown.

Indeed, as late as 1960 Stanley Chadwick, former editor of *Rugby League Review*, was crediting Bulmer with the try in *Sport International*. One journalist credited the try jointly to Bartle and Bulmer, an extraordinary, and possibly unique, judgement. In an article in the *Rugby Leaguer* of 14 February 1953, *Casca* recalled the 1903 Challenge Cup Final 50 years after it took place. He quoted from a poem written immediately after the Final by "a pro-Halifax bard", who wrote:

"John Morley and Joe Riley o'er the line had rushed the ball
Then Bulmer dropped upon it there, and Hadwen kicked the goal."

However, the post-match investigations came down on the side of Ike Bartle as the scorer and it is Bartle who is now set in history as the match-winner of the 1903 Challenge Cup Final. The try is captured on film in the remarkable Mitchell and Kenyon collection and, as far as is currently known, is the first try of a Challenge Cup Final to be so documented. Although the action is indistinct, Billy Bulmer must be depicted on that historic celluloid.

Billy was rewarded for his burgeoning prowess with selection for Yorkshire against Northumberland & Durham at South Shields on Tuesday, 14 April 1903, the last county game of the season. He was Halifax's only representative in the match, which Yorkshire won 8–0. Three of the Yorkshire three-quarters were Welshmen while in the pack was Alec Laidlaw (Bradford), who was a Scot.

The 1903–04 season saw Halifax drop precipitously from top of the league to ninth, but serious consolation was obtained when the Challenge Cup was retained with an 8–3 victory over Warrington in the final at Salford on 30 April 1904. Billy Bulmer thus picked up a second Challenge Cup winners medal, not yet having reached his 23rd birthday.

On the day, Warrington had no answer to the power and obduracy of Billy and his fellow forwards. Critics reckoned Halifax deserved to triple their score, so pronounced was their dominance.

Athletic News cartoon of the 1903 Challenge Cup Final.

Detail from cartoon on page 114, showing the try which won the Cup for Halifax. Ike Bartle eventually got the credit in preference to Billy Bulmer. The cartoonist was fortunate that shirt numbers had not yet been invented.

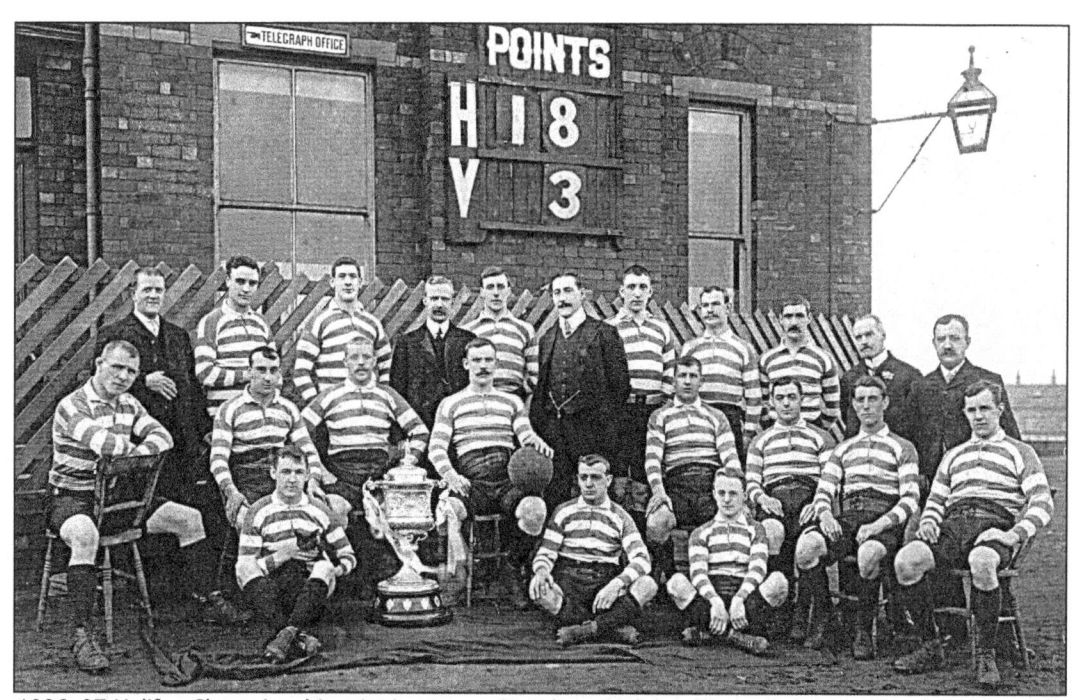

1906–07 Halifax Championship winning team. Standing: Midgley (Trainer), WW Williams, Wedgwood, Dodd (President), Bulmer, Ricketts (Secretary), Robinson, Bartle, Brearley, Foster, Morris; Seated: Swinbank, Atkins, Littlewood, Riley (captain), Langhorn, WJ Williams, Ward, H Morley; Front: Grey (holding Smut), Hilton, Eccles

Billy played in all the previous Cup rounds as Halifax beat St Helens (home) 15–0, Barrow (away) 11–6, Leeds (home) 8–2 and Hunslet 7–2 in the semi-final at Wakefield.

The season was also notable for the Northern Union's experiment with 12-a-side rugby in representative matches. Looking to speed the game up and enhance spectator appeal was a continuing obsession for the sport's leaders and remains so to this day. In 1903–04, the County Championship was therefore designated a 12-a-side competition, teams consisting of a full-back, three three-quarters, two half-backs and six forwards. Such a game would clearly be played at a faster pace than the 15-a-side version and, with three fewer men in teams, there would potentially be a sizable cut in a club's expenditure if the transformation became permanent.

For ambitious forwards, however, selection for representative sides would be harder to attain. Such forwards would have to be quick, athletic and endowed with exceptional stamina. Billy Bulmer fitted the bill. He was chosen for Yorkshire's County trial match at Craven Street, Hull on 12 October, 1903, figuring in a 16–11 victory for the Possibles over the Probables. Four of the Possibles' six forwards were Halifax players – Billy, Jack Riley, Fred Mallinson and Jack Swinbank, while Billy Little was the team's full-back.

Billy Bulmer had never scored a try in first-class rugby and must have been delighted to break his duck, at the 64th attempt, when he claimed one of his side's four tries. The weather in Hull had been so foul that the Yorkshire Committee decided that the trial had been unfair to the players and ordered a replay at Huddersfield on 21 October, when the Probables emerged 16–8 winners. Billy and the other four Halifax men played again for the Possibles and all except Jack Riley were in the Yorkshire XII that defeated Northumberland & Durham 25–13 at Wakefield on 28 October. Billy Bulmer was selected for the remaining Yorkshire fixtures against Cumberland, Lancashire and Cheshire, but missed the last because of injury.

The Northern Union had a further innovation set for New Year's Day, 1904. The game's first international match was to be played at Oldham between England and Other Nationalities with the sides playing in the same formations as for the County Championship matches. Billy Little, Jack Riley and Billy Bulmer were selected for the England team for this historic encounter. Unfortunately, the game was postponed because of a severe frost. It was ultimately staged on Tuesday 5 April 1904, and the venue was changed to Wigan's Central Park. For the players selected in the original sides the postponement must have been a blow. They would have to wait three months before finding out whether they would be able to participate in such a momentous event. Loss of form or injury could deprive them of an honour which may never present itself again.

On the appointed day Bulmer, Little and Riley were all in the England side which took the field at Wigan and so was Billy Bulmer's best friend, Johnny Morley. Morley was fortunate in that the make-up of the teams had been changed. This time the sides would comprise a full-back, four three-quarters, two halves and only five forwards. James Lomas had been selected at half-back in the New Year's Day XII, but moved to centre for the Wigan game, allowing Morley to take his vacated position. Ironically, Lomas arrived late for the match and England started with only 11 men. The England team showed only minor changes from the side originally selected while the Other Nationalities team had been altered dramatically with only four of the original choices turning out. Two of the 12 were Scots, the rest Welshmen, although one, half-back, Peter Brady (Huddersfield) was actually English-born. In the event it hardly mattered as the Other Nationalities won 9–3, despite their rejigged side.

In truth it was not the best time to stage such a prestigious and innovative fixture. A Tuesday afternoon in Wigan provided a crowd of only 6,000. The match was squeezed into an overflowing fixture glut, quite usual in April for most of the years winter rugby existed, as clubs sought to clear the backlog of postponed games and fit in the most important Challenge Cup rounds. Halifax, for example, played four fixtures in the first week of April, on the first, second, fourth and seventh. Bulmer, Little and Morley played against Hunslet on 4 April, the day before the international, as did four Oldham players (two English and two Other Nats) against Swinton.

They were the lucky ones. Pity the three Broughton Rangers men, Bob Wilson, Andy Hogg, and Sam James, and Bradford forward Alec Laidlaw, all of whom were forced to withdraw from this most historic occasion as it clashed with their clubs' third round replay in the Challenge Cup at Park Avenue. The first tie had finished scoreless and so did the replay, before Bradford ran away with the second replay 15–0 at Headingley three days later. It was no wonder that clubs sometimes elected to play grossly under strength sides when progress in the Cup-ties and the resultant prestige and financial rewards were at stake. Halifax and Warrington, the eventual Cup finalists, were both fined £10 by the Northern Union on 8 April for fielding weakened teams in the run-up to the semi-finals.

For the 1904–05 season, the 23-year-old Billy Bulmer replaced his fellow chorister Johnny Morley as captain of Halifax. Johnny had given up playing to concentrate on his career, but returned to the colours in January 1905. Tragically a broken leg soon after his return ended his playing career. Billy Bulmer was a suitable and well-received choice for the captaincy, one journalist writing of his "characteristic good humour and genial joviality, as well as for his undoubted capabilities as a player. More, he is also a notable leader, being resourceful and a popular 'article' with the boys."

The season proved to be the last of two divisions until the system was briefly re-introduced in 1962. Billy's campaign at the helm was not particularly successful. His team finished 10th in the First Division, winning 15 and drawing two of their 34 games. They surrendered their two-year possession of the Challenge Cup when they went out 5–2 at Wigan in the second round on 25 March 1905. However, Billy passed two significant milestones during the season. On Christmas Eve he made his 100th appearance for Halifax, when his side lost 6–0 at Widnes. A month later, on 21 January 1905, he finally scored his first try for Halifax in a 6–0 home win over Leigh - his 107th match for the club. When he led his team to a 23–2 home victory against St Helens in the last game of the season on 29 April, Billy had seemingly played his own last game for the club. He was still only 23 and the rugby world appeared to be his oyster.

Billy had other ideas though. His entrepreneurial streak was pushing him in other directions and he did not tread the Thrum Hall turf at all in 1905–06. Billy had taken a job as an improver with TS Dodd, a building contractor. He was in fact the last joiner that Mr Dodd employed. When Mr Dodd decided to give up his business in 1905, Billy Bulmer bought his employer's plant with the money he had been saving assiduously from his rugby earnings and his singing engagements.

Billy's first job as his own boss was to repair a counter for Mr Albert Hind, a well-known citizen of the town, who sold pianos in Waterhouse Street. Bizarrely, perhaps, Mr Hind also sold cycles. It was reported that Billy carried the counter on his back from the shop to his work place. The business was clearly a success and within three months, Billy Bulmer was employing 25 men. His premises were the Carpet Street Joinery Works and he presented himself as "Joiner, Builder, Shopfitter and Undertaker". Surprisingly perhaps, there was nothing unusual about that combination of trades. Halifax had many such businesses.

By 1905 Billy owned the freehold of 63, Essex Street, just down the road from Thrum Hall, and had two more properties on Conway Street, a few hundred yards further away.

With his business prospects burgeoning, Billy must have felt confident enough to have another tilt on the rugby field. Halifax supporters were overjoyed when he decided to start the 1906–07 season after his year off... and what a season it turned out to be. Joe Riley was appointed captain of a team, which contained plenty of Billy's former colleagues. However, there had been significant additions in his absence. Two truly exceptional wingers in Percy Eccles and Billy (WJ) Williams had been unearthed, both of whom would win international caps. Billy Bulmer would probably have bonded with the pair for other reasons than mere playing ability. Eccles, nicknamed "the mighty atom", was a leading light in the Halifax Amateur Operatic Society, while Williams was from Pontypool and all (sic) Welshmen love singing! Although the sainted Archie Rigg and Johnny Morley had been consigned to history, a wonderful new half-back pairing blossomed in the small shapes of Tommy Grey (formerly of Swansea rugby union) and Jimmy Hilton (formerly of Leigh). Even though their combination was relatively short, followers of the club, who lived long enough, could only compare them to the fabulous Dean 'n' Kielty duo of the 1950s.

Some of the Halifax pack were familiar to Billy – old colleagues such as Ike Bartle, Jack Swinbank, Joe Brearley and George Langhorn. However, new blood had been injected in locals Harry Morley and Asa Robinson, while Fred Littlewood had been imported from Huddersfield. Morley was Johnny's brother and had flitted between the pack and three-quarters before settling as a fast moving forward. Robinson, signed from the local Thrum Hall amateur club, went on to enjoy an extraordinarily long and successful career from 1904 to 1923, winning test caps against the first Kiwis and the first Kangaroos and being awarded the Military Medal in the First World War. At 6 feet 2 inches and 14 stone 10 pounds, Asa was a veritable giant for the period.

Even if most of the players he rejoined were familiar to him, the game to which Billy returned was definitely different. The game in 1906–07 was revolutionised. Thirteen-a-side rugby was introduced, referees were allowed to play advantage instead of blowing up for infringements on every occasion and the sport's trademark play-the-ball law was established, replacing the scrum, which had previously been employed when a tackle was completed.

Additionally, the Northern Union decided that the Championship would be decided by a top four play-off, establishing a model the game has persisted with, except for a few short periods, in some shape ever since.

If Billy Bulmer had loved the old game, the new game suited him down to the ground. Packs of six forwards allowed for a faster, more open style of play compared to the claustrophobic regime when eight-man packs ruled the roost. His first game under the new laws brought him two tries as Halifax downed Huddersfield 20–10 on 1 September 1906 at Thrum Hall – twice as many as he had scored in his entire Halifax career under the old laws. By the season's end he had eight tries to his credit as Halifax's forwards gathered 42 between them, a hitherto unheard of number and a new club record.

The opening of the campaign was certainly unusual, for, besides the innovations in the game itself, there was a great deal of attention taken up with a tram strike in the town. Bewilderment was exacerbated by the weather. It was just too hot for playing rugby. Temperatures reportedly reached 121 degrees and afternoon games were played in the comparative cool of the early evening as a result. The new rules did not help for it was reported in the *Courier* that "the pace is a real cracker". The heat and the tram strike and the new rules were too much for Halifax's veteran and venerable forward Jack Riley, who retired after two games. He had been with the club for 14 years and won most of the honours open to him. His county career had spanned a dozen seasons – Rugby Union and Northern Union – and he had captained Yorkshire. On retirement he had set up a record of 368 appearances for Halifax.

Jack Riley and Bob Winskill enjoyed a testimonial game when Halifax met Bradford on 20 October; 15,000 turned up to pay those two grand old forwards their due. Riley and Winskill were spectators, but Billy Bulmer starred in Halifax's 12–6 victory. The gate realised £220 and a collection raised £11 and two shillings.

By that stage in the season Halifax were top of the league and looked a good bet for the Yorkshire Cup. However, a 6–4 loss at Bradford in the semi-final on 17 November put paid to that aspiration. It was also the last game Billy Bulmer played until 19 January, 1907, an absence of 11 matches.

That Billy had successfully adapted to the new game was demonstrated by his selection for the Possibles against the Probables in Yorkshire's county trial at York on 17 October, when five Halifax men turned out. Billy's team lost 30–28, an indication of how open the game had become. He was selected as reserve to travel for Yorkshire's game against Lancashire at Salford on 3 November. Joe Riley, Jimmy Hilton and Ike Bartle all figured in the side which lost 19–0 to the Red Rose. Halifax could have done with their four county men as they lost for the first time, going down 10–4 at Leeds, despite leading 4–2 with only five minutes remaining. Halifax were the last team to lose their season's unbeaten record.

During the time Billy Bulmer was unavailable, a strange thing came to pass at Halifax. Following their defeat against Bradford in the Yorkshire Cup semi-final on 17 November, Halifax did not suffer another until 23 February 1907. In the interim Halifax won 16 and drew one of the next 17 fixtures. Beside the undoubted and considerable skills of the players, Halifax had acquired an additional aid in winning matches. This was 'Smut', a black cat that had taken up residence at Thrum Hall and was believed to have brought good luck in large dollops with her. Smut gained nationwide fame, which increased as Halifax's successful run gathered momentum.

Frank Williams wrote in his 1954 history of Halifax RLFC, "The cat was photographed and paragraphed from one end of the country to the other ... and received a handsome gift of a silver collar from the Black Cat Cigarette Company." He could have added that it was it was caricatured, locally, for years, and nationally. In fact, Smut became a symbol for Halifax, or

Thrum Hall, in cartoonist Charles Howarth's work for the *Halifax Courier* right up to the start of the Second World War, when the Saturday *Green Final* was abandoned for the duration of the hostilities. A pub was named after Smut and postcards and greetings card companies did a roaring trade on the back of the lucky black cat's celebrity.

Billy returned to action on 19 January, when Halifax beat Salford 11–9 at Thrum Hall in what was described as "a nasty match". On the following Wednesday Halifax won their 13th game in a row, beating Broughton Rangers 12–8 at Wheater's Field. Rangers provided a rare tussle for the 'Black Cat Brigade', who had Jack Swinbank sent off in the second half. After the match Arthur Widdeson, a Rangers three-quarter in their double-winning side of 1901–02, said of the Thrum Hallers, "Halifax quite merit their high position on the register. They are a splendid side, and I see no reason why they should not secure dual honours once more. They play the game for what it is worth – a bit more on occasions, for they have a few tricks in the way of obstruction and time-killing ... noticeable to the close observer – and their football is good."

A 21–4 win at Bradford consolidated Halifax in top place in the league and on 2 February Leeds visited Thrum Hall. The Loiners were second in the table and Smut had to exert all his influence to gain Halifax a somewhat fortunate 11–11 draw. Jimmy Hilton's drop goal three minutes from time only intensified the unwavering belief of the Halifax supporters that Smut was the Bringer of Fortune. Earlier 10,000 people saw Percy Eccles score two tries to break Archie Rigg's club record of 21 tries in a season. A week later slippery Percy added four more in a 29–5 home win against Dewsbury, while Billy Bulmer also claimed a try.

February 12 was set for a clash with the powerful Warrington side and their great wingman Jack Fish had ideas about breaking Smut's spell. The local reporter provided this information, "Jack Fish tells me he is bringing over a running dog of the same name as your cat, with a view to putting an end to your black cat, and at the same time checking the remarkable sequence of victories your team have recorded." However, whether Fish's black dog could have shattered Smut's mystical influence will forever remain a mystery as the game was postponed.

A hard game was won 10–7 at Hunslet on 16 February, following which Halifax's luck finally ran out, albeit temporarily. On 23 February an under-strength side travelled to Salford hoping to make their unbeaten run stretch to 18 games. Wintry weather prior to the game had prompted Salford to cover the pitch but, apart from an icy cold wind, the conditions were ideal. When *Rocket*, the Halifax reporter, and the Halifax supporters passed no fewer than six funeral processions *en route*, it seems likely that Smut had bitten off more than he could chew, funeral processions at that time being a well-known antidote to the power of black cats and so it proved.

The *Salford Reporter* commented, "Incidentally it may be added that the black cat was not with the team, the omission to bring that lucky animal being no doubt afterwards regretted. In this place a drawing of puss was nailed to the door of the visitors' dressing room, but this particular mouser wore a red ribbon round its neck and a most decided wink." Perhaps more pertinently the Salford journalist added, "Halifax are notoriously unlucky on the Salford ground and have not won a match there for something like quarter of a century."

The Halifax forwards were mastered and three goals from James Lomas proved the difference, as Salford won 9–5 before a crowd of 12,000 who forked out £289.

Worse ensued the following Saturday. Runcorn, second in the table, won 6–3 at Thrum Hall. The police were summoned after a demonstration against the referee, Mr Priestley of Salford, and Runcorn's star half-back Jim Jolley was struck by an irate spectator. Interestingly, the Runcorn players only received 10 shillings each for their famous victory. On 9 March Halifax suffered their third defeat in a row when Oldham completed a double at Watersheddings in a cracking game before 18,000 onlookers. Tommy Grey, who had missed most of the season, made his reappearance at stand-off. It was noted of him, "Grey is a good catch - that is clear. He plays with his head". Grey, however, could not prevent Oldham's 10–5 victory, which was secured five minutes from time, when winger George Tyson's try was converted by Joe Ferguson.

In spite of these three defeats, Halifax were still top of the league above Runcorn and Oldham. Four league games remained and Halifax won them all. First up were Jack Fish's Warrington, who were dispatched 35–0 at Thrum Hall. No mention was made as to the whereabouts of the black dog, but Smut must have returned to the fold. The first round of the Challenge Cup on 16 March provided some light relief as Millom were crushed 45–3 at Thrum Hall, Bulmer scoring one of 11 tries, while wingers Eccles and Williams each claimed three.

Billy Bulmer was missing the following week, as were Jimmy Hilton and Fred Littlewood, for the second round tie which was greeted with apprehension as Oldham were Halifax's visitors. The two teams were joint-favourites to lift the trophy and 20,000 spectators filled Thrum Hall, paying a massive £429 at the gates. Halifax must have thought victory was theirs when a late try by George Cottrell gave them a 5–2 advantage. Three and a half minutes remained when half-back Arthur Lees scored a try, which Joe Ferguson converted to give Oldham a 7–5 lead. Bert Avery rubbed salt into Halifax's wounds by scoring a last minute try and Oldham had triumphed 10–5, going on to reach the final.

Halifax won their last three league fixtures: 5–3 at Warrington, followed by a huge double against York by 49–14 (away) and 58–0 at Thrum Hall. The new-fangled top-four finished thus:

	P	W	D	L	F	A	%
1 Halifax	34	27	2	5	649	229	82.35
2 Oldham	34	26	1	7	457	227	77.94
3 Runcorn	30	23	0	7	546	216	76.66
4 Keighley	24	17	1	6	431	231	72.91

Halifax consequently met surprise packages Keighley in the Championship semi-final on 6 April. A Thrum Hall crowd of 9,500 (8,365 paying £179/9/-) saw an unexpectedly strong Keighley side perform heroics in holding Halifax to a narrow 9–4 victory. In the last few minutes Driver, the Keighley centre, sustained a broken shin, while Billy Williams received a severe knee injury, which ruled him out of the final and most of the following season. In the other semi-final Oldham accounted for Runcorn 11–3.

The first Championship Final was staged at Fartown on 20 April, 1907 before a crowd of 13,200, paying £772/7/0. Oldham were confident of victory, having thrice defeated Halifax during the season. Halifax were lacking Billy Williams and had to draft in forward Harry Morley on the wing, while Fred Atkins was a surprise selection at centre, ahead of Billy Wedgwood, Ernie Ward and George Cottrell. Oldham too had a forward in their three-quarters, Bert Avery filling in at centre for 'Birdie' Dixon. This historic event was to be a fitting end to Billy Bulmer's career in rugby.

From start to finish Halifax were dominant. Billy Bulmer and his fellow packmen were far superior in the scrums and in the loose, while Oldham's backs were uncharacteristically weak. Halifax took the lead after 10 minutes when Avery lost the ball around half-way. Asa Robinson pounced on it, broke clear and sent Ike Bartle hurtling over. Billy Little kicked the goal and Halifax never lost the lead. Joe Ferguson scored a try for Oldham from a breaking scrum to reduce the deficit to two points, but that was as good as it got for the Roughyeds. Before the break Halifax scored again when the ball rebounded from the Oldham goal-post and – shades of the 1903 Challenge Cup final – Bartle and Bulmer touched down almost simultaneously, the try being credited to Billy. By the 54th minute, the scoring had been completed. Halifax added tries from Harry Morley and Joe Riley, while Billy Little potted a penalty and a conversion. An 18–3 score-line was deemed by most critics to be flattering to Oldham.

Billy Bulmer thus bade farewell to the game on the best possible note. He was not yet 26 years old and it is tempting to speculate what more he might have achieved in the sport, had he even played until he was 30. The next few years saw the birth of test rugby, the All Golds (1907) and the Kangaroos (1908 and 1911) arriving on British shores for the first time and a Northern Union tour to Australasia departing in 1910. Billy Bulmer could reasonably have been expected to be involved in those developments. Instead, he chose to retire to concentrate on business and this time he meant it.

His first-class rugby career had been brief. He had played five seasons for Halifax, making 137 appearances and scored nine tries. He had been a vital member of Challenge Cup-winning sides in 1902–03 and 1903–04 and Championship-winning teams in 1902–03 and 1906–07. He had represented Yorkshire (four caps) and England (one cap) and there would undoubtedly have been more representative honours if he had played on. There was no great fuss when Billy decided to give up the game. The nearest approach to an announcement appeared in the *Evening Courier* on Friday, 6 September 1907, when, as the new season got under way, *Rocket* observed, "Bulmer does not seem inclined to turn out". Doubtless, many of the Thrum Hall faithful took the news with a pinch of salt.

Billy Bulmer did not do things by halves and the new world he entered was a far cry from the fields of the Northern Union. In 1907 he "started taking contracts for building throughout, specialising in skating rinks." He built one in Manningham in three weeks and another in Guernsey in two weeks, which was considered quite staggering. He then turned his attention to constructing cinema theatres, which had become the rage in Edwardian times. One of his projects was Teddington Picture House in London, which reportedly took him 35 days from "first sod to opening!"

The *Halifax Evening Courier* of 1 August, 1908 ran the following advertisement:
Tel 962   JW BULMER
JOINER, BUILDER, SHOP
FITTER AND GENERAL
CONTRACTOR
CARPET-STREET JOINERY WORKS
OFF ALMA-STREET, HALIFAX
Residence 159, SPRING HALL-LANE
Prompt attention to repairs. Estimates free.

The 1911 census, taken on 2 April, shows that Billy Bulmer still resided at 159, Spring Hall Lane, which was almost on the doorstep of Thrum Hall. He was still single and his occupation was listed as builder and contractor and the census return added that he was an employer. Billy was the head of the household, although his mother Hannah (50 years old) was living with him, as were his sisters, Florence (26), Clara Ellen (25) and Hilda (7), and his youngest brother Horace (17). His younger brother Arnold was no longer present. Billy's aunt Sarah Ellen Holdsworth (43), a domestic housekeeper, was also a member of the household. Billy's star was clearly rising. He had disposed of his two previous properties on Conway Street and replaced them with four more, clearly trading upward.

His circumstances changed on Wednesday, 19 July, 1911, when Billy married Florence Lumb at St John's Wesleyan Chapel, Halifax. Florence was born on 4 February 1888 in Elland and was six and a half years younger than Billy. She was the younger daughter of Mary and James Lumb, of 1, Heathfield Terrace, Halifax, otherwise grandly known as The Hermitage.

The *Halifax Evening Courier* ran a substantial report of the wedding and, bafflingly, failed to mention his rugby connections. His prowess as a "well-known baritone vocalist" was, however, worthy of comment, as was his bride's singing talents. The only hint of a previous life as a rugby player was the presence of Harry Morley as best man. Billy's marriage was a sure sign that he was trading upwards. The Hermitage was a big house with eight rooms, and 100 guests attended the reception there, with music supplied by Messrs Priestley & Sutcliffe's band. James Lumb, Billy's father-in-law, was a man of substance. He had been a brass founder before establishing a successful firm as a steam engine and machine maker. Billy and Florence spent their honeymoon in London and the south before returning to live at Elder Grove, Dunkirk Lane, within easy walking distance of his business premises.

There were also dramatic changes in Billy's business affairs. He abandoned the building trade and entered the world of worsted spinning. Apparently, he had inherited a fascination for the textile trade from his mother's side of the family. He began in earnest in 1912 when he put down a worsted spinning plant at Keighley Mills, Halifax, installing 2,000 spindles, which he started running in 1913. In the same year the firm of Smith, Bulmer and Co was founded at Holmfield Mills, Halifax.

At one point Billy Bulmer controlled Holmfield Mills, Keighley Mills, Hare Street Mills, Woodfield Mills (Cullingworth), Branxholme Mills (Bailiffe Bridge), offices and warehouses in Bradford for the wool and top trade, and a central warehouse in Akroyd Place, Halifax.

In 1914 he and his partner Sam Smith dissolved their partnership by mutual consent. The Great War had caused orders for worsteds to plummet, but Billy saw another opportunity and launched into supplying khaki cloth for the army. His workers were able to produce a million yards every 10 weeks. He had restricted his own profit and did not make any speculative gains on the wool he purchased. It was crucial for his reputation that he maintained his integrity as he contributed to the war effort.

Billy Bulmer was a member of the Board of Control of Wool Textile Production. He was also a member of a small committee, appointed by the Home Secretary, which was entrusted with the task of examining the highly confidential information relating to the movement of ships having wool in their cargo and of advising the War Office as to quantities that would be available for civilian production. In essence he had to check everything concerning the production and consumption of wool handled by the government on behalf of the wool trade. Billy was rewarded with a knighthood. On 3 June, 1922 *The London Gazette* published the latest Honours List. Billy's entry read, "James William Bulmer, Esq. Head of the firm of Smith, Bulmer & Co, Worsted Spinners, of Halifax. Served on the Wool Statistical Committee and on the Wool-Textile Control Board. Chairman of Executive of the Yorkshire National Liberal Council. For public services."

For his contribution to the war effort and for his services to business, Billy was duly knighted at Buckingham Palace on 8 July 1922. He was henceforth Sir William Bulmer. It was said of him, "He rose by sheer grit and perseverance from humble circumstances to be honoured with a knighthood." For a boy who had left school before his 11th birthday, he had certainly, to put it in the vernacular, "done good". Moreover, he was not finished yet.

On the day of his elevation *The Yorkshire Post* commented that Sir William was "a bass vocalist of some distinction". It added "as Chairman of the Yorkshire Coalition Council, he entertained Mrs Lloyd George recently at his home at Cullingworth". Perhaps the latter remark hinted at the controversy which surrounded the bestowal of honours by Liberal/Coalition Prime Minister David Lloyd George, who would be forced from office a few months after Billy received his knighthood. Billy's local newspaper, *The Halifax Courier* was more interested in "our new knight's ... possession of The Grange, Cullingworth – a fine place and fifty acres of picturesque surroundings adjoining that much advertised Yorkshire pleasure ground Goit Stock". Billy's household consisted of his wife, two daughters, his son and five servants. There was some indignation that other publications appeared to think that Cullingworth was near Harrogate, rather than Halifax. Unsurprisingly, none of the coverage of Sir Billy's ennoblement mentioned his Northern Union connections.

Weirdly, another Northern Unionist received a knighthood in the same Honours List. Sir Edwin Airey (1878 to 1955), Governing Director of William Airey & Son, Engineers and Contractors, quarry owners and brick makers of Leeds and Barton-on-Humber, received his honour "for services to the Ministry of Munitions and the Ministry of Health". Airey was also heavily involved in organisations for social welfare and education. In 1923 he became Chairman of Leeds Rugby League Club, a position he held until 1955. He was Lord Mayor of

Leeds in 1923 and Chairman of the Rugby League Council in 1952–53. He was largely responsible for the vast improvement of the Headingley grounds which took place under his chairmanship of Leeds.

Six years before Bulmer and Airey were knighted, Glynn Hamilton West had been similarly honoured. Knighted in 1916, West (born 24 September 1877) was the Deputy Director General of Munitions Supply, a key post during the Great War. Between 1897 and 1899 he had been a regular in the Leeds NU team (55 games, five tries), appearing at centre, wing, half-back and latterly in the pack. West was a native of York. At the time of Billy's knighthood West was Chairman of Sir WJ Armstrong Whitworth & Co and lived at 8, Bryanston Square, St Marylebone, London with his wife, a butler and six maids. Three knighthoods for three Yorkshire-born Northern Unionists within six years – strange times indeed!

In 1924 Billy's interest in the rayon trade led him to form the Bulmer Rayon Company Ltd, for the manufacture of viscose silk, and he became chairman and managing director. In 1927 he installed a preliminary acetate spinning plant, and, after carrying out research and demonstration work, produced an acetate silk. To produce this on a large scale, a company called the British Acetate Silk Corporation was formed in 1928, with a nominal capital of £2,700,000. It was not really a surprise when Sir William Bulmer was appointed managing director at a salary of £5,000. He received that for one year only, however, and spent it on setting up a research department in London.

In 1931 Sir William and Lady Bulmer, still resident in Cullingworth, joined the firm of Ambler & Lumb Ltd, worsted spinners of Prospect Mills, Wibsey. The firm was soon renamed Bulmer & Son, Ltd. After a few months Mr Roland Lumb retired and was replaced by Mr JH Oates, who had been associated with Billy's Halifax business for 10 years. Sir William was again appointed chairman and managing director. Apart from his positions in the textile industry, he held the chairmanship of Staincross Colliery, Mapplewell, near Barnsley. The Bulmers had lived at The Grange for at least 10 years, as they were there in the 1921 Census, when they had five live-in servants.

Beyond the business world Sir William Bulmer maintained a passionate interest in music, as did his wife, Florence. For many years he was President of the Halifax Competitive Music Festival and presented the Lady Bulmer Trophy for mixed voice choirs. The pair were heavily involved in the affairs of the celebrated Leeds Music Festival.

In politics Billy was a staunch Liberal, but during the First World War was a strong supporter of the Coalition Government. He became President of the Yorkshire National Liberal Association at its inception. However, in 1923 he resigned from the National Liberal Council, of which he was also President, as he opposed David Lloyd George's policies on trade tariffs and unemployment. A Freemason, he was a member of St John's Lodge, Blackwall, Halifax. That he moved comfortably in the highest circles is evident from the innumerable accounts of his business and social life in the newspapers of the 1920s and 1930s. He appears to have been forever in the company of royalty, the aristocracy, the judiciary and major politicians.

However, to a degree he still retained the common touch. In 1916 he joined a committee of Halifax players and supporters to raise money for his old playing colleague Fred Mallinson. Fred, a miner from Wyke, had joined the Royal Engineers, been blown up twice and then lost three fingers of his right hand when a shrapnel shell wrecked his billet, a barn, 30 seconds after he had entered it. Discharged from the Army, Fred was granted a pension of one shilling and sixpence per day for his services to King and country. The committee raised £52 and five shillings for their 42-year-old former forward and Bulmer made Fred a personal gift of a handsome gold watch.

Among many other things, Billy was President of the Holmfield Gala Association and, according to *The Leeds Mercury* in 1923, was reported to play cricket with his employees at Holmfield Mills. He was described as "always on good terms with his employees and looked after their conditions". In private life he was a member of the Royal Automobile and Union Clubs, among others. His charitable donations included £1,000 to the Royal Halifax Infirmary in 1922.

Surprisingly perhaps, Sir William's sporting interest following The Great War was directed to rugby union and he did much to re-establish that game in Halifax, where it had all but died out after the advent of the Northern Union. After the First World War there was a tremendous surge in the formation of new rugby union clubs. The Halifax RU club was born out of that surge, going through several incarnations and grounds between 1919 and 1923. By the time it put roots down at Ovenden Park in 1925, the Halifax Rugby Union Football Club had re-entered the world of first-class rugby union after a 30-year hiatus provoked by Bulmer's old club joining the Northern Union. He was wise – and bullet-proof – enough to persuade two of his old Thrum Hall comrades to become trainers at the Halifax RUFC. It was hardly possible that the sporting enthusiasts of Halifax did not recognise those trainers – Archie Rigg and Joe Riley.

Nor was it any more likely that the Yorkshire rugby union fraternity was not aware of their identities. Blind eyes were turned in all directions as Sir William Bulmer and his cohorts drove a coach and horses through the anti-professional laws of rugby union!

Billy was President of Halifax RU Club from the early 1920s until his death. He did not, however, appear on the list of members of the Yorkshire RU in the Yorkshire RU annual handbook until 1923, just after he had been knighted. Even if Joe Riley and Archie Rigg could somehow get away with coaching a first class rugby union team, it should have been self-evidently inconceivable that any 'convicted' former Northern Union player of Billy's eminence could become President of a rugby union club. Clearly his knighthood opened doors which otherwise would have been barred to him. He had broken most of the anti-professionalism laws of the Rugby Football Union. He had accepted hundreds of pounds for playing for Halifax and had received gold medals for winning Championships and Challenge Cups – practically hanging offences.

No matter. The rugby union authorities did not cavil as Halifax RU club quickly became a major force under Sir William's very hands-on presidency. Halifax RU won the Yorkshire Cup, the original and genuine "t' owd tin pot", in 1926, 1927, 1928, 1930, 1933 and 1935, and were runners-up in 1931. Halifax RL club also saw the benefits of Billy's enterprise. Six members of those earliest Halifax RU Yorkshire Cup-winning sides turned professional with the Thrum Hallers – three-quarters Fred Adams and Wilson Smith, half-backs Arthur Gledhill and Herbert 'Gillie' Hanson, and forwards Herbert Smith and Bernard Newman. Adams, Hanson and Newman were in the 1931 Wembley-winning Halifax team. A seventh member of those Halifax RU sides, forward Bill Chalcroft later became a director at Thrum Hall.

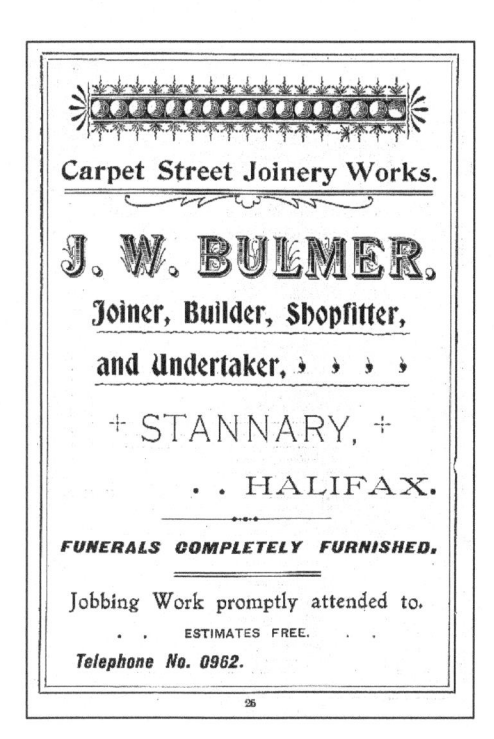

Left: Advert for Bulmer's business in the 1906 *Halifax Guardian Historical Almanack*
Right: Sir William Bulmer *circa* 1923

Almost annually Billy presided over celebratory dinners at the White Swan Hotel after Halifax RU's various Yorkshire Cup triumphs. He may well have paid for the functions too. In 1926 following victory over Otley the *Courier* reported, "He had seen the desire of his heart attained ... He had a feeling of happiness and satisfaction ... It had been a magnificent game. He had got more pleasure than when helping to win trophies in his own days as a Rugby player. It had been the type of forward game calculated to delight the old Rugger man." Billy declared, "There was no finer amateur side in the world than Halifax". The world had indeed turned upside down and Billy knew how to handle his audience, which included giants of the original Halifax (RU and NU) club such as James Pearson, one of the club's founding players, Jimmy Dodd, Tom Scarborough, Harry Wilkinson, Archie Rigg and Joe Riley.

Billy Bulmer may have been bullet-proof, as far as avoiding the retribution of the Rugby Football Union was concerned, but he was not immune from making bad decisions in business in his later years. When he had exchanged his building business for the textile trade he had £400 in capital. Within a few years his capital had catapulted to £381,000. Yet in 1932 he was declared bankrupt with liabilities amounting to £160,475. He had built up a fortune, was reputed to have been a millionaire and had at one time been offered £400,000 for his business. However, depreciation in his own shares and his venture into the rayon industry led to his downfall. Still, he was not defeated. A year later, on 11 July 1933, his discharge from bankruptcy was granted at Bradford County Court. *The Yorkshire Post* observed, "Latterly, Sir William's business ability was once more gaining him a place in the Bradford trade, and his enterprise was never hampered by the setbacks which he suffered."

Nonetheless, on Friday, 26 June 1936, *The Halifax Daily Courier & Guardian* ran the following headline: "SIR WILLIAM BULMER'S BANKRUPTCY". Lightning had struck twice. This time it was reported, "Shares valued at nearly £50,000 were the subject of a 'motion of considerable importance', which came before Judge McCleary at Bradford County Court yesterday." Smith Bulmer & Co Ltd was indebted to the National Provincial Bank to the tune of £47,107. The request to extend the time-limit to settle the debt was refused.

That information was imparted on page six of the *Courier & Guardian*, which was an evening paper, daily printing several different editions. Later editions added the tragically stunning news, on page seven, that Sir William Bulmer had died early that morning. The obituary was headlined:
"JOINER WHO BECAME A LEADER OF THE WOOL INDUSTRY
DEATH OF SIR JAMES WILLIAM BULMER
ROMANTIC CAREER OF A HALIFAX MAN
DYNAMIC AND VERSATILE PERSONALITY"

Billy had died at his home, at 14a, Park Drive, Heaton, Bradford. It explained that he had been "ill with heart trouble for about 10 months but had resumed business for a short time, two or three months ago. He had a relapse and died about 7am today." He was 54 and left his wife, Florence, two daughters, Mary and Joan, and a son, William. His funeral was at St Barnabas' Church, Heaton. He was buried at Nab Wood Cemetery on Monday, 29 June 1936.

The death notice in the *Courier & Guardian* stipulated "no flowers and no mourning". The request for no flowers was probably a wise one, bearing in mind that the florists of the West Riding would have been hard pressed to supply the demand. In attendance were literally hundreds of representatives from major and minor textile firms in the west of Yorkshire, as well as staff and employees from Bulmer & Lumb. Halifax RLFC were represented by their president, Councillor Eli Butterworth, JP, and club secretary, Arthur Archbell. Among Billy's old Thrum Hall team-mates present were Archie Rigg, Joe Riley, George Kitson, Johnny Morley, Fred Hammond, Joe Brearley, Herbert Hadwen, and Billy Wedgwood. Halifax RUFC were represented by their chairman, C Walker, and secretary, N Collins, while notable Halifax RU players Harry Eastwood, Bill Chalcroft, Jack Wood, Clifford Morton, Jim Preston, Jim Pendleton, Fred Adams, Herbert "Gillie" Hanson and Wilson Smith also attended.

Billy Bulmer died bankrupt and intestate. The man who had been hailed as a giant of the wool trade, made a fortune for himself and others, and been knighted by George V for his services to the nation, left effects of only £155.

He was a man once truly famous, but is now long forgotten.

Appendices

1. A chat with the Northern Union Football Champion: Mr Archie Rigg of Halifax

Boys Own Paper (BOP) 3 February 1900
By a *BOP* Special Correspondent

As is well known, the Rugby Union has been splendidly organised by Mr George Rowland Hill, a robust Churchman, who says "Professionalism is illegal." For many years, excellent progress has been made along lines that are full of promise of solidarity for our national pastime.

But there are some who said: "We cannot afford to lose the half-days we give to the game, and if the Rugby Union will not help us we will have a Union of our own." Hence the rise of the Northern Union, comprising the best clubs of Yorkshire and Lancashire, and the gradual extension of their programme.

One of their champions is Archie Rigg, whom I had the pleasure of meeting at Halifax, and he consented to tell me about the Northern Union for the BOP.

He is a lover of the Rugby game, and has taken high honours in it. But although living a careful and abstemious life, he could not afford to give up his time and lose money.

But the Rugby Union refused to consider this, and so the Northern Union was formed for the purpose of paying broken time to those who elected to play football under its auspices; and now it has gone in entirely for professionalism. But there is no place in it for the man who wishes to play football on the Saturdays and lounges his time away the rest of the week. The object of the controlling authorities is to leave such a one no place in the Northern Union.

"But how can this be carried out?" I asked.

"We believe that the payment of men openly allowed will tend to make men honest in their transactions, open and above board in all their dealing with players and funds; and any club offending is sharply dealt with."

"And what constitutes professionalism?"

"Professionalism is legal with us, and a professional is a player who actually receives remuneration over and above travelling expenses actually paid. All professionals must be registered on a form to be supplied by the Secretary of the Union. Each form, after all the particulars have been filled in, must be signed by the professional and returned to the hon. Secretary within five days of such signature. A professional is not allowed to play until this rule has been complied with, and the secretary of the club registering the player shall have received the acknowledgement on the official form from the Secretary of the Union. Players may be transferred from one club to another. The secretary of every club has to supply the secretary of the Union with a complete list of all his club's players, their present addresses, and the names of the firms for whom they work. Such particulars have to be supplied by September 1 next."

"But how do you keep out the pot-hunting, gold seeking player?"

"Why, knowing that the player must have a good deal of leisure, every professional in our Union must be in *bona fide* employment, and is not allowed to play unless in such employment. And there are situations that do not count as *bona fide* employment – viz. 'billiard markers, waiters in licensed houses or any employment in connection with a club.' We have quite made up our minds that the footballer who spends his leisure in public-houses is not the man who is a credit to any team. It may be said if a man plays well, what more is required? The answer is, that public opinion – a most healthy censor – demands that those who contend in the national games shall be honourable and of good repute. And, indeed, only such will elevate sport."

"But suppose a player is thrown out of work, Mr Rigg?"

"Then the case is covered by a rule which says a professional player thrown out of work through fire, lock-out, or strike, may be given permission to play football at the discretion of the Northern Rugby Union Committee; and if a player changes his situation the secretary of the club to which he is attached must notify the fact to the hon. secretary of the Union, and such player must not play football until he is again in *bona fide* work, full particulars of which have been given to the secretary of the Union. Then, during the cricket, or close season, no professional is allowed to receive pay of any description, and he must not serve on the Committee of the Union, or represent his own, or any other club at any meeting of the Union. Such, in substance, are our rules; we do all we can. Some have wished that the Union had fixed the maximum amount of payment to a player. In the past season the club has had to find six shillings a day at least, One evil is, that there is bound to be a limit to the number of men any club can take on, and rising clubs cannot compete against the man who has a big purse. But there ought to be a maximum salary, or big clubs will find bigger clubs outbidding them for a player, and then we may have a similar state of affairs to that which now exists in the Association world."

The Northern Union has been started three or four years, and each season has made progress. It has over a hundred affiliated organisations, chiefly in Yorkshire and Lancashire; but now Cumberland and Westmoreland have joined.

As to the laws of the game, Archie Rigg says there are few alterations; but the differences have a material effect upon the play. One rule prevents a half-back from getting in front of the rearmost forwards, and is likely to be adopted by the Rugby Union. The line-out is abolished, the punt being substituted, and the innovation has worked well. Success is achieved by points, and it is only a question of time before the parent union adapts it.

There is already a County Championship and Challenge Cup competition, and of the latter it may be said that it has proved overwhelmingly popular. Batley were the holders last year, and they only obtained the position by plucky, determined and skilful football. The conspicuous harmony which has attended the working of the Northern Union is due to the fact that every member of the Executive is animated by the desire to further the objects of the sport; and so long as this good feeling prevails there is not likely to be much alteration.

The Northern Union, says the great Halifax player, has received very cordial recognition at the hands of the press– and chiefly from the *Athletic News*, a paper that refuses to insert anything about horse-racing or betting; and the journal has attained amazing success, until it is sold all over England.

Personally, the Halifax man is confident that, to play long, a man must leave beer alone, and live a very steady life. He lives on a simple diet, and, in the summer, plays cricket. As to the crowds that are often drawn together on a Saturday afternoon, their numbers do not grow greatly, and it is really the only leisure that many have. Some of the Yorkshire manufacturing towns are badly off for open spaces, and that is a drawback to the game, which, owing to science and recent modifications, gets less and less dangerous every year.

As I left Rigg, my conviction was confirmed that football all over the country is undergoing a great change for the better. Public protest against drunken debauchees, etc., has done its work and a good character is now one of the first essentials. It is well that it is so, and with the united influence of Press, Platform, Pen and Pulpit, our great winter game will become, what it ought to be – pure and honourable in the sight of all men.

Archie Rigg says that, as a boy at school, he was a devoted admirer of the *BOP*, and was delighted to hear of its continued great popularity.

The *Boy's Own Paper* (1879 to 1967) was a massive selling weekly and later monthly magazine aimed at the boys of Britain and the British Empire. Stanley Baldwin, leader of the Conservative Party (1923 to 1937) and thrice Prime Minister, famously wrote, "Boys who are nurtured on the *Boy's Own Paper* will turn out men and neither prudes nor prigs".

2. Club career records

Albert Goldthorpe

Hunslet Rugby Union

	A	T	G
1888–89	34	0	17
1889–90	37	7	71
1890–91	29	7	37
1891–92	30	0	61
1892–93	33	11	40
1893–94	38	4	38
1894–95	30	0	36
Totals	231	29	300

The above figures are taken from page 100 of Bryan Smith's *Four Cups to Fame*, published in 2008.

Hunslet Northern Union

	A	T	G	P
1895–96	39	4	27	79
1896–97	29	5	24	80
1897–98	33	1	66	135
1898–99	33	8	66	156
1899–1900	30	1	29	61
1900–01	28	2	44	94
1901–02	33	1	43	89
1902–03	34	1	48	99
1903–04	34	4	34	80
1904–05	31	3	42	93
1905–06	28	2	49	104
1906–07	31	5	74	163
1907–08	41	5	101	217
1908–09	34	3	41	91
1909–10	2	0	3	6
Totals	460	45	691	1547

Note: The above figures are derived from the Rugby League Record Keepers' *Teams and Scorers* booklets (1895 to 1910). They differ slightly from Bryan Smith's figures for Albert Goldthorpe's Northern Union career with Hunslet, listed on page 103 of *Four Cups to Fame*. There the figures amount to 445 appearances, 46 tries, 692 goals and 1552 points.

Attempts to reconcile the differences would undoubtedly be problematic. Suffice to say that in his entire first team rugby career in both codes, including representative matches, Albert racked up just over 700 appearances in which he claimed around 80 tries and kicked just over 1,000 goals.

Archie Rigg

Halifax Rugby Union

	A	T	G	P
1891–92	6	2	0	4
1892–93	29	8	1	19
1893–94	30	21+	0	63
1894–95	27	11	4	41
Totals	92	42	5	127

+ Club record in rugby union

Halifax Northern Union

	A	T	G	P
1895–96	37	16	5	61
1896–97	29	18	23	110
1897–98	24	16	9	66
1898–99	18	5	7	29
1899–00	16	6	3	24
1900–01	23	15	2	49
1901–02	24	4	1	14
1902–03	37	9	1	29
1903–04	23	2	0	6
1904–05	12	0	0	0
1912–13	1	0	0	0
Totals	244	91	51	388

Rigg also played three games for Halifax in 1915–16, which are not included in official records.

Bradford Northern

	A	T	G	P
1908–09	16	3	0	9
1909–10	24	7	0	21
1910–11	17	4	0	12
1911–12	1	0	0	0
Totals	58	14	0	42

3. Yorkshire County records

Yorkshire scores first

Albert Goldthorpe

Rugby Union (8 caps)

14 Nov 1891	Durham	Hull	17–7	3 goals
6 Feb 1892	Cheshire*	Birkenhead	12–13	2 goals
20 Feb 1892	England	Headingley	4–0	
19 Oct 1892	Devon	York	31–5	2dg, 2 con
12 Nov 1892	Durham	Hartlepool	13–7	try, 2 con, pen
16 Nov 1892	Glamorgan	Fartown	5–5	con
19 Nov 1892	Northumberland	Headingley	17–12	try, 2dg, con
26 Nov 1892	Lancashire	Manchester	2–2	

*captain

Summary: Won 5, drew 2 lost 1. 2 tries, 17 goals.
Yorkshire were County Champions in both the seasons Albert played for the county.

Northern Union (6 caps)

29 Feb 1896	Lancashire	Fartown	3–8	
7 Nov 1896	Cheshire	Hull	17–10	pen, con
29 Oct 1898	Cheshire	Manningham	14–2	goal
5 Dec 1898	Lancashire	Salford	20–9	
28 Jan 1899	Cumberland	Leeds PC	8–5	
5 Nov 1903	Cumberland	Workington	11–0	try

Summary: Won 5, lost 1. 1 try, 3 goals.
Yorkshire were County Champions in 1898–99.

The game against Cumberland in 1903 was played under experimental 12–a–side rules. It was the only game he played at half–back for the county under either code, all his other Yorkshire appearances were at centre.

Archie Rigg

Rugby Union (19 caps)

14 Jan 1893	Somerset	Bradford	29–0	try
21 Jan 1893	Cheshire	Halifax	19–5	2 tries
30 Jan 1893	Middlesex	Richmond	14–5	2 tries
16 Feb 1893	Cumberland	Carlisle	17–2	try
25 Feb 1893	England	Fartown	2–0	
11 Nov 1893	Durham	Headingley	18–0	
18 Nov 1893	Northumberland	Newcastle	9–0	try
25 Nov 1893	Lancashire	Bradford	11–3	
13 Jan 1894	Somerset	Weston	27–0	try
15 Jan 1894	Glamorgan	Swansea	3–0	
27 Jan 1894	Cheshire	Birkenhead	16–6	try
3 Mar 1894	England	Headingley	9–15	2 tries
31 Oct 1894	Glamorgan	Fartown	31–0	
10 Nov 1894	Durham	Hartlepool	16–5	
17 Nov 1894	Northumberland	Headingley	19–5	
24 Nov 1894	Lancashire	Manchester	26–10	try
11 Feb 1895	Midlands	Leicester	3–3	
7 Mar 1895	Devon	Plymouth	12–5	try
8 Apr 1895	England	Headingley	21–3	try

Summary: Won 17, drew 1, lost 1. 14 tries.
Yorkshire were County Champions in all three seasons Archie played for the county.

Northern Union (13 caps)

25 Nov 1895	Cheshire*	Headingley	5–9	
7 Dec 1895	Lancashire*	Oldham	8–0	try
29 Feb 1896	Lancashire*	Fartown	3–8	
7 Nov 1896	Cheshire*	Hull	17–10	
21 Nov 1896	Lancashire*	Oldham	3–7	
6 Nov 1897	Cheshire*	Stockport	22–3	2 tries
20 Nov 1897	Lancashire*	Bradford	7–6	
29 Oct 1898	Cheshire*	Manningham	14–2	2 tries
5 Nov 1898	Lancashire*	Salford	20–9	try
28 Jan 1899	Cumberland*	Leeds PC	8–5	try
28 Oct 1899	Cheshire*	Birkenhead	8–9	try
30 Nov 1901	Cheshire	Stockport	3–13	
1 Nov 1902	Cumberland	Headingley	29–2	

* captain

Summary: Won 8, lost 5. 8 tries.

Yorkshire were County Champions in 1897–98 and 1898–99.
Archie captained Yorkshire on 5 Feb, 1898 when Cumberland were beaten 8–0 at Hunslet. No caps were awarded for this match, which was a preparation for Cumberland's entry into the NU County Championship in the 1898–99 season.

All Archie's appearances for Yorkshire under both codes were at half-back, apart from his final two, when he played at centre.

Amazingly, Albert Goldthorpe and Archie Rigg only played five times together for Yorkshire. Three of those games were in the Championship-winning campaign of 1898–99. The others were against Lancashire at Fartown in 1896 and against Cheshire at Hull in 1896.

4. Appearances in major finals

Albert Goldthorpe

Yorkshire Challenge Cup Final (RU)
Hunslet 21 Leeds 0 (HT 0–0)
23 April 1892 at Fartown, Huddersfield

Hunslet: W Goldthorpe; J Goldthorpe, AE Goldthorpe, Wright; Lapping (capt), Townsend; Gilston, Kaye, Rathmell, Groves, Bennett, Liversedge, Mossley, Moore, Skirrow
Tries: J Goldthorpe 2, Rathmell, W Goldthorpe, AE Goldthorpe, Kaye
Conversions: AE Goldthorpe 3
Leeds: Wilkinson; Place, Summersgill, Walker; Potter (capt), Watts; Lorriman, Donaldson, Fletcher, Naylor, Munro, Cousins, Watson, Lewthwaite, Pickles
Referee: WH Humphreys (Durham County) **Crowd:** 15,484 **Gate:** £847

Yorkshire Senior Competition Championship Play–off
Hunslet 5 Bradford 2 (HT 0–2)
30 April 1898 at Headingley

Hunslet: Mitchell; W Goldthorpe, AE Goldthorpe (capt), Wright, Hannah; Robinson, Gillings; Kaye, O Walsh, Deacon, Barraclough, Young, Bowley, Leach, Ramage
Try: Ramage
Goal: AE Goldthorpe
Bradford: Patrick; Dobson, Cooper, W Murgatroyd, F Murgatroyd; Calvert, Prole; Broadley (capt), Robinson, Fearnley, Holt, Holden, Kelsey, Foulds, Robertson
Goal: Cooper
Referee: PF Farrar (Halifax) **Crowd:** 3,088 **Gate:** £111/10/–

Northern Union Challenge Cup Final
Hunslet 9 Oldham 19 (HT 9–5)
29 April 1899 at Fallowfield, Manchester

Hunslet: Mitchell; Hannah, AE Goldthorpe (capt), W Goldthorpe, Wright; Robinson, Fletcher; O Walsh, Young, Rubrey, Leach, T Walsh, Ramage, Harrison, Wilson
Try: W Goldthorpe
Goals: AE Goldthorpe 3
Oldham: Thomas; Williams, S Lees, Fletcher, Davies; A Lees (capt), Lawton; Bonsor, Moffatt, Telfer, Broome, Ellis, Barnes, Frater, J Lees
Tries: Williams 2, Moffatt, S Lees, J Lees
Goals: Thomas, S Lees
Referee: TH Marshall (Bradford) **Crowd:** 15,762 **Gate:** £946/16/1

Yorkshire Challenge Cup Final
Hunslet 13 Halifax 3 (HT 4–3)
2 December 1905 at Park Avenue, Bradford

Hunslet: Place; C Ward, Eagers, W Goldthorpe, W Ward; AE Goldthorpe (capt), Everson; Shooter, Jukes, Wray, Brooks, Wilson, Wilcox, T Walsh, Glew
Try: W Ward
Goals: AE Goldthorpe 3, W Goldthorpe 2
Halifax: Little (capt); Hartley, Wedgwood, Williams, Drummond; Joe Riley, Hilton; Jack Riley, Morton, Langhorn, Winskill, Bartle, Swinbank, Hammond, Norton
Try: Drummond
Referee: W McCutcheon (Oldham) **Crowd:** 18,500 **Gate:** £465/13/6

Yorkshire Challenge Cup Final
Hunslet 17 Halifax 0 (HT 4–0)
21 December 1907 at Headingley

Hunslet: Place; Farrar, C Ward, Eagers, Batten; AE Goldthorpe (capt), Smith; Wilson, Brooks, Jukes, Randall, T Walsh, Wray
Tries: Batten, AE Goldthorpe, Smith
Goals: AE Goldthorpe 2, Ward, Eagers
Halifax: Little (capt); H Morley, Atkins, E Ward, Joe Riley; Hilton, Grey; Robinson, Langhorn, Brearley, Littlewood, Hammond, Sunderland
Referee: W McCutcheon (Oldham) **Crowd:** 15,000 **Gate:** £397/2/10

Northern Union Challenge Cup Final
Hunslet 14 Hull 0 (HT 7–0)
25 April 1908 at Fartown, Huddersfield

Hunslet: Place; Farrar, Eagers, W Goldthorpe, Batten; AE Goldthorpe (capt), Smith; Wilson, Brooks, Jukes, Randall, Higson, T Walsh
Tries: Smith, Farrar
Goals: AE Goldthorpe 3, Eagers
Hull: Taylor (capt); Parry, Cottrell, Cook, Rogers; Wallace, Anderson; Holder, Herridge, Fulton, Kilburn, Owen, Carroll
Referee: JH Smith (Widnes) **Crowd:** 18,000 **Gate:** £903

Northern Union Championship Final
Hunslet 7 Oldham 7 (HT 7–4)
2 May 1908 at Salford

Hunslet: Place; C Ward, W Goldthorpe, Eagers, Batten; AE Goldthorpe (capt), Smith; Wilson, Brooks, Jukes, Randall, Higson, T Walsh
Try: AE Goldthorpe
Goals: AE Goldthorpe 2
Oldham: Thomas; GW Smith, Dixon, Llewellyn, Tyson; White, Beynon; Ferguson (capt), A Smith, Avery, Wilkinson, Wright, Longworth
Try: Wright
Goals: White 2
Referee: R Robinson (Bradford) **Crowd:** 14,000 **Gate:** £690

Northern Union Championship Final Replay
Hunslet 12 Oldham 2 (HT 7–0)
9 May 1908 at Wakefield

Hunslet: Place; Farrar, Eagers, W Goldthorpe, Batten; AE Goldthorpe (capt), Smith; Wilson, Jukes, Randall, Higson, T Walsh, Smales
Tries: W Goldthorpe 2
Goals: AE Goldthorpe 2, Place
Oldham: Thomas; Tyson, Dixon, Llewellyn, Oldershaw; White, Beynon; Ferguson (capt), Avery, A Smith, Longworth, Wright, Wilkinson
Goal: White
Referee: E Tonge (Swinton) **Crowd:** 14,054 **Gate:** £800

Yorkshire Challenge Cup Final
Hunslet 5 Halifax 9 (HT 0–7)
28 November 1908 at Wakefield

Hunslet: Place; Batten, Hoyle, Eagers, Farrar; AE Goldthorpe (capt), Smith; Jukes, T Walsh, Higson, Wilson, Randall, Cappleman
Try: Randall
Goal: AE Goldthorpe
Halifax: Little; Williams, Joe Riley, Ward, Thomas; Hilton, Grey; Robinson, Langhorn (capt), Swinbank, H Morley, Hammond, Mallinson
Try: Hilton
Goals: Little 3
Referee: JH Smith (Widnes) **Crowd:** 13,000 **Gate:** £356

Archie Rigg

Yorkshire Challenge Cup Final (RU)
Halifax 8 Batley 2 (HT 5–2)
22 April 1893 at Headingley

Halifax: Dodd; Toothill, Keepings, Firth; Rigg, Arnold; Fletcher (capt), Watson, Wilkinson, Wilson, Webster, JW Mellor, B Mellor, Dickenson, Winskill
Try: JW Mellor   *Conversion:* Keepings
Penalty: Winskill
Batley: Joseph Naylor; Simms, Goodall, Shaw; James Naylor, Elliker; Lowrie (capt), Shackleton, Stubley, Thornton, Haigh, Farrar, Oldfield, Scott, Squires
Try: James Naylor
Referee: WH Humphreys (Durham County) **Crowd:** 17,288 **Gate:** £820/6/10

Yorkshire Challenge Cup Final (RU)
Halifax 38 Castleford 6 (HT 10–3)
21 April 1894 at Headingley

Halifax: Bromwich; Firth, Keepings, Jackson, Chorley; Rigg, Arnold; Fletcher (capt), B Mellor, Wilson, Knowles, Ripley, Dickenson, Robertshaw, Jack Riley
Tries: Firth 3, Rigg 2, Keepings, Ripley, Jackson
Conversions: Keepings 5, Robertshaw 2
Castleford: Rowlands; Donynge, Bellerby, Jepson, Smith; Shaw, Burns; Speed (capt), Walton, Nowell, Starks, Hambleton, Townend, Rhodes, Hanson
Tries: Hambleton, Shaw
Referee: H Hutchinson (Wakefield) **Crowd:** 16,093 **Gate:** £747/15/6

Northern Union Challenge Cup Final
Halifax 7 Salford 0 (HT 0–0)
25 April 1903 at Headingley

Halifax: Little; Wedgwood, Williams, Rigg (capt), Hadwen; Joe Riley, Morley; Jack Riley, Bartle, Mallinson, Swinbank, Morton, Hammond, Bulmer, Winskill
Try: Bartle
Goals: Hadwen 2
Salford: Smith; Norris, Messer, Lomas (capt), Bell; Harter, Griffiths; Rhapps, Williams, Heath, Tunney, Brown, Buckler, Shaw, Shore
Referee: J Bruckshaw (Stockport) **Crowd:** 32,509 **Gate:** £1,834/16/6

5. Halifax's League and Cup Double season 1902–03
Captains: George Kitson, Archie Rigg.
CC: Challenge Cup. **Bold:** home fixtures

6 Sep	**Hull KR**	11–0	
13 Sep	Hunslet	5–2	
20 Sep	**Wigan**	8–4	
27 Sep	Widnes	7–0	
4 Oct	**Bradford**	9–0	
11 Oct	Huddersfield	5–0	
18 Oct	**Warrington**	2–2	
25 Oct	**Brighouse R**	5–2	
1 Nov *	**St Helens**	8–0	
8 Nov	Runcorn	5–3	
15 Nov *	**Batley**	12–6	
22 Nov	Salford	0–12	
29 Nov	Swinton	3–3	
6 Dec	**Leigh**	13–0	
13 Dec	Hull	3–0	
20 Dec	Oldham	0–11	
25 Dec	**Hunslet**	3–4	
27 Dec	Broughton R	0–5	
1 Jan	Brighouse R	10–0	
3 Jan	Hull KR	0–6	
24 Jan	**Widnes**	3–2	
31 Jan	Bradford	2–6	
4 Feb	Wigan	2–0	
7 Feb	**Huddersfield**	7–0	
14 Feb	**Salterhebble**	34–0	CC 1st round
21 Feb	Castleford	0–0	CC 2nd round
24 Feb	**Broughton R**	7–0	
25 Feb	**Castleford**	10–3	CC 2nd round replay
28 Feb	St Helens	3–7	
7 Mar	**Brighouse R**	0–0	CC 3rd round
10 Mar	Brighouse R	8–2	CC 3rd round replay
14 Mar	Batley	11–3	
21 Mar	Runcorn	2–0	CC 4th round
26 Mar	**Runcorn**	8–0	
28 Mar	**Swinton**	13–0	
4 Apr *	Hull	8–5	CC semi–final at Fartown
10 Apr *	Warrington	0–2	
11 Apr *	**Hull**	8–0	
16 Apr	**Salford**	5–5	
18 Apr	**Oldham**	10–0	
25 Apr	Salford	7–0	CC final at Headingley
27 Apr	Leigh	11–0	

League matches	P 34	W 23	D 3	L 8	Pts 199–85
Cup matches	P 8	W 6	D 2	L 0	Pts 69–10
All matches	P 42	W 29	D 5	L 8	Pts 268–95

Archie Rigg played in 37 games, missing five, which are denoted *.

6. Hunslet's All–Four Cups season 1907–08

Captain: Albert Goldthorpe
YC: Yorkshire Cup, CC: Challenge Cup, Ch: Championship

7 Sep	**Dewsbury**	11–0			1G
14 Sep	Hull	9–8			3G
21 Sep	**Keighley**	15–5			3G
28 Sep	Batley	10–0			2G
5 Oct	Leeds	10–5			2G
12 Oct	**Salford**	12–12			3G
16 Oct	**Bramley**	25–9			2G
19 Oct	Halifax	10–8			2G
26 Oct	Huddersfield	17–11			3G
2 Nov	**York**	29–12			7G
9 Nov	**Bramley**	50–0	YC 1st round	2T	8G
16 Nov	Bradford N	9–6			2G
23 Nov	Leeds	17–10	YC 2nd round		4G
30 Nov	Hull KR	37–8			8G
7 Dec	**Wakefield T**	10–0	YC semi–final		2G
14 Dec	**Huddersfield**	9–7			
21 Dec	Halifax	17–0	YC final at Headingley	1T	2G
25 Dec	**Halifax**	8–6			1G
26 Dec	**New Zealand**	11–11	Tour match		4G
28 Dec	**Wigan**	12–11			3G
1 Jan	St Helens	24–8		1T	5G
8 Jan	York	2–0			1G
11 Jan	**Bradford N**	10–2			2G
18 Jan	Hull KR	11–23			3G
25 Jan	Salford	6–7			–
27 Jan	Merthyr Tydfil	9–13			3G
1 Feb	**Wakefield T**	5–9			1G
8 Feb	Keighley	2–7			–
15 Feb	Wakefield T	11–0			2G
19 Feb	Bramley	21–11			3G
22 Feb	**Leeds**	3–0	Abandoned (16 minutes)		
29 Feb	Leeds	14–5	CC 1st round		1G
7 Mar	**St Helens**	21–6			
14 Mar	**Oldham**	15–8	CC 2nd round		dnp
18 Mar	**Leeds**	10–4			dnp
21 Mar	**Hull**	17–3			dnp
23 Mar	**Merthyr Tydfil**	5–3			1G
28 Mar	Barrow	8–0	CC 3rd round		1G
1 Apr	**Batley**	4–3			2G
4 Apr	Dewsbury	8–5			
11 Apr	Broughton R	16–2	CC semi–final at Wigan		2G
13 Apr	Wigan	0–36			dnp
18 Apr	**Broughton R**	28–3	Ch semi–final		5G
25 Apr	Hull	14–0	Cup final at Fartown		3G
2 May	Oldham	7–7	Ch final at Salford	1T	2G
9 May	Oldham	12–2	Ch final replay at Wakefield		2G

Season's record: P 46, W 36, D 3, L 6, Abandoned 1, Pts 611–285
Yorkshire League record: P 24, W 21, D 0, L 3, Pts 300–152

Albert Goldthorpe's record–breaking century of goals is listed on the extreme right.
dnp indicates Albert missed that fixture. He played in 42 of Hunslet's 46 matches, scoring 217 points (101 goals and 5 tries). Of his goals, 27 were dropped. He dropped goals in 22 of the matches in which he appeared.

More Rugby League books

Ahead of his time – Roy Francis and Rugby League
By Peter Lush. The first biography of Roy Francis, the first black player to play for Great Britain. He played for Wigan, Barrow, Dewsbury, Warrington and Hull. He was a very successful and innovative coach at Hull, Leeds and Bradford. He also coached in Australia. Published in April 2022 @ £14.95

The Dragons versus St George – England versus Wales in rugby league 1908 to 1996
By Graham Williams. The historic rivalry of England and Wales. Although not as well known as its counterpart with matches at Twickenham and Cardiff Arms Park, English and Welsh rugby league players had a professional series from 1908 until rugby union went open in 1995. That series may be less well-known, but those matches mattered just as much to the players involved. Published 25 October 2023 @ £14.95

From The Valleys to Headingley – Leeds Welsh rugby league players
By Neil Jones. Comprehensive history of the Welsh players who have played for Leeds. Includes club legends such as Lewis Jones, Frank 'Bucket' Young, Dickie Williams, Iestyn Harris and Joe Thompson. Published in August 2022 @ £13.95

There are more rugby league books on our website. All above on Amazon & Abe Books, or from London League Publications Ltd, www.llpshop.co.uk Order by post from: LLP, PO Box 65784, London NW2 9NS, cheques payable to London League Publications Ltd; credit card orders via www.llpshop.co.uk More information: email: peter56nw@gmail.com or phone 07973-845285

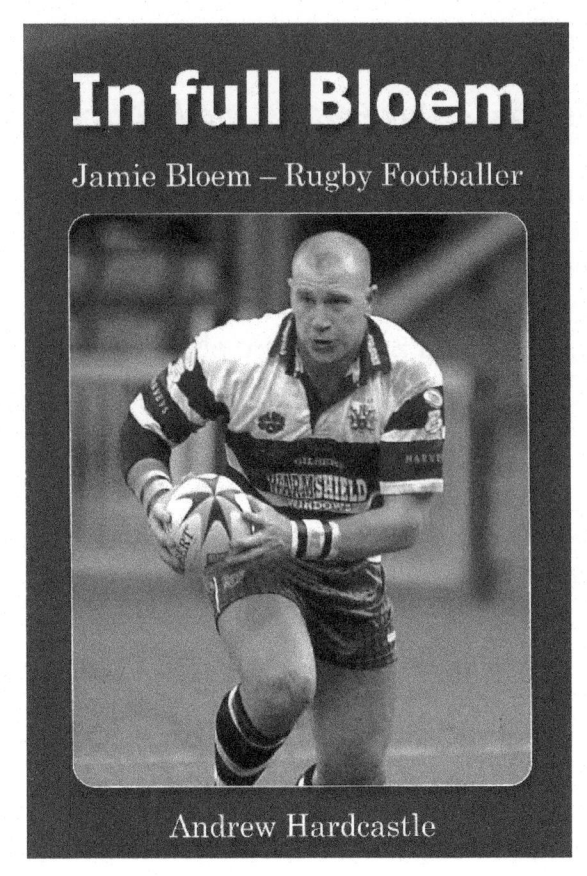

In full Bloem
Jamie Bloem – Rugby Footballer
Andrew Hardcastle

From being a young South African rugby union player, Jamie Bloem developed into a star rugby league [layer. From 1992 to 2005he played every position on the field in a career that took in Castleford, Oldham, Doncaster, Widnes and Huddersfield, but primarily Halifax. He later became a coach, commentator and Grade 1 referee.

He was never far from the headlines, be it for drug taking, an accusation of biting Lee Briers, charges of abusing referees, declining pay cuts, or even sometimes for scoring spectacular tries or kicking touchline goals.

In this authorised biography, he lifts the lid on everything that has happened to him, giving a frank account of when he was in the wrong and when he was not.

Andrew Hardcastle has had a lifelong association with Halifax RLFC, where he is the club historian and timekeeper. He has written widely about rugby league.

Hardback book, published in January 2013 @ £14.95.

Available on Amazon & Abe Books, or from London League Publications Ltd, www.llpshop.co.uk
Order by post from: LLP, PO Box 65784, London NW2 9NS, cheques payable to London League Publications Ltd; credit card orders via www.llpshop.co.uk   More information: email: peter56nw@gmail.com or phone 07973-845285